Interacting with Broadband Society

Participation in Broadband Society

Edited by Leopoldina Fortunati / Julian Gebhardt / Jane Vincent

Volume 1

PETER LANG
Frankfurt am Main · Berlin · Bern · Bruxelles · New York · Oxford · Wien

Leopoldina Fortunati / Jane Vincent /
Julian Gebhardt / Andraž Petrovčič /
Olga Vershinskaya
(eds.)

Interacting with Broadband Society

Bibliographic Information published by the Deutsche Nationalbibliothek
The Deutsche Nationalbibliothek lists this publication in the Deutsche Nationalbibliografie; detailed bibliographic data is available in the internet at http://dnb.d-nb.de.

ISSN 1867-044X
ISBN 978-3-631-58393-7
© Peter Lang GmbH
Internationaler Verlag der Wissenschaften
Frankfurt am Main 2010
All rights reserved.

All parts of this publication are protected by copyright. Any utilisation outside the strict limits of the copyright law, without the permission of the publisher, is forbidden and liable to prosecution. This applies in particular to reproductions, translations, microfilming, and storage and processing in electronic retrieval systems.

www.peterlang.de

Acknowledgements

The editors wish to thank Peter Lang AG, Berlin for their support in establishing a new series on new ICT and society called Participation in Broadband Society.

This publication is supported by COST Office and their staff is acknowledged for their assistance together with the COST Action 298 Chair Bartolomeo Sapio and Vice Chair Tomaz Turk. The members of COST Action 298 Working Group "Humans as e-actors" are thanked for their support during the production of this book. These are: Leopldina Fortunati, Julian Gebhardt, Hajo Greif, Sander Limonard, Claire Lobet-Maris, Andraž Petrovčič, Lilia Raycheva, Panayiota Tsatsou, Olga Vershinskaya and Jane Vincent.

COST – the acronym for European *CO*operation in the field of *S*cientific and *T*echnical Research- is the oldest and widest European intergovernmental network for cooperation in research. Established by the Ministerial Conference in November 1971, COST is presently used by the scientific communities of 35 European countries to cooperate in common research projects supported by national funds. Web: www.cost.esf.org

ESF provides the COST Office through an EC contract

COST is supported by the EU RTD Framework programme

COST 298 – Participation in the Broadband Society

Table of Content: Interacting with Broadband Society (Volume I)

Leopoldina Fortunati, Jane Vincent, Julian Gebhardt, Andraž Petrovčič and Olga Vershinskaya
Introduction: Approaching the notion of humans as e-actors interacting with Broadband Society 9

Theme I: Conceptual perspectives on e-actors interacting with broadband society

Leopoldina Fortunati
From ICT User to Broadband e-Actor 27

Gregor Petrič, Andraž Petrovčič and Vasja Vehovar
Communication Technology Use as a Structuration Process:
Exploring the Communicative Portraits of Active Users 47

Hajo Greif, Oana Mitrea, and Matthias Werner
Usability vs. Functionality? Mobile Broadband Technologies
and User Agency 73

Giuseppina Pellegrino
Mediated Bodies in saturated environments:
Participation as co-construction 93

Theme II: Emerging Interpersonal Communications among e-actors

Amparo Lasen
Mobile Culture and Subjectivities: an Example of the Shared Agency
between People and Technology 109

Julian Gebhardt
Alfred Schütz and the media: The intersubjective constitution
of mediated interpersonal communication in everyday life 125

Jane Vincent
Me and My Mobile 143

Theme III: Exploring the notion of e-actors within the information society

Vsevolod M. Zherebin
Information Society as the Law-governed Result
of the Evolution of Information 161

Olga Vershinskaya
Theoretical Approach to the Concept of Humans as e-Actors 175

Theme IV: E-actors in the institutional context: Policies and regulations from e-actors' point of view

Lilia Raycheva
Television: The Good, The Bad and the Unexpected Challenges of ICT 187

Panayiota Tsatsou
Digital Divides in Greece: The Role of Culture and Regulation
in Internet Adoption. Implications for the European Information Society 207

Vesna Dolničar
Regulating on an informed basis: Integrative methodological framework
for monitoring the digital divide 227

Authors 257

Leopoldina Fortunati, Jane Vincent, Julian Gebhardt, Andraž Petrovčič and Olga Vershinskaya

Introduction: Approaching the notion of humans as e-actors interacting with Broadband Society

This book aims to focus on the specific dimensions experienced by people in their participation in the broadband society[1]. It explores the concept of the e-actor and discusses the different ways in which individuals, social groups, institutions, operators, manufacturers, policy makers, designers and others in socio-technical systems contribute to human interaction in broadband society. The recent diffusion and implementation of new generations of information and communication technologies (ICTs) and of new trajectories of uses create the need to capture more profoundly the characteristics of contemporary users. The term 'e-actors' underlines the idea that human beings are playing a more powerful role in experiencing and developing ICTs (Vershinskaya 2003; Raycheva 2008; Höflich & Gebhardt 2005). The notion of humans as e-actors refers to the confluence of many different roles and situations that people experiment with in their relationships with ICTs. These different roles include those of user, citizen, customer, consumer, co-designer, and stakeholder, but also those of drop-out and non-user (Gebhardt et al. 2010). The book covers four theoretical and empirical areas of research: Firstly the conceptual perspectives of e-actors; second the emergence of new forms of agency, subjectivity, and mediated interpersonal communication; third the exploration of the broadband society through the eyes of the e-actors; and fourthly the shaping policies and regulations in the broadband society.

The first area debates and challenges different notions and theories of ICTs users and their activities within the broadband society. The chapters presented in this section deal with the development and promotion of an anthropocentric perspective in developing broadband ICTs. In other words how such ICT development should be user-pulled rather than technology-pushed (see also Fortunati 2005). Any such anthropocentric perspective requires one to reflect upon the end user as often being the main target, beneficiary and 'raison d'être' of ICTs (Gebhardt 2008).

---

1 The term "broadband society" is used to characterise a society in which information has not only become the primary economic commodity, as it defines the information society, but where people's instant access to a wide variety of modes of information and communication (made up of sounds, images, texts) is becoming a common and – to a certain extent, in certain contexts – indispensable feature of their everyday lives.

The second area focuses on how agency, subjectivity, and identity change in relation to the new trajectories of mediated interpersonal communication as it reconfigures itself in the broadband society. This is very significant for issues of social cohesion and re-organization of social structures as well as for different types of relationship. In addition, the ways in which e-actors are managing their electronic identities and the way they can access ICTs in public and private spaces are seen as crucial for the integration of these new media in the everyday life. This section concludes by mapping the emerging research areas relevant for understanding uses and relationships with ICTs (e.g. cognitive complexity, group decision making, ethical aspects, etc).

The third area addresses issues concerning the electronic portraits of individuals that are raised by the concept of humans as e-actors. What type of electronic information do people deal with, how do they exchange and make use of it in order to present themselves in and through digital devices? What are the styles and modalities of self-presentation in the new technological environment where the analogue and digital technologies converge, diverge, or complement each other? Given that humans use, produce, store, disseminate and retrieve information, these particular processes have been studied in order to understand the production of the electronic self and its social consequences in the digital broadband society.

The fourth area analyses how the broadband society deals with policy and regulation issues regarding new media, and it addresses the conceptual and methodological aspects of the digital divides (Vehovar et al. 2005; Raycheva 2006) that are being produced by new forms of social exclusion, and how these might be overcome. Reflections on the political understanding of ICT scenarios in which e-actors are involved are presented in this section in their various guises as users, consumers, customers, citizens, innovators (Haddon et al. 2005), as well as observations on the current agenda of the debates on the policy about the broadband society.

Overview of Book

The book addresses the issue of e–actors interacting with broadband society by bringing together the work of a group of international researchers who are part of a global community researching ICTs and peoples' participation in the broadband society. The chapters of this book represent a very important moment of dialogue and discussion within this community, as it emerged from an international conference organized by the European network COST 298 in Moscow in May 2007. This conference was unique in the degree to which it was an international and interdisciplinary event focusing on a broad theme – Participation in the Broadband

Society – and in the ways it tried to produce a true conceptual integration of different approaches and disciplines. The subject matter was explored from the perspective of various disciplines, including social sciences, computer and engineering sciences and design. The common focus of attention were the processes in which personal and social relationships, devices, signs and communication practices and its users are mutually shaped.

This book presents the discourses of leading scholars in the form of originally published material that was presented in the "Humans as e-actors" strand of the Moscow conference.[2] Within this context, the chapters that are presented and discussed here include the development of theoretical frameworks as well as current research projects and different methodological approaches in analysing people's practices and experiences of ICT use and their social implications. The present aim is to build upon the dialogues and networks that have grown from this conference, crossing and integrating many different cultures as well as conceptual perspectives, with a view to developing a new theoretical position on humans as e-actors to emerge from this collective work.

Central Themes

The empirical research and conceptual work presented here is organised according to the four areas outlined above. The chapters in the four sections of this book shall contribute to a better understanding of the notion of humans as e-actors by examining their interaction with, and the outcomes of their participation in, the broadband society The concept of the e-actor is introduced with the purpose of helping scholars, policy makers, designers, etc. to adequately conceptualise both the complex and crucial role these e–actors play in the broadband society and the enormous potentialities they represent for the development of the knowledge society. In the following sections we outline the various chapters that comprise the aforementioned research areas.

Theme 1: Conceptual perspectives on e-actors interacting with broadband society

In this section the authors discuss theories on humans as e-actors based on empirical findings gathered from studies carried out in Italy, Austria and Slovenia. Key

---

[2] Other chapters presented in the same strand are collected in the book "Experiencing Broadband Society", edited by Gebhardt et al. (2010).

to these chapters is the emphasis on the way that the interdependence between humans and those features of ICTs that are meant to empower them as social actors is shaping their different forms of participation in the broadband society. The increasingly high penetration of broadband technologies and services leads to unforeseen tensions between users and technologies, and these aspects are explored in the first four chapters, with emphasis on the pull from the user rather than the push from the technology.

Leopoldina Fortunati in her chapter *From ICT User to Broadband e-Actor* looks at the new way in which the traditional ICT user could and should be conceptualised. Her chapter aims at analysing the shift that is now occurring from ICT users to broadband e-actors, who are 'augmented' users. The research question explored in this chapter is: In the face of the broadband penetration, are the roles and identities of e-actors changing? If so, in which direction and with which modalities? The thesis that Fortunati discusses here is that broadband actors are subjected to increasing social control, social negotiation, and power conflict. The use of the new media is configured more and more, not as a generic activity, but as a veritable labour, which is immaterial labour. In this conceptual framework, ICT use should be understood as a political domain, in which the control and dominion over people's everyday life will be confronted by a strong process of self-determination and valorisation by people themselves. Through broadband technologies, e-actors have accelerated and invigorated the process of acquisition of a new power by means of which they re-configure the world of information and communication on the basis of their subjectivity. The author tries to show that it is on the base of its intrinsic, political value that technology use is increasingly becoming a political domain in itself.

However, the elaboration of the concept of e-actors also may start from other points of view. *Gregor Petrič, Andraž Petrovčič and Vasja Vehovar*, in their chapter *Communication Technology Use as a Structuration Process: Exploring the Communicative Portraits of Active Users,* view the notion of the e-actors through the lens of the convergence of the usage of different ICTs. The authors advance the notion of an active user as a central notion for improving the current understanding of how shared ways of achieving communication goals through various interpersonal communication channels are related to people's socio-cultural embeddedness, and their active role in experiencing the social consequences of (un)mediated modes of communication. This chapter argues that the active use of communication devices should be conceptualised as a structuration process within which users' awareness of media interactional affordances, expectations of media-related social outcomes, their innovative appropriation and deliberative selection of media are embedded in socio-cultural arrangements and socio-technical systems that set the framework of evolving usage patterns. In order to identify such patterns, a research project was conducted by Petrič, Petrovčič and Vehovar on a representative sample of the Slovenian population which yielded four groups of users of communication technologies with distinctive communicative patterns and socio-cultural features. These groups were identified by means of a cluster analysis and labelled as techno-ascetics, cyber-communicators, techno-rationalists and mobile-traditionalists. The chapter concludes with an analysis that details the social consequences of emerging communicative portraits, demonstrating how these four clusters differ in the size of their social support networks and levels of social participation associated with the specific configuration of their use of communication technologies.

The reflection on e-actors might also start from the vantage point of design, as in the third chapter by *Hajo Greif, Oana Mitrea, and Matthias Werner,* entitled *Usability vs. Functionality? Mobile Broadband Technologies and User Agency.* Their argument starts from the observation that, while providers hope that mobile broadband devices and applications will define the future of telecommunications, and while the dissemination of devices is increasing, real-world usage does not live up to the promise of the widespread adoption of newly available services. One possible reason for this discrepancy is that both the convergence of functions and applications in mobile broadband devices, and the everyday uses intended by their designers, imply trade-offs between the norm of usability and the ease and intuitiveness of accessing the functions of a device with the norm of functionality and the control over, and in-depth access to the functions of a device. The working hypothesis in this chapter is that the way in which these possible trade-offs are addressed in design depends on developers' preconceptions of users' expectations and actions. On the background of a discussion of the notion of user agency, the two norms mentioned are critically compared by Greif, Mitrea, and Werner, with respect to their value as conceptual tools for analysing the case in question. In a second step, three different design strategies towards the issue of functionality and usability, and the notions of user agency they imply, are matched against findings from a recent Austria-wide survey on the usage of advanced mobile applications. Users' perceived needs and adoption strategies appear to suggest that different degrees of specialisation and adaptability of functions should be available. Finally they question the seeming disjunction between the norms of usability and functionality.

The discussion on the notion of e-actors is further advanced by examining strategic issues pertaining to the understanding of the evolution of socio-technical systems in contemporary societies. It is within this framework that *Giuseppina Pellegrino* in her chapter *Mediated Bodies in saturated environments: Participation as co-construction* deals with the issue of e-actors, elaborating further on powerful features of current socio-technical systems such as the notion of a saturated environment. The chapter starts from the observation that social interaction is increasingly intertwined with technological artefacts. Such a process changes the characteristics, definitions and expectations related to participation. According to Pellegrino, the issue of participation can be interpreted in the light of the convergence of bodies and environments under the mark of an increasing dependence on technology. ICTs in particular mediate and contextualise both interaction and action towards other actors/systems. Indeed, social actors are more and more required to use complex socio-technical systems in their everyday life. As users, they are required to manage new contexts and especially the crucial combination of mobility and proximity in order to be skilled social actors and competent communicators. Pellegrino argues that to participate means to become engaged in patterns of co-construction involving mobile, convergent and saturated communication environments. This implies that participation is linked to access to infrastructures and resources of connectivity, even if this does not automatically guarantee a better connection between actors and environments. Connection and connectivity cannot be considered the same: saturated environments represent both catalysts and constraints to effective participation by users.

In summary, this first section proposes to move from the established concept of ICT users to the new notion of e-actors, in order to face the new usage dimensions of information and communication technologies in the broadband society. It therefore tries to include and to elaborate upon several research traditions. Firstly, it encompasses the user-centred research approach, which has produced a considerable number of studies on the domestication (see, for example, Silverstone & Hirsch 1992) and social representation of ICTs (Contarello et al. 2008; Fortunati & Manganelli 2008). Secondly, this section draws on science and technology studies and social informatics inquiries into the role of users in technology development (Bijker & Law 1992; Oudshoorn & Pinch 2003, 2008; Kling et al. 2005), and thirdly, it refers to media studies which have proposed the notion of the "active" user (Livingstone 1999; Blumler & Katz 1974). These different traditions contribute to identifying the main aspects of what makes up the e-actor: the integration of identities, the integration of ICT uses, the role of human beings in design and the contradictions posed to them by technologically saturated environments. The chapters address different new technologies, although the main focus is on mobile technologies.

Theme 2: Emerging Interpersonal Communications among e-actors

Understanding the communications, inner feelings and subjectivities of e-actors and how they integrate their personal ICTs into the intimacy of their everyday lives is at the heart of this section. It provides new insights to the definition of e-acting and social interaction in public and private media spaces. This is echoed for example in the emergence of new forms of agency (see also Greif et al. in Theme 2 of this volume), subjectivity, and mediated communication as new integral parts of the developing broadband society.[3] Such issues are becoming increasingly important for all users of ICTs. All three chapters in this section examine the social fabrication of mediated communication in the context of both new digital media and devices which e-actors are using to establish and maintain their social contacts and relationships.

The first chapter in this section, *Mobile Culture and Subjectivities: an Example of the Shared Agency between People and Technology* by *Amparo Lasen,* discusses the role of mobile culture in the transformation and production of e-actors as subjects, understood here as changing and heterogeneous entities both in a material and an informational sense. The author shows how mobile phones play an ever more important role in the constitution of subjects and subjectivity (in what she terms "subjectivation processes"), both in the shaping of the self and how the self is perceived by others. This phenomenon is reflected in the example of how subjectivity is related to the processes of co-production between people and their technological devices. Lasen's analysis is situated within contemporary theoretical approaches that challenge the views on the status of objects and subjects. In this regard she discusses a recent contribution of the Italian philosopher Giorgio Agamben (2007), who revisits Foucault's concept of the *dispositif* and its role in answering such questions. Her theoretical analysis is illustrated by an example drawn from ethnographic and qualitative research about mobile phone use among couples and how this leads to a trans-personalisation of this device. Since the personalisation of mobile phones is a way of individuation, self-representation and recognition, it not only concerns the single individual but also other entities, such as couples and other dyadic relationships. At the same time it reveals how mobile phone usage is embedded in specific power relationships, reciprocal control and monitoring and how this, in turn, helps to identify and consolidate the relationships of the couples investigated.

While Lasen's chapter deals with the subjectivity of e-actors and the way in which they expand it in situated contexts which are emerging in the use of broadband devices such as third generation mobile phones, *Julian Gebhardt* draws on the social, inter-subjective, pre-conditions of these processes. The title of his chapter is *Alfred Schütz and the media: The intersubjective constitution of mediated interpersonal communication in everyday life.* The theoretical foundation

---

3 For more-in-depth analyses of the concept of human agency in the context of ICTs by authors present in this volume see Lasen (2005, 2007); Lobet-Maris et al. (2008); Lobet-Maris and de Terwangne (2007); Lobet-Maris and Gallez (2009); Grandjean et al. (2008), Greif et al. (2008).

employed here is the socio-phenomenological concept of the "life-world" as it has been developed by Alfred Schütz (1967) and subsequently elaborated by Alfred Schütz and Thomas Luckmann (2003). These studies inquire into one of the most fundamental problems of any kind of social (inter-)actions and consequently of any types of mediated communicative activities: the problem of inter-subjectivity, which may be described here as the problem of co-ordinating reciprocal communicative actions, i.e. such activities in which at least two people are orientated towards each other. Gebhardt first draws on Schütz' notion of communicative actions as "expressive", "meaningful" and "goal-directed" acts of working. Based on Schütz' concept of everyday life tools as meaningfully constituted artefacts, he then conceptualises communication technologies as communicative working tools, whose interpersonal usage is based on reciprocal orientations, rules and mutually established social practices. In conclusion, the author shows how Schütz's work can help us to better understand the constitutional processes of using and adopting communication tools not only in their technological, but also, and especially, in their social and inter-subjective dimensions.

The analysis of e-actor's agency in this section is completed by the reflections of *Jane Vincent* entitled *Me and My Mobile.* The author discusses the question of how the identity of e-actors and their emotions, mediated by new technologically advanced devices like the mobile phone, are closely related to the issue of situated (inter-) subjectivity (Vincent & Fortunati 2009). Based on various empirical research projects conducted by the author and the Digital World Research Centre (DWRC) since 2003, Vincent's chapter examines the ways in which people have appropriated the mobile phone into their everyday lives. From the theoretical perspectives of the interactionists Goffman and Hochschild, the author explores people's use of the mobile phone as a means of maintaining social interaction between family, close friends and work colleagues. In contrast to situated individual-to-individual connectivities, Vincent's research also highlights the me-to-machine relationship that many people, particularly children, have now established with their mobile phones. This is exemplified by the ways in which they explore and play with these devices, their technological capabilities and their convergence with other broadband technologies. The author goes on to describe how such individual-to-individual and me-to-machine relationships have given rise to a specific emotional discord – both with regard to users' emotions to all that the mobile phone enables and with regard to the demands that are placed upon them, such as to be available at any time and to respond in ways that are different from how they feel at a certain point in time.

In summary, this second section is devoted to developing a deeper understanding of e-actors and agency as it becomes visible in the relationship between people and technology. Drawing on the lessons from such theorists as Foucault and

Agamben, Schütz and Luckmann, and Goffman and Hochschild, the discourse developed here deepens the understanding of both the limitations and the opportunities that the use of the new ICTs and, in particular, the mobile phone implies in the domain of (inter-)subjectivity, personal identity and emotion in situated contexts across different cultures in countries such as Spain, Germany and the UK.

Theme 3: Exploring the notion of e-actors within the information society

This third section presents current research from Russia that examines the very notion of the emergence of the e-actor from within the information society. Starting from the concept of the noosphere, theoretical perspectives are developed that offer a new approach to scrutinising the ways in which humans are interacting with ICTs, thereby combining the biological, technological and social realms. This section is composed of only two chapters, both offering a significant contribution to this still under-exposed debate.

This section is opened by *Vsevolod M. Zherebin*, who presents a chapter entitled *Information Society as the Law-governed Result of the Evolution of Information*. Zherebin approaches the phenomenon of information from the perspective of the process of its evolution, from its emergence to the modern social forms and formation of the information society. The thesis Zherebin vindicates here is that information, contrary to the accepted conception, is not an attribute of matter in general, but appears only together with the animate life and represents an inherent part of it. The process of the evolution of information and current concepts of it are considered from the point of view of the general information theory. Since the evolution of information, the development of concepts relative to it and the growth of informational possibilities in society are interconnected, these are examined in parallel fashion in this text. Discussing the natural history of information, the author takes an untypical stance towards an evergreen topic that has inspired a huge corpus of scholarly literature, but that, in its capacity of being the regulator principle of the post-modern societies, has also inspired policy-makers, professionals, consultants, public administration managers and many other social actors, as the literature especially at European level shows.

The second chapter *Theoretical Approach to the Concept of Humans as e-Actors* is authored by *Olga Vershinskaya* and reflects on the fact that e-activity is one of the possible perspectives with which to study change in the relationships between society and ICT. For her, the emergence of the notion of e-actors is a direct consequence of the fact that the dissemination, adoption, and appropriation of the new technologies have posed the problem of overcoming the fragmented images of digital users and their portraits. According to Vershinskaya, there is still no holistic theory that studies users and the social influence of ICT dissemination. She thus discusses the formation of an action-oriented multidisciplinary approach to research, based on other theories and approaches: semiotics, noosphere theory, the theory of sociocultural reproduction, domestication theory, and the social portrait genre. From Vershinskaya's point of view, there are different options "to draw" e-portraits: an e-portrait may be a part of the social portrait, or a list of e-activities performed, or a type of user and so on. The pragmatic value of e-portraits is also considered, since they can be used in many different ways: to monitor the transformation of the service sector, to measure social differentiation and stratification, or to study lifestyles and other issues involved in measuring users' behaviour at quantitative and qualitative levels. It is also argued that the importance of cultural, informational, and psychological aspects of the social dynamics is growing. In this framework, e-activity is analysed as part of the computer culture in general.

This third section offers a fascinating glimpse at the current debate on e-actors that takes place in Russia, where next to rural areas still characterised by a limited diffusion of the internet, urban areas are conversely 'informatised' at an astonishing pace. Under these specific conditions, a specific school and type of scholarship evolves with regard to the diffusion of computers and information systems – a scholarship whose importance to research on issues regarding the information society and e-actors should not be underestimated.

Theme 4: E-actors in the institutional context: Policies and regulations from e-actors' point of view

The broadband society is dependent on a variety of European policies and regulatory regimes to ensure ubiquitous and equitable opportunities for e-actors to participate in this society. These policies and regimes are of course the fruit of sometimes hard negotiation processes between the different e-actors involved, understood as users, consumers, citizens and so on. Unfortunately, the results of these negotiation processes are not always in e-actors' favour. Therefore it is necessary to analyse the legislation corpus very carefully and be aware of its relevance to people's lives. Policies may be attentive to people's different needs and social and economic situations, so as to enable them to contribute to the arenas in which they participate. However, as it turns out, policies may also be found to be pushed by industry's interests, either forcing people to live according to new standards, thus in a certain sense designing the modes and ways in which they and next user generations may participate, perhaps leaving out large sectors of the population, or failing to achieve any goal in the first place. In particular, the following chapters examine the ways in which researchers from some Central- and South-Eastern

European countries – namely Bulgaria, Greece, and Slovenia – address some of these issues, with special attention to the transition to digital television service as well as to the means of avoiding digital divides within European societies.

This last section is opened by *Lilia Raycheva's* chapter *Television: The Good, The Bad and the Unexpected Challenges of ICT. In this chapter, the author argues that t*he rapid progress of the information and communication technologies has intensified the issue of their influence on the global/regional/national/local communication environment. According to Raycheva, that progress stimulates the mass media to pass from an extensive into an intensive phase of development. A market-driven technological convergence is taking place across the media industries. The combination of terrestrial broadcasts with cable and satellite TV to the households in EU countries is expected to grow into a strongly competitive environment, allowing for programmes, technical and financial backups. The type and pace of these changes may present challenges to both EU citizens and the European governments, policy-makers, regulators and broadcasters. Digital compression of the spectrum has already given access – continues Raycheva – to the widest possible range of programmes by offering many commercial and public services. Broadband TV which enhances the possibility of the individual selection of programs, is now on the agenda. Meaning that, television actively moves towards diversification of the services on offer. It is becoming a service itself. At the end of her chapter, Raycheva examines the contemporary European audiovisual policy developments, particularly in terms of the digital switchover. The transformation processes that involve television are a sensitive issue, given that TV use is embedded in the everyday life of millions of people, and given that the transformations illustrated by Raycheva are more technologically driven than user pulled.

Not only television, but also the Internet is a key component of the everyday life of millions of people. This issue is addressed by *Panayiota Tsatsou* in her chapter *Digital Divides in Greece: The Role of Culture and Regulation in Internet Adoption. Implications for the European Information Society.* Tsatsou looks at digital divides in Greece from a cultural and regulatory perspective, with the aim of making a contribution to the theme of the participative role of e-actors. The chapter first draws on the scholarly literature on digital divides as a phenomenon embedded into a social context in which various other kinds of social exclusion take place as well. Then, the author argues that the existence of digital divides in Greece is to a significant extent a result of both culture and regulation. Based on the discussion of various policy schools and paradigms, and highlighting the tensions between the ideology of the information society and the power of the market, the state and resistant citizens, Tsatsou's chapter opens up a discussion about how we should view the relationship between culture and regulation in the Greek case. In particular, she poses the question: 'Can culture be regulated in the Greek information society?' Moreover, data and evidence concerning the Greek puzzle of digital exclusion allow Tsatsou to apply her general socio-cultural and regulatory account to a case-study that is of particular interest, since it entails significant implications for future research on digital divides in Europe.

The issue of digital divide, analysed by Tsatsou in a particular case study – Greece – is also taken up by another author, *Vesna Dolničar*, in her chapter *Regulating on an informed basis: Integrative methodological framework for monitoring the digital divide*. The author points out that, when analysing the dynamics of the digital divide, the answer to the seemingly simple question 'Is the digital divide increasing, decreasing, or is it constant?' is not straightforward. Dolničar introduces an integral methodological tool that could comprehensively address this question.

This new methodological approach is based on the assumption that none of the established statistical measures – absolute measures, relative measures and S-time-distance are considered here – truly communicates the essence of a certain digital divide phenomenon. Even the simultaneous reporting of all three measures is insufficient. In order to monitor and interpret the dynamics of the digital divide it is thus very important to explicitly take into account future scenarios of ICT diffusion among the subjects observed (e.g. population segments, countries…). Dolničar has developed these scenarios within the broad framework of the diffusion theory of innovation (Rogers, 1962/2003), but with a critical view on two of its implicit assumptions that amount to a deterministic conceptualisation of the diffusion process: the form of the diffusion function and the anticipated level of the final penetration rate. The author argues that the proper measure – that could be easily integrated in the process of benchmarking, monitoring and regulating the basic digital divide on the national and international levels – can only be provided if we anticipate and take into account the full distribution functions of the compared subjects or population segments and the location of the subject at a certain point.

In this fourth and last section, European policies and regulation regimes as well as methodological issues related to measuring the different forms of digital divides are thoroughly discussed. The two socio-technical systems under consideration here are television and the computer/internet. At the European level, humans as e-actors are confronted with policy-makers, regulators and media groups engaged in dismantling the socio-technical system of the analogue television that had been co-constructed by all these social actors. Raycheva's chapter illustrates very well what is at stake in the transformation of television nowadays. With regard to the Internet, Tsatsou introduces the culture variable into the debate on the digital divide, and thus introduces an anthropological sensitivity into that debate that had been missing so far. To that same debate, Dolničar contributes a new methodological instrument designed to properly measure the otherwise elusive dynamics of the digital divide. The major common concern of these three final chapters is not to conceptually cope with the observation that humans are lagging behind the technological developments, for the latter's sheer rapidity and market-drive. The chapters also point towards solutions to this problem. In the face of the developments provided by scientific and technical research, more attention should be paid to the public's best interests by policy-makers, NGOs, and consumer associations.

Conclusions

Putting together and integrating different disciplinary perspectives, this book presents highly differentiated cross-cultural approaches and theoretical elaborations that are helpful in thoroughly understanding the relationships between humans and technology, the social meanings and functions of the new media, and the development of socio-technical systems.

One main focus of this book is on what one may call the "normalisation" of ICT uses in everyday practice, or the fact that uses become embedded in personal and social rituals and daily rhythms (Licoppe & Smoreda 2006). We refer, in contrast to studies emphasising innovative uses, to the way in which devices, applications, functions and services are embedded in the socio-technical environment as a part of the normative system that frames users' everyday social practices and which also embodies bottom-up innovations. This topic is approached from two different angles: Firstly, the ways in which 'active' users select and adapt new technologies, and, secondly, the ways in which social actors do not recognize a need for using these technologies, either ignoring or being indifferent towards them, or even actively choosing not to use them. These dimensions serve to reveal key aspects of the agency of what we define as e-actors. We analyse different technologies, and explore the notion of e-actors on different levels of activity, as well as we pinpoint the idea that access to some technology, in itself, does not warrant some actors' general agency as social beings.

Another main outcome of this book is that the notion of the e-actor in the broadband society cannot be defined simply in relation to a device, service or application, or to a certain set thereof, but only in its relation to the socio-technical systems that are co-constructed by e-actors and in turn shape them in the course of adoption, diffusion, appropriation, domestication and use. Thus it is evident both from the empirical findings and from the theoretical reflections presented here that one should look at a technology not merely as a material object, but as a node in a network of social relationships and human-machine relationships that mutually shape each other. This allows us to look at the e-actor as a multidimensional and multidisciplinary notion that comprises all the negotiations, the tensions and the conflicts in which actors are involved. For example, this notion of e-actors might make policy-makers aware of the fact that they should not confound the concept of the Internet user with that of the citizen because they are not equivalent. Moreover, it enables us to look at the power relationships between different e-actors and to understand how the dynamics between them are evolving.

In terms of future directions of research, the conceptual framework introduced in this volume may serve firstly as a starting point for further empirical research that can be used for developing new applications, devices, features and so on. In this way, our approach may be of service to the development of new technologies or services in both private and public sectors. A second task for future research would be to connect the dimensions of agency developed here with existing theoretical discussions and research in the fields of Science and Technology Studies, technology policy, and technology assessment, from which either side may benefit. Lastly, while the chapters in this book already indicate the complexity and the importance of the phenomenon of the e-actor, a further step is required in developing new methodological approaches to that phenomenon, helping to identify and describe its properties and implications more accurately both on an institutional and interpersonal level.

References

Agamben G. Qu'est-ce qu'un dispositif? Paris: Rivages (2007)

Bijker W. E., Law J. Shaping Technology/Building Society. Studies in Sociotechnical Change Cambridge, MA: MIT Press (1992)

Blumler J. G., Katz E. The Uses of Mass Communications: Current Perspectives on Gratifications Research. Annual Reviews of Communication Research Volume III Beverly Hills: Sage (1974)

Contarello A., Fortunati L., Gomez Fernandez P., Mante-Meijer E., Versinskaya O., Volovici D. 'ICTs and the human body: An empirical study in five countries' eds. Loos E. Haddon L., Mante-Meijer E. The Social Dynamics of Information and Communication Technology Aldershot, Hants: Ashgate (2008) pp. 25-38

Fortunati L. 'The Mobile Phone as Technological Artefact' eds. Glotz P., Bertschi S., Locke C. Thumb Culture: The Meaning of Mobile Phones for Society. Bielefeld: Transcript Verlag (2005) pp. 149-160

Fortunati L., Manganelli A. 'The social representations of Telecommunications' Personal and Ubiquitous Computers 12 (2008) pp. 421-431

Gebhardt J. Telekommunikatives Handeln im Alltag. Eine sozialphänomenologische Analyse interpersonaler Medienkommunikation Wiesbaden: VS Verlag (2008)

Gebhardt J., Greif H., Raycheva L., Lobet-Maris C., Lasen A. Experiencing Broadband Society Berlin: Peter Lang (2010)

Grandjean N., Cornélis M., Lobet-Maris C. 'Sociological and Ethical Issues in Facial Recognition Systems: Exploring the Possibilities for Improved Critical Assessments of Technologies?' ISM 2008 Proceedings Conference held in Berkeley (15-17th December 2008)

Greif H., Mitrea O., Werner M. 'Information und technologische Handlungsfähigkeit' eds. Greif H., Mitrea O., Werner M. Information und Gesellschaft. Technologien einer sozialen Beziehung Wiesbaden: VS Research (2008) pp. 49-71

Haddon L., Mante E., Sapio B., Kommonen K-H, Fortunati L., Kant A. eds. Everyday Innovators: Researching the Role of Users in Shaping ICTs Dordrecht: Springer (2005)

Höflich J., Gebhardt J. eds. Mobile Kommunikation. Perspektiven und Forschungsfelder Frankfurt am Main: Peter Lang (2005)

Kling R., Rosenbaum H., Sawyer S. Understanding and Communicating Social Informatics: A Framework for Studying and Teaching the Human Contexts of Information and Communications Technologies Medford, NJ: Information Today (2005)

Lasen A. Understanding Mobile Phone Users and Usages Newbury: Vodafone R&D Group (2005)

Lasen A. 'Mobile culture and Subjectivities. Mobile Phone Trans-Personalisation in Young Couples' Proceedings Towards a Philosophy of Telecommunications Convergence Budapest (2007) pp. 175-180 URL: http://www.socialscience.t-mobile.hu/2007/prepro2007_szin.pdf (accessed September 2007)

Licoppe C., Smoreda Z. 'Rhythms and Ties: Towards Pragmatics of Technologically Mediated Sociability' eds. Kraut R., Brynin M., Kiesler S. Computers, Phones, and the Internet: Domesticating Information Technology Oxford: Oxford University Press (2006) pp. 296-313

Livingstone S. 'New media, new audiences?' *New media and society* 1 (1999) pp. 59-66

Lobet-Maris C., de Terwangne C. 'De l'E-gouvernement au gouvernement en reseau: questions pour la recherche en sciences sociales' Terminal 99-100 (2007) pp. 11-26

Lobet-Maris C., Cornelis M., Grandjean N. 'Human Sciences and System Design From Expertise to Situated Deliberation' ACM/ICMI 2008 Proceedings Conference held in Chania, Greece (20-22nd October 2008)

Lobet-Maris C., Gallez S. 'Les pratiques numériques des jeunes, catalyseurs d'une certaine fracture générationnelle' eds. Burnay N., Klein A. Figures contemporaines de la transmission Namur: Presses Universitaires de Namur (2009)

Oudshoorn N. E. J., Pinch T. J. How Users Matter: The Co-Construction of Technologies and Users Cambridge: MIT Press (2003)

Oudshoorn N. E. J., 'Pinch T. User-Technology Relationships: Some Recent Developments' eds. E.J. Hackett, O. Amsterdamska, M. Linch, J. Wajcman The Handbook of Science and Technology Studies Cambridge, MA: MIT Press (2008) pp. 541-566

Raycheva L. 'Tracing the Digital Switchover in Enlarged Europe' eds. Urban A., Sapio B., Turk T. Digital Television Revisited. COST Action 298 Participation in the Broadband Society (2008)

Raycheva L. 'Television in Bulgaria on the Net' ed. Leandros N. The Impact of Internet on the Mass Media in Europe Bury St. Edmunds, Suffolk, UK and USA: Abramis (2006) pp. 503-513

Rogers E. The Diffusion of Innovations New York: Free Pess (1962; 5th edition 2003)

Schütz A. The Phenomenology of the Social World Evanston, IL: Northwestern University Press (1967)

Schütz A., Luckmann T. Strukturen der Lebenswelt Frankfurt: Suhrkamp (2003)

Silverstone R., Hirsch E. eds. Consuming Technologies: Media and Information in Domestic Spaces London: Routledge (1992)

Vehovar V., Sicherl P., Hüsing T., Dolničar V. Methodological Challenges of Digital Divide Measurements The Information Society 22 (2005) pp. 279–290

Vershinskaya O. 'Information and Communication Technology in Russian Families' ed. Katz J. Machines that Become Us. The Social Context of Technology New Brunswick, New Jersey: Transaction Publishers (2003) pp.117-126

Vincent J., Fortunati L. eds. Electronic Emotion. The Mediation of Emotion via Information and Communication Technologies. Oxford: Peter Lang (2009)

Theme I:
Conceptual perspectives on e-actors interacting with broadband society

Leopoldina Fortunati

From ICT User to Broadband e-Actor

Evolution of user labels and the relationship between people and technical systems

After dedicating a long period of time to empirical research on the social use of information and communication technologies ('ICTs') on the European level (Actions COST[1] 248, 269, A20, 298), it is time to 'rethink technology' (Maldonado 2007). In fact, at this point in time the gap between the technique experienced as discourse and the technique experienced as situated and local practices in which the conditions of existence of artefacts and socio-technical systems are realised risks expanding (Langenegger 1990). To bridge the distance between discourse and practices, I will try to operate a liaison between 'mediated and 'immediate' techniques by outlining the concept of e-actors. I wish to do this not by discussing important theories such as the actor-network theory ('ANT') (Callon & Latour 1991) that have brought this definition, but by expanding this definition in the light of the many different research projects conducted on the use of ICTs at the social level.

The need to reflect upon e-actors is also imposed by the present circumstance that on one hand sees the strong, innovative development of the ICT sector and, on the other, the prudent appropriation of broadband in Europe. In addition to increasing e-actors' capability (Haddon et al. 2005; Mante-Meijer et al. 2008), the diffusion of broadband technology has underlined a process of continuous transformation both of the re-configuration of ICTs and the role of e-actors (Fortunati & Manganelli 2003). As to the latter aspect, users' roles have become increasingly complex in the information society because of users' empowerment towards and through technology (Williams et al. 2005). As to the former aspect, the reconfiguration of ICTs has been enabled by design variants introduced by users and by a convergence between media. The recent development of convergence is made possible by the diffusion of broadband and at the same time gives meaning to this diffusion. Media convergence is enriching the single device to the extent that one talks of 'augmented' media. The evolution of complex relations between users and

---

1 COST stands for European Co-operation in the field of Scientific and Technical Research. Cost 248 was a network studying 'The Future European Telecommunications User', COST 269 'User Aspects of ICTs', COST A20 'The Impact of Internet on the Mass Media in Europe' and COST 298 'Participation in the Broadband Society'.

technical systems can be found in the continuum of user labels which are related to different social realities, contexts and practices: user, non-user[2], drop-out, buyer, customer, consumer, co-designer, stakeholder (Gaglio 2004; Glotz et al. 2005). I propose that we summarise all these labels in the one word 'e-actor' and that we see them as all converging in individuals.

In the last few decades, the literature on the various labels with which people are defined in terms of their social relations with technology has become very rich. First, it has followed a logic that is inherent to the debate. In the scientific community, the problem of a more precise definition of users has trailed behind for a long time. Technological innovation has become so rapid that the scientific community has had difficulty keeping up with and arriving at a shared and comprehensive definition of users. In fact, an incredible amount of disciplines and sub-disciplines study the use of technology. Hard and social disciplines (such as engineering, information science, designers, sociology, psychology, anthropology, economics and so on) are working on this topic from different perspectives. Second, the literature on users' labels has expanded over time because the European Commission has bet on the social im-plementation of communication and information technologies. The European Commission was and is in fact still convinced that technological innovation is the only added value that can help win in the area of global competition. So the notion of ICT users is quite present on the European political agenda. In European reports such as the Bangemann Report (1994) or the e-Europe programme (1999), users are mentioned as a key factor of implementation of the information society. In the following eEurope report users are mentioned in a very generic way (Bastelaer 2005). In general, despite the important investments the European Commission has made in ICTs the way in which users are mentioned in the political and normative body of reports, agreements and so on is often firmly connected with stereotypes, and the approach to technology is marked by strong technological determinism and rhetoric (Nye 2007). Third, specific literature on users' labels has grown because it was necessary to produce a most comprehensive understanding and description of ICT users in order to follow the evolution of the relationship between people and technical systems. Here I do not refer to evolution of the relationship between users and technical systems as depicted in the famous book *Diffusion of Innovations* by Rogers (1962), where users are defined as innovators, early adopters, early majority, late majority and laggards. Despite the suc-

---

2 It might be surprising to find 'non-user' and 'drop-out' in the continuum of user labels, but they are the other faces of users (Oudshoorn & Pinch 2008). Socio-technical systems are also designed by those who are not interested or cannot afford some new technology and by those who have been disappointed by it because their numerosity matters in suggesting the dimension of investments and the social and institutional attention paid to the technology in question.

cess of his book, Rogers's analysis has been criticised for its representation of the diffusion of technologies and for its concept of users as being overly simplified. According to such criticism, users are only seen by Rogers as a dependent variable of the technological process. Instead, when considering a phenomenon such as the diffusion of innovations we should take into account that probably the main factor influencing innovation adoption rates is that users often adapt technology to their own needs or desires, transforming the technological artefact in both its purpose and meaning and, ultimately, when passing from the early adopters to the majority, also in it design. In this case, the device very probably radically changes both its material and immaterial characteristics (Ling 2008).

Starting from this framework, the evolution of the relationship between people and technical systems should be understood more as a negotiation between users and a series of actors such as operators, manufacturers, authorities, and so on. This process of negotiation is so active in shaping the quality of the relationship in itself that we talk of the co-construction of society and technology within a power relationship (Oudshoorn & Pinch 2003). Through technical systems a continuous re-engineering of society is assured. The social organisation and order are re-shaped, social and individual discipline are implemented at a higher level, social and individual control are developed, command over labour is obtained in a more sophisticated way and becomes command over everyday life, including the domestic sphere. Like many other power relations, this relationship often changes following the modalities of negotiation between two parties. But, in this case, the negotiation is more complex and also ambiguous because it is implicit. In fact, there is not an official and formal negotiation between peoples and telecoms, public bodies, government representatives and so on. Two aspects are problematic in this implicit negotiation: the fact that the labour supplied by e-actors is immaterial labour and the fact that this labour is supplied in the domestic sphere where there are no official contracts or negotiating procedures. This negotiation between society and technology is based on a reciprocal understanding and knowledge on the part of the subjects involved, which is not easy. This makes all stages of the negotiation very uncertain. Over the last few decades, for several reasons this power relationship between society and technology has changed. It has changed in correspondence with the empowerment of people towards telecoms and manufacturers. Secondly, this relationship has changed as a reflection of the empowerment of people towards and through technology. Finally, it has changed as a consequence of the political counterpower of e-actors. What is at issue here is some kind of dialectic relationship. The power relation has shifted in favour of e-actors although the technological re-engineering of society has been marked by making e-actors' labour more immaterial, informal and domestic. These three points will now be discussed in the following three sections.

Empowerment of people towards telecoms and manufacturers

Let us start this section by briefly illustrating the progressive change of people's role in their relationship with telecoms and manufacturers. We can distinguish at least four stages of people's empowerment. The first stage describes the rise of people's empowerment towards telecoms and corresponds to the shift from the notion of user to that of customer (who is a user who should also be seen as a buyer and consumer[3]). The second stage represents the shift from customer to consumer/co-designer, the third from co-designer to stakeholder while, fourthly, from stakeholder to intercultural e-actor.

In the first stage, European telecoms were companies with absolute monopoly. Communi-cative technologies were only run by these great state companies that had an obligation to guarantee a service – telephony – which by being an element of infrastructure was considered an essential good for citizens. But irrespective of whether such a company was successful or not in guaranteeing these services to citizens, it continued to be in charge of this duty. Even when it was unsuccessful, it was very reluctant to become customer-oriented. It is no surprise that the transition from the concept of user to that of customer (in practice, a customer is a user with many more rights) was neither easy nor painless. The privatisation of these companies aimed to push the transition from user to customer and emerged for several reasons such as the hope to reduce the costs of the service by developing free competition in the sector, the strong protests of users[4], and the need to change the testing procedures of technological products. The user was in fact involved in the process only after a new product was launched on the market. But it was always too late to go back and put things right if the customer did not like it or complained about defects. The shift from the concept of user to that of customer was due both to the need to oppose a technocratic vision of users and to overcome a conception of user that was basically derived from the design of the machine. Those who used a machine were simply qualified and defined by using it and thus became users. In the scientific debate, this emphasis on use relegated all the other aspects such as, for example, purchase and consumption, into a kind of twilight zone. But in this stage users, who in their everyday practices play an unpredictable role in the success or failure of a product, began to be seen as an independent variable of

---

3   Customers have traditionally been seen in their capacity to buy rather than in their role of consumers. Little attention has been paid to the different modalities and styles of consumption in daily life or the symbolic and affective meaning attributed by consumers to technological objects.
4   See, for example, http://www.repubblica.it/online/tecnologie/telefonini/reazioni/reazioni.html or http://clarence.dada.net/contents/tecnologia/speciali/smstrike/

the consumption process[5]. Consequently, the debate on users benefited from the complexity of the general debate on consumption. An important notion in consumption studies was its conception as an activity (De Certeau 1992; Baudrillard 1968). This conception was expanded when the consumption of values of use, that is products, including technologies, began to be seen as labour directly involved in the production and reproduction of individuals themselves (Fortunati 1981). I allude here to the domestic sphere where individuals reconstruct their energies after work and where new generations of workers are produced. In this stage, some studies focused on the criteria for buying a mobile phone (Gaglio 2005), on its life span, on one's feelings when it is left behind somewhere or lost and so on (Vincent 2006).

In the second stage, that is the shift from customer to co-designer, consumption research has been further implemented in studies inspired by the theories of Bijiker & Law (1992) regarding the role of the user in the re-elaboration of technologies and their design. These studies represent another point of contact and mutual fertilisation for research on ICT. This approach has also helped view ICT consumption as an important element of the co-construction of these devices by users/customers (Akrich 1992). After this merging, the literature, for example, on the mobile phone began to register various aspects of that co-construction (Fortunati 2005). Without doubt, this line of inquiry on the use/consumption/co-construction of the mobile phone has made it possible to observe how the process of the development of design concepts and implementation of technologies does not stop in front of factory walls but is immersed in a much wider circuit, which also includes the domestic sphere. The domestic sphere is the main place where the mobile is bought or rejected, tried out in its available or possible functions, in its more or less latent meanings and in its hierarchy of performances, that depends on the trajectories of the use of services and functions that one is able to activate in his/her technological artefact. In other words, it is here that the mobile phone and its functions are adjusted and implemented, that is, redesigned. The customer becomes a co-protagonist of the production process of this technology, contributing to all steps in the design of the technological aspects and services (du Gay et al. 1997). Ideas, imagination, suggestions from customers shape the new products that increasingly correspond to customers' tastes, needs and desires. In this process, customers become true co-designers since they work side by side with designers, guiding and influencing the entire design process. From this stage onward socio-technical systems become more organically the result of the co-construction

---

5   It might be worth recalling with this proposal that Raymond Williams began to look at television audiences as an independent variable of the consumption process in 1974 (Williams 1974).

by operators, manufacturers and users/customers/consumers. This innovation process from below can be more easily understood if we point out what technology is. As Nye argues (2007, 9), 'technology is not a working out or an application of scientific principles. For most of human history, technology came first; theory came along later and tried to make sense of practical results'. In other words, technology has arisen from problems posed to technicians in their experience of the behaviour of matters and mechanisms. However, given the ownership and use of ICTs by the mass population, it is not surprising that ideas and suggestions that re-design a technology come from users. However, the process of co-construction does not only produce the transformation of the customer into a co-designer since at the same time it also produces the transformation of the other member of the relationship: telecoms. In fact, while it is often stressed how the subjectivity of the user/customer is able to transfigure the technological device during its use, it has already been underlined how users' behaviours have forced telecoms to reconfigure themselves, especially the organisation of their research work, planning and marketing (Fortunati & Manganelli, 2003). Slowly but surely, customers' power has been recognised not only as mere spending power but also as the power of influencing the market, whereby customers/users, potential co-designers, have acquired new importance within the process as a whole.

In the third stage, which corresponds to the shift from co-designer to stakeholder, the progressive opening of the citadel of engineers to women has been one of the basic premises that has enabled the development of a technology that tries to include the taste, desires and needs of the various social stakeholders involved in the purchase, use, consumption and co-design of ICT. Here I am referring to the feminisation of research teams. Historically, telecoms have always been places chiefly inhabited by male engineers on the basis of the equation 'technology = engineer = male'. Yet the 1990s showed that inside the telecoms there was a need to create broader areas of competence in order to cope with a market that was increasingly articulated and conscious of its power. Women with different competencies – psychologists, communication scientists, designers – started to be taken on, mainly at the levels of research and planning. The acceptance of women's judgement, needs and requirements has changed the debate, rhetoric, routine and organisational structure of research work (see the recent shift from the concept of usability to that of acceptability) inside telecoms. However, it was not easy for the women in the teams to express their womanhood and oppose the inertia produced by the long-standing male-dominated culture. Yet in this period mobile phone design was, for example, subjected to a feminisation process. It became more attractive, assumed more round forms and colours and corresponded more with a woman's body. In fact, the keys became higher to allow women with long fingernails to easily use the keyboards. This process of reshaping technology makes the technological artefact more flexible to users' needs. During this third stage, the appropriation of technology by people has been developed significantly. This means that the amount of freedom obtained through technology use is becoming much more than was foreseen at the beginning. In a certain sense, the ability of powerful institutions/actors to dominate people's lives through technology is encountering its limits, although the big problem which remains is the expropriation of stakeholders' creativity. By involving stakeholders in their capacity as co-designers all around the world and in many respects, telecoms and operators have begun to act as expropriators of the design work supplied by stakeholders. This phenomenon is well known in the economic sphere and also involves other productive sectors such as fashion. Here, as Ted Polhemus (1994) critically remarked, this expropriation is organised on a grand scale. Street style hunters go around the world observing how people dress and what are the ideas, solutions, combinations and styles that people are introducing into their daily lives. Of course, this process is a rationalisation process in which the capitalistic dominion is less effective but still continues to act. Instead, it is reinforced by this mass creativity since it does not remunerate this creative labour at all. This is the dialectic relationship I alluded to before: co-designer empowerment goes hand in hand with the expropriation of its very fruits by the forces of capitalism (Manovich 2001).

The last shift is from stakeholders to intercultural e-actors. I use the e-actors notion upon proposing the following definition: e-actors is a term that defines social actors viewed under the lens of their relationship with ICT. They are individuals who are analysed through the lens of their social relationship with ICT. They possess a common cognitive reference framework with regard to technology, have a specific competence, share common attitudes and social practices, and share common language and communication resources. They are therefore recognisable as stable social figures since they form a kind of wholeness for others and for themselves, and they share a common life world and a common social reality (Stockinger 2006). Moreover, they are much more intercultural than in the past since globalisation makes it inevitable to articulate on a world scale the process of negotiation between societies and ICT. Globalisation tries, and sometimes succeeds, to impose relevant changes in the organisation of everyday life as well as in the production and diffusion of communicative technologies. However, global societies (Law et al. 2006) negotiate the quantity and quality of the technology they need and/or which they in any case accept to metabolise. In particular, the negotiation of ICTs has always been quite complicated. But, in turn, their penetration has made it possible to have, or has made more acceptable, social processes of the outmost relevance such as diasporas, migrations, short-range mobility, transformation of the organisation of labour in a post-Fordist manner, the formation of virtual communities of various kinds, and the maintenance of a continuity between the world of labour and the domestic sphere. If we focus our attention on the globalisation process through the lens of the mobile phone, a contradiction immediately emerges: current Western policies on ICTs are elaborated and developed by taking into consideration the knowledge of Western e-actors, their attitudes, opinions and behaviour as a starting point, rather than users on a global level, but the reference frames and resources are not the same for everyone, everywhere. For example, at the beginning of diffusion of the mobile phone this kind of device was the fruit of a lengthy negotiating process between operators/telcos (telecoms) and Western societies (states, political bodies, users and so on). However, Western operators/ manufacturers have aimed to be involved and are effectively more and more involved in serving foreign markets. Clearly, the technological products that are exported come from, and belong to, Western culture. Nevertheless, these cultural objects undergo a re-semanticisation process by local users. The limited possibility of pre-defining communication and in-formation technologies becomes, in this sense, an advantage. As Longo (1999-2000) argues, ICTs display some analogy with mammals, even humans: they are born flexible and incomplete and develop in the course of time through an interaction with users and learning by users. The adaptation and transformation of the meaning of ICTs might generate new processes of creation of services and functions, which should be understood and implemented by operators and manufacturers. At this point, ICTs should be so flexible in their design as to be able to incorporate mentalities of different people and cultures. In order for this to happen, it is necessary for users from different cultures to be embodied in the design process (intercultural design) to guarantee that ICT platforms, which are in principle interpretively flexible, can be really inclusive. Manufacturers and operators cannot continue to think locally and to simultaneously want to serve the world. Further, in the West we have already made a transition from ICT mass production to the diversification of communicative devices, follow-ing a strong tendency present in all productive sectors: to pass from a mass market via a segmented one to a 'dedicated' market. It is well known that the globalisation of markets is never a slavish imitation of the first phase of diffusion processes when it takes place in a second stage and in countries different from those in which the diffusion first appeared. Innovations and novelties have a power of attraction that is so strong as to make the recapitulation of any historical process impracticable. Global development proceeds in leaps and bounds and has no difficulty leaping immediately to the most recent innovation. The themes that continue to be discussed in the background of this debate are manifold: what might be a good strategy for the intercultural e-actor? What is a good answer to the needs of e-actors in both China and Latin America etc.? When operators/manufacturers have to deal with billions of customers, is it feasible to continue the diversification of products and services or would a return to mass production be better? In order to make production on a global scale successful, in perspective the intercultural design of devices will become increasingly important. ICTs of the future must include global e-actors by integrating different cultures, languages, ethnic groups, genders and generations. This is a very strong point not only for democratising the use of these technologies but also for democratising democracies all over the world.

Empowerment of people towards and through technology in the broadband society

ICT use as a creative process

In broadband socio-technical systems the complex identity of e-actors is marked by different characteristics and behaviours to be found not only among, but also within, e-actors. These different labels are faces of the same coin but their co-existence might give birth to tensions since, beyond the different user labels, there might be different personal, social and cultural trajectories. The historical reconstruction of the formation of e-actors might also have a heuristic function. As Östlund (2001) writes, as citizens e-actors claim civil rights, as customers they have the power to drive the market, as users they perform different levels of capability in the practices of the use of ICTs and are co-designers of technologies and innovators, as consumers they are productive actors and so on. But what is important, too, is that the complex fabric of e-actors is also defined by the area of non-users and drop-outs. These two categories are often misunderstood as information socio-technical systems have the ability to represent themselves as absolutely desirable by every individual. So, a person who is not part of the most advanced socio-technical systems is often seen as someone who would like to possess and access a technology but who, for educational or economic or other reasons, cannot fulfil his/her desire. Consequently, he/she is seen as a socially excluded person. But this area should also be seen as a place of social resistance expressed by people who at a certain point reject or are not interested in some technology. These people, too, contribute to shaping the notion of e-actors, even if in negative terms, as they should be considered as a critical awareness of socio-technical systems and evident proof of their limits. They are generally constituted by the weakest part of a population, but not always; areas of technological rejection might also include very affluent people.

Unfortunately, telecoms and manufactures, but also public bodies such as the European Commission, never worked seriously on non-users and drop-outs (Katz & Rice 2002; Nosengo 2003), although it is well known that contemporary cultural production is not separable from processes and products of technique (Maldonado 2007, 208). Public bodies pretend to make a lot of commitments to non-users and drop-outs, but then they leave the very non-users and drop-outs to the mercy of social learning. Within this logic, operators are condemned to never really understand the technological device because they are not interested in understanding the reasons and motives for its non-use and/or abandonment. Research on users and drop-outs could yield precious information on the limits and defects of a technology and so allow its improvement. In particular, telecoms' indifference to non-users and drop-outs derives from the fact that they are still more conditioned by the pressure of their R&D departments than by e-actors' indications. The non-consideration of the non-user and drop-out has had the serious consequence that failed technologies have also never been studied *a posteriori*. Technological failures are rapidly metabolised without allowing for any reflection or debate. The impression is that inside telecoms the regulation of innovation is often lacking. The logic of the market and the ever narrower profit margins exert pressure to configure technological devices only for immediate buyers.

All the souls of e-actors have a different 'nature' since the same individual is sometimes a buyer, always a customer, with a certain frequency a user and a consumer etc. But the important point is that all these figures in everyday life merge in the individual. So if one wants to study the process and try to analyse all of these figures as they are, that is in a united sense, we should look at the individual as a whole and talk of the individual. And when moving over to talk of the individual we must take into account that he/she is a fantastic convergence agency as he/she generally uses more than one medium (Petrič et al., in this volume). This means that not only in the individual do multiple uses converge, but also that the individual elaborates strategies to optimise these uses (Greif et al., in this volume). In everyday life e-actors incorporate not only different roles and functions but also merge things belonging to very different universes. In reality, individuals mix food and technology, fashion and environment, urbanity and mobility and so on (Miller 1987). In other words, they mix different dimensions, conditions and contexts of everyday life in a situation in which they own the means of immaterial (re-)production. This ownership might enhance their possibility of access to information, knowledge, entertainment and self-valorisation. Certainly, intellective machines (as Maldonado 2007 calls them) such as radio, TV, computer, the Internet, telephone and mobile phone are still 'primitive' given that, apart from the telephone/mobile and the computer/Internet, they have been unidirectional or only modestly interactive. Moreover, they might be used for surveillance and control at a social level and so they could imply negative consequences. But one cannot underestimate their potentiality because of them becoming more sophisticated with digitalisation. Especially in the last decade there has been a spread of technological appropriation from the bottom through multiple processes of social learning. In this appropriation, at the beginning the world of work was the drawing power but immediately after that the family and, in general, the domestic sphere became another true drawing power. In the practices of the use of these technologies, the social learning process (Williams et al. 2005) also emerged as an innovation process on the part of e-actors (Haddon et al. 2005).

In the seven years since Britt Östlund's paper entitled *Users Wear Different Hats* (2001), the discussion, which resumes the content of e-actors' identity and its theoretical and disciplinary premises, has as mentioned above become related to the diffusion and adoption of broadband technology. This technology allows us to overcome the fragmentation of the different aspects of users' identities and to produce a better recomposition and integration of them all. To give just a few examples, broadband allows users to easily become content and service producers, to communicate among themselves and organise their networks also as political subjects, to acquire more information and control on new products and their costs as consumers, and so on. From the analysis of the four stages I depicted in the two previous sections it emerges that the growing empowerment of people towards technology has radically changed the relationship between society and technology. First, having ownership of these instruments of information, communication and knowledge gives great power to people. Second, people can have devices that correspond better to their needs and desires. As buyers they are able to drive the market much more than in the past; as co-designers, e-actors contribute to realising what they would like to have. And where they are not in a position to define the technological artefact beforehand, they transform it during its use to the extent that, and this is the third point, e-actors now are stronger than before in the relationship with telecoms, manufacturers, and authorities. This process has become deeper with the diffusion of broadband technology since broadband allows even greater complexity of e-actors. In fact, during the shift to the broadband society the e-actor has also become a citizen, member of audiences, creative worker, learner, teacher, photographer, journalist, director and so on. But all of these roles cannot remain fragmented images of e-actors in a situation in which the principle of fusion, which is the prevailing logic of globalisation (Featherstone et al. 1995), puts various technologies together in the one device. Broadband technology, with its high levels of convergence between sound, image and written words, makes the negotiation between them even more crucial (Haddon 2004). The convergence of technologies urges us to look at e-actors from a more holistic viewpoint and to put all the different pieces of the mosaic together. The task of recuperating a conceptual integration among the different approaches and to produce a new transdisciplinary reflection on the identity of ICT users is also increasingly required for the scientific debate (Östlund 2001). We are confronted with a new scenario in which several limitations of the previous socio-technical systems have been overcome.

ICT use and body gestures.

One of the limitations of the past is that, with traditional media, the consumption of cultural and technological objects was mainly mediated by the eye and the ear. The satisfaction of these two senses does not require the movement of an individual's body. In addition, in effect the consumption of the old media mainly amounted to immobile reception. Yet immobile reception does not mean passive consumption since consumption always presupposes co-operative work on the part of the consumer. At least, it implies the work of interpretation and elaboration of meanings but, in reality, users also are used to attribute to their reception other aims than those designed inside the cultural object. It may be sufficient to think of a newspaper that is used to package things or clean windows, or of a TV being used as a baby-sitter or a sleeping pill and so on.

But the gestures involved in the use of the old media were reduced to a minimum. The immobility of the body during consumption was a relevant aspect of the social discipline and command undergone by users/audiences. People had the right to relax, amuse and inform on the condition that they were immobile. The old media imposed a rigid time discipline, restricted movements inside the house and the loss of decision-making in the sense they effectively took away agency from people, dictating the rules for more efficient living. Freedom of communication and expression and the production of knowledge were paid for with a new slavery: the near immobility of the body in many moments of everyday life (Williams 1974). People lost control over movement of their own bodies. This immobility gives a precise idea of users' impotence. With broadband the involvement of the body is greater since the new media (computer/Internet, digital television etc.) allow at least micro gestures. The mobile phone is even better because it allows micro gestures while people are moving. These micro gestures are a great difference. The control lost by people regarding their movement in this case is perhaps partially coming back into their hands. Empowerment on the physical level, by virtue of the mobility and interactivity of the technologies in question, *may* open up opportunities for empowerment in a wider, social and political sense.

Beyond the talk of thumb culture (Glotz et al. 2005), I would argue that the hand (and arm) is beginning to assume a more lively role in the broadband society. Certainly, the technology of writing has always been closely linked with the human body, especially the hand/arm. However, compared to handwriting the bodily skills required are *different* (developing a 'quick' and 'sure' thumb rather than good and quick handwriting) involving a loss of traditional writing skills. Further, the increased propensity to write shown by contemporary e-actors has probably been sustained by both an increasing general education level and the possibility supplied by ICTs to exercise this skill in an unusual way. Yet using more parts of the body is meaningful with regard to another quality of consumption/use. Simmel (1985, 230) is particularly relevant here. He argues that gesture is not simply a movement of the body but is an expression of the soul. With their gestures human beings spiritually appropriate part of the space. Use of the new media requires many more gestures than when using the old media, even if they are micro gestures whose trajectories are short since they occur in a micro space. Think, for example, of use of the mouse or the bodily gestures needed to take a mobile phone from a pocket or bag. In the case of computers, these micro gestures occur while the body is generally sitting down but in the case of mobiles, they can occur while the body is in motion on the macro scale.

In general, use of the new media occurs near to hand. The involvement of the hand brings with it a reduction of the distance between the e-actor and ICTs in consumption. Now these technologies are continuously touched in their use, while the cultural product is continuously modified. The screen of the computer is much closer to the user than a television screen or a radio, and the mobile phone is even present on the surface of the human body. The degree of activity and involvement of users/audiences is much higher. It is obvious that e-actors, touching the device continuously during its use, are more able to produce modifications of these technologies. Of course, the morphology of the new media is also different from the old media. While in the traditional development of ICTs indication devices tended towards hypertrophy and control devices towards atrophy, the computer and the mobile phone present an opposite logic. Their interface largely consists of keys, which are controlling devices. Today the degree of command and control over the device's functioning has increased greatly (Fortunati 2005). Users' command over the machine is continuous and very detailed and carried out through the hand and fingers. In a certain sense, although it only allows limited command over the television the remote control also responds to the same logic of power of control over the machine. Invented by Adler in 1956, the remote control has significantly supported the consumption of TV. It is not by chance that some mobile phones can also work as remote controls. In reality, an important reason for the convergence between these two technologies might obviously be found in the 'rapture' of power, which both of them endow to their users. This rapture of power, with all the pleasure that it implies, goes some way towards explaining the huge popularity of these devices. It emerges from this analysis how clearly the use of the hand is connected to power. Further, on a symbolic level the hand in effect expresses the idea of labour, as well as that of potency and dominion (Chevalier & Gheerbrant 1987).

Self-valorising conduct in the new media.

Thus, with broadband technologies e-actors acquire more structural power (although this major expressive and intellectual power is paid for by e-actors in terms of eyestrain, tendonitis, back and neck problems and so on – see Tenner 1997). The reduction of distance implies, first, a bigger degree of psychic and affective intimacy between e-actors and technology. The mobile phone is the most intimate device since it implies an even more intimate relationship with the bodies of e-actors. Second, this reduction of distance implies the possibility of overcoming some limitations of traditional mediated communication. The possibility to put images (as pictures and videos) alongside text allows users to bring the body back to the centre of mediated communication. This is exactly what Lieves Gies (2007) calls 're-embodiment'. Consequently, mediated communication opens more possibilities to add production and vision of images to reading, writing and hearing. If we agree that cinema is the art of the 20th century, this process of acquisition is in a certain sense a process of the aesthetic modernisation of electronic consumption. Third, the user is slowly also learning to be a producer. As Staudenmaier argues (1985), technology consists of tools and skills. Broadband technology is undergoing experimentation by e-actors as they develop many different skills. It is a slow process in which e-actors are learning, for example, how to take a picture or a video of an important event or how to write a news item. Virtual communities of interest testify how social learning related to the use of photography, video, film and TV is constructed collectively. The YouTube phenomenon is an example of the process of the development of mediated communication languages. Several videos collected at this website have allowed us to 'look' inside the realities of everyday life that were hitherto excluded from common knowledge and sensitivity. YouTube has become an unforeseen observatory of bullying in schools, for example. Obviously, the expressive ability is not homogeneous on a formal level but e-actors are experimenting with their performance in many directions. The reader who becomes a journalist or reporter, by capturing images of events that later receive media broadcast, has become a widespread phenomenon. We-journalism (Gillmor 2004) is a reality that is equally important, being able to build up counter-information about wars and conflicts or important events such as 9/11. As an important research carried out by Euro RSCG Magnet and Columbia University in

2005 showed, blogs of information have become an important source of news for journalists on the international level.[6]

The impotence and discipline of users/audiences in the consumption of the old media has been broken with the formation of e-actors. Today consumption implies the greater involvement of the e-actor. As Hjorth correctly observes, there is a rhetoric of prosumers from which it is suitable to stay away (Gebhardt et al 2009). But it is a matter of fact that e-actors have more communicative, social and political power than users/audiences of the traditional media. Yet this power remains quite limited and unused for the moment (Hindman 2008). Several scholars who have studied the new media have put great emphasis on interactivity and intertextuality (Petrič et. al., in this volume), although those who have empirically studied the practices related to this phenomenon have observed that these practices are still deficient in broadband-related cultural products such as online newspapers (Oblak 2005). Current interactivity allows only modest openings from below towards the world of e-participation.

The political counterpower of e-actors

The fact that these different figures (buyer, user, customer, consumer and so on) are increasingly finding a synthesis and a fusion in the same individuals who buy, use, re-create, consume, reject or are indifferent to a device has accelerated and strengthened the process of the acquisition of this new power by e-actors. Subjects who embody all these figures and roles are *potentially* 'political' subjects with strong power to re-configure the world of information and communication technology on the basis of their subjectivity. E-actors are individuals who act and supply *immaterial labour* (Lazzarato 1997; Arvidsson 2006) by putting their body in the front line (Fortunati et al. 2003; Katz 2003). The figure of e-actors can be elucidated by looking at the actor in the theatre. Actors doing their performance work at an immaterial level. The body is the main instrument with which actors work so in their performance actors perfectly embody the unity of mind and body (Negri 2006). Broadband ICT use is clearly a performance in which the body or the re-embodiment has begun to come back to the centre of the stage. The body is not only the main instrument with which actors work, but today it is a crucial, political terrain of struggle, resistance, creativity and self-determination. At a time when technologies are mediating the flux of immaterial labour this aspect is becoming ever more relevant. The intellectual aspects of daily life are re-organised through computer/Internet use in a sort of a super-societal subject (Longo 2003).

---

6   http://www.eurorscgpr.com/index.php?s=_thought (accessed January 2008).

In post-modernities the previous atomisation and isolation of these processes in private homes are now reorganised in a kind of virtual factory made up of social networks. Virtual communities make up an important connective tissue between a powerful thrust towards individuality and the increasingly weak sense of national societies. Yet mediated immaterial labour has a strong power of re-shaping information, communication and knowledge on the basis of people's initiatives. Talking of labour and power in fact means talking of social conflicts, collective negotiation and mass movements. This provides the link between the argument developed so far about physical empowerment and the dialectics between users, as e-actors, becoming more powerful while being subject to the forces of the global economy to which they creatively contribute. For this reason it is worth outlining the profound, political transformation that is now occurring as regards broadband e-actors. Broadband technologies are machines or applications that might enhance communication, information and knowledge, but also might support the power of self-determination of e-actors in the everyday life sphere. What kind of power do e-actors have? It is a communicative, cognitive, performative and innovating power. At the heart of their activities and engagement there are political issues and strategies such as determining the artefacts, re-configuring the world of information and communication on the basis of e-actors' subjectivity and opening up the discussion about the final aims of broadband and its social and political meaning. In conclusion, e-actors are becoming important political subjects who might potentially appropriate control over important parts of everyday life.

Conclusion

By analysing the evolution of user labels and the relationship between people and technical systems, I hope to have shown the process of people's empowerment both towards telecoms/manufacturers and towards and through technology in the broadband society, along with the potential for the development of a political counterpower of e-actors. The use of broadband technology should be considered within a political framework since it is a terrain of confrontation for the control and dominion on e-actors' everyday lives. This is the main conclusion of the analysis I have developed in this paper. In this new political frontier mass behaviour is acquiring an intrinsically political value, also in cases where actors do not talk expressively about politics. At the same time, it is very important to also take the complexity of e-actors on a methodological level into account since e-actors are users, consumers, producers although often mainly observers. Hence, researchers should be aware that the object of their observation is in turn an observer of the phenomena investigated. Further, research generally looks at some aspects of ICT use or even exclusively at the use of one information and communication technology. This is understandable since research must navigate within precise limits. But the discussion of the results should now also consider the whole picture and should be articulated in respect of the rich identity of e-actors in the broadband society.

References

Akrich M. 'The description of technological objects' eds. Bijker W. & Law J. Shaping technology/building society Cambridge: MIT Press (1992)

Arvidsson A. "Quality Singles': Internet Dating and the Work of Fantasy' New Media and Society 8 (2006) pp. 671-690

Bangemann M. et al. Europe and the Global Information Society, Recommendations to the Council Of Europe Brussels (1994)

Bastelear B. 'Assessment of the eEurope Initiative Regarding User Aspects of ICTs' ed. Fortunati L. e-Citizens in the arena of social and political communication. COST 269 Report (2005)

Baudrillard J. Le système des objets. Paris: Gallimard (1968)

Bijker W. E., Law J. Shaping Technology/Building Society. Studies in Sociotechnical Change Cambridge, MA: MIT Press (1992)

Callon M., Latour B. La Science telle qu'elle se fait Paris: La Découverte (1991)

Chevalier J., Gheerbrant A. Dizionario dei simboli vol. II Milano: Rizzoli (1987) pp. 61-66

De Certeau M. The Practice of Everyday Life Berkeley: University of California Press (1992)

du Gay P., Hall S., Janes L., Mackay H., Negus K. Doing Cultural Studies: The Story of the Sony Walkman London: Sage (1997)

eEurope: An Information Society for All. Brussels (1999) URL: http://europa.eu/scadplus/leg/en/lvb/l24221.htm (accessed May 2008)

Featherstone M., Lash S., Robertson R. eds.: Global Modernities London: Sage (1995)

Fortunati L. L'arcano della riproduzione. Venezia: Marsilio (1981) (English Trans. The Arcane of Reproduction. New York: Autonomedia (1995)

Fortunati L. 'The mobile phone as a technological artefact' eds. Glotz P., Berschi S., Locke C. Thumb Culture: The Meaning of Mobile Phones for Society Bielefeld: Transcript Verlag (2005)

Fortunati L., Katz J. E., Riccini R. Mediating the Human Body: Technology, Communication and Fashion Mahwah: Erlbaum (2003)

Fortunati L., Manganelli A. 'From the GSM to the UMTS: is it a Path Towards Women?' eds. MacKeogh C., Preston P.: Strategies of Inclusion: Gender in the

Information Society, vol. II: Experiences from private and voluntary sector initiatives Trondheim: Centre for Technology and Society (NTNU) (2003)

Gaglio G. ed. 'Nouvelles technologies et consommation' Consommation et sociétés 4 (2004) URL: http://www.consommations-societes.net/numero4/ (accessed May 2008)

Gaglio G. 'Are Ostentation and Distinction Relevant Concepts for Dealing with Materials Culture? Illustration through the Mobile Phone and Its Social Trajectory' ed. Kim S.D. When Mobiles Came. The Cultural and Social Impact of Mobile Communication Seoul: Communication Books (2005)

Gebhardt J., Greif H., Raycheva L., Lobet-Maris C., Lasen A. eds. Experiencing the Broadband Society Berlin: Peter Lang (2010)

Gies L. 'How Material Are Cyberbodies? Envisaging the Internet as a Medium of Re-embodiment' Paper presented at the conference 'The Good, the Bad, and the Unexpected. The User and the Future of Information and Communication Technologies' Moscow (2007)

Gillmor D. We the Media: Grassroots Journalism by the People for the People Sebastopol: O'Reilly (2004)

Glotz P., Berschi S., Locke C. eds. Thumb Culture. The Meaning of Mobile Phones for Society Bielefeld: Transcript Verlag (2005)

Greif H., Mitrea O., Werner M. 'Usability vs. Functionality? Mobile Broadband Technologies and User Agency' (in this volume)

Haddon L. Information and Communication Technologies in Everyday Life: A Concise Introduction and Research Guide London: Berg (2004)

Haddon L, Mante E., Sapio B., Kommonen K.-H., Fortunati L., Kant A. eds. Everyday Innovators: Researching the Role of Users in Shaping ICTs Dordrecht: Springer (2005)

Hindman M. The Myth of Digital Democracy. Princeton: Princeton University Press (2008)

Hjorth L. 'Beyond the Frame: The Place of Mobile and Immobile Media' (in this volume)

Katz J. Machines that Become Us New Brunswick: Transaction Publishers (2003)

Katz J., Rice R. eds. Social Consequences of Internet Use: Access, Involvement, and Interaction Cambridge, MA: MIT Press (2002)

Langenegger D. Gesamtdeutungen moderner Technik Würzburg: Königshausen & Neumann (1990)

Law P., Fortunati L., Yang S. eds. New Technologies in Global Societies Singapore: World Scientific Publisher (2006)

Lazzarato M. Lavoro immateriale [Immaterial labour] Verona: Ombre corte (1997)

Ling R. New Tech, New Ties. How Mobile Communication is Reshaping Social Cohesion Cambridge: MIT Press (2008)
Longo G.O. 'Mente e tecnologia' Pluriverso 4 (1999-2000) pp. 135-146 (2000)
Longo G.O. 'Lo scenario: uomo, tecnologia e conoscenza' eds. Apuzzo G.M., Araldi S., Barbieri Masini E. Uomo, tecnologia e territorio Trieste: Area Science Park (2003)
Maldonado T.: Memoria e conoscenza. Sulle sorti del sapere nella prospettiva digitale Milano: Feltrinelli (2007)
Manovich L. The Language of New Media Cambridge, Mass.: MIT Press (2001)
Mante-Meijer E., Haddon L., Loos E. eds. The Social Dynamics of Information and Communication Technology Aldershot: Ashgate (2008)
Miller D. Material Culture and Mass Consumption Oxford: Basil Blackwell (1987)
Negri A. Movimenti nell'impero: passaggi e paesaggi Milano: R. Cortina (2006)
Nosengo N. L'estinzione dei tecnosauri. Storie di tecnologie che non ce l'hanno fatta Milano: Sironi (2003)
Nye D. Technology Matters: Questions to live with. Cambridge: MIT (2007)
Oblak T. 'The Lack of Interactivity and Hypertextuality. Online Media' Gazette 67 (2005) pp. 87-106
Östlund B. 'Users Wear Different Hats'. COST 269 Report (2001)
Oudshoorn N. E. J., Pinch T. J. How Users Matter: The Co-Construction of Technologies and Users. Cambridge: MIT Press (2003)
Oudshoorn N., Pinch T. 'User-Technology Relationships: Some Recent Developments' eds. E. J. Hackett, Amsterdamska O., Linch M., Wajcman J. The Handbook of Science and Technology Studies. Cambridge, MA: MIT Press (2008)
Petrič G., Petrovčič A., Vehovar V. 'Communication technology use as a structuration process: Exploring the communicative portraits of active users' (in this volume)
Polhemus T. Street Style. London: Thames & Hudson (1994)
Rogers E.M. Diffusion of Innovations. New York: The Free Press (1962; 4th ed. 1995)
Simmel G. La moda e altri saggi di cultura filosofica. Milano: Longanesi (1985)
Staudenmaier J. M. Technology's Storytellers: Renewing the Human Fabric. Cambridge: MIT Press (1985)
Stockinger P. Semiotics of Culture and Intercultural Communication. Paris: ESCOM (2006) URL: http://www.chass.utoronto.ca/epc/srb/cyber/stockinger1.pdf (accessed December 2007)
Tenner E. Why Things Bite Back: Technology and the Revenge of Unintended Consequences. New York: Vintage (1997)

Vincent J. 'Emotional attachment and mobile phones'. Knowledge, Technology, and Policy 19 (2006) pp. 39-44
Williams R. *Television: Technology and Cultural Form.* London: Fontana (1974)
Williams R., Stewart J., Slack R. Social Learning in Technological Innovation. Cheltenham: Edward Elgar (2005)

Gregor Petrič, Andraž Petrovčič and Vasja Vehovar

Communication Technology Use as a Structuration Process: Exploring the Communicative Portraits of Active Users

Introduction

People's access to various forms of new information and communication technologies ('ICTs') – computers, the Internet, mobile phones – has recently become widespread in all developed countries. The further advancement of broadband transmission possibilities and telecommunication services is paving the way for a society in which contact between people is becoming literally independent of space and time constraints, giving them the opportunity to keep up their spatially dispersed social bonds and remotely arrange their everyday activities within various spheres of everyday life (Ling & Campbell 2008). The proliferation of portable ICTs (i.e., mobile phones, lightweight laptops, PDAs) and Internet-based communication services for interpersonal communication (i.e., email, instant messaging, social network sites) has given a strong impulse to a continuing trend of greater demand for ubiquitous, geographically extended, faster and more personalised social interaction.

The evolution of these ICTs for interpersonal communication is neither accidental nor technologically-driven, but seems to be part of a complex response to the intensification of a social reflexivity process which is accompanying structural changes in late modernity and which is implying a more vigorous attitude of human actors to the social system (Giddens 1990). The disembedding of the individual from social structures demands his/her active involvement in (re)building a resourceful social circle, which can be efficiently achieved through the use of the many ICTs available today. New technologies are thus increasingly becoming indispensable and inseparable elements of everyday life in a network and broadband society. However, since they do not enter everyday life as intruders, as external objects, but are appropriated by individuals in line with their socially, culturally and individually structured purposes and expected goals of communicating with others, they also imply the more active engagement of users when integrating them into the domain of social practices and cultural representations.[1]

---

[1] The domestication theory advanced by Silverstone and Haddon (Haddon 2003) is a seminal example of the research tradition that has focused on social, cultural and ideological reverberations of the creative involvement of users in relation to technology.

In this context we want to investigate the notion of *active use* that is implied in the research on humans as e-actors thoroughly addressed in this volume. The notion of the active use of communication devices originally appeared in the uses and gratification approach to mass media research (Blumler & Katz 1974). Although this tradition offers a rich insight into the ways communication devices can be used, we believe that its theoretical focus should be complemented with some sociological input in order to more comprehensively understand how and to what extent users have actively appropriated the interactive affordances of ICTs. We contend in this paper that the active use of technology can be conceptualised as a structuration process in which "actors draw upon the modalities of structuration in the reproduction of systems of interaction, by the same token reconstituting their structural properties" (Giddens 1984, 28-29). As Stillman (2006) observes, one modality of structuration includes patterns of communication in which human motives can be satisfied by the use of various technological devices. These uses are on one hand socially structured while, on the other, they are an objectified expression of the creative human agency of intervening in one's living social conditions.

On the theoretical level we shall explore various notions of an active user and propose a definition of the concept that encompasses various meanings of being active in terms of ICT use, simultaneously considering the user's embeddedness in technical, social and cultural contexts. The theoretical discussion is then narrowed down to three specific research questions which were analysed through comprehensive empirical research of users of interpersonal communication channels in Slovenia. An insight is offered into the communication patterns of a subpopulation of users who have simultaneous access to mobile phones, short text and multimedia messages (SMS/MMS), fixed telephones and the Internet. Also investigated is whether these people cluster together with regard to their choice and purposes of using these communication channels and if these expected clusters correspond to a specific socio-technical background, as well as experiencing similar social consequences with regard to their social support networks and social participation.

These questions concerning the interpenetration of various communication technologies with their users and surrounding social environments have already been comprehensively studied in various temporal and cultural contexts (e.g. Fischer 1992; Glotz et al. 2005; Katz & Aakhus 2002; Katz & Aspden 1997; Ling & Campbell 2008; Ling & Pedersen 2005; Pool de Sola 1977), offering detailed pictures of users' activity and innovativeness in shaping communication technologies. However, it is the suggestion of Papacharissi (2005) that these ICTs are leading to an increasingly complex and entwined media ecology which would be better apprehended with an integrative approach. Following this we seek in our empirical research to transcend particular medium-focused studies and analyse in a single representative study based on a nation-wide survey the general regularities that appear between the purposes of use of different communication devices, their socio-technical embeddedness and their social consequences. This study should not be understood as predicting technology uses and the related consequences, but rather as an exploratory study that aims to shed some light on the commingling of all of these elements.

E-merging media and socially embedded users

It is undisputable that people can be very creative with the ICTs available to them in today's broadband society. Many different communication goals can be achieved through various channels and the same device can be put to totally different, sometimes unimaginable uses. Especially within the uses and gratification approach (Blumler & Katz 1974) which has lately seen a revival of its success (Flanagin & Metzger 2001; Ruggiero 2000), rich empirical documentation can be found concerning the different purposes which are satisfied through the communication channels available today. It has already been documented that the fixed telephone can be used for social (i.e., to keep family contacts, achieve a permanent sense of security, overcome loneliness, show affection to others) and instrumental purposes, including making appointments, exchanging news, co-ordinating work matters and the like (Fischer 1992; Fortunati & Manganelli 1998; Noble 1987; Perse & Courtright 1993). With the arrival of the Internet and its services for interpersonal communication, many studies highlighted its suitability to achieve a variety of communication goals. Namely, research conducted in the organisational field (e.g. Trevino et al. 2000) assessed that email was successfully being adopted as a work-coordinative communication channel for accomplishing tasks. Functions like establishing and maintaining relationships, expressing affection and personal needs were ascribed quite early on to Internet communication services (Cummings et al. 2002; Papacharissi & Rubin 2000) and later often confirmed (e.g. Flanagin 2005; Wei & Lo 2006). The Internet has also opened up possibilities to satisfy a set of needs that result in socially problematic behaviour such as flaming, trolling (Burnett & Buerkle 2004) and harassment (Barak 2005). Later on, mobile-based communication (voice calls, SMS/MMS, video calls, mobile emails) also created many opportunities for social interaction that both compete with and complement other media. At the end of the last decade, young people changed the primary function of the mobile phone from its original role as a business tool to a communication device for relational use. Recently, studies investigating usage patterns of mobile phones confirmed that also among other age cohorts new communication practices have emerged that embrace not only functional (micro-coordinative) but also hyper-coordinative, expressive and symbolic purposes (Ishii 2006; Ling 2004; Ling & Yttri 2002; Thulin & Vilhelmson 2007; Wei & Lo 2006).

Social and communicative facets of active use

The notion of *active use* has several different, but not unrelated meanings. It was the uses and gratification approach (Blumler & Katz 1974) that initially addressed the idea of an active individual in relation to technology (in the form of mass or interpersonal communication media). This approach implies two interrelated meanings of active. First, people can be active in considering the various purposes that can be achieved through the same communication device and sometimes appropriate technology in an unprecedented way to find new ways of relating to others. This idea also appears in the context of the COST 298 action programme (2005) as a dimension of the notion of 'e-actor'. It is assumed that users are 'aware of the interactional affordances created by various communication channels' (Rettie 2007, 261). Users consider the totality of technologically extended forms of interpersonal communication and even take part in the creative, experimental discovery of new forms of communication. Goggin (2006) provides us with a nice example of how users change the behaviour patterns that are implied in a technological device: SMSs were conceived by designers as a possibility for technicians to send each other short written notes during work. The function was in no way advertised by mobile phone carriers yet it has been discovered and activated on a large scale by young people who have transformed SMS' original (technical) purpose of use and enthusiastically adopted it to flirt and ask their coevals to go on a date (Ling & Yttri 2002).

Second, the uses and gratification approach also considers the notion of being active as a process of selecting a media for interpersonal communication on the basis of expectations of which communication goals a certain medium can offer (Blumler & Katz 1974; Katz et al. 1973). Active in this context relates to the sheer process of selection in which a single communication device needs to be chosen in order to satisfy a certain communication goal. In contemporary, technologically saturated environments, people are obliged to be active in this process since they have to decide which technology to use according to their interactional affordances and communication contexts. In the contemporary media environment the use of communication devices is not limited to characteristic social contexts like it used to be. On the contrary, an individual is confronted in the same social context with many communication channels and none of them is any less accessible than another. If, for example, one wishes to arrange a meeting with a co-worker there are many options to choose: meet them in-person, call them by mobile phone, send them a text message, call them by fixed phone, write them an email, poke them on Facebook, Skype them etc.. With the new hybrid communication formats, multitasking devices and converging technologies that are expanding rather than reducing interactional diversity, such decision-demanding situations are becoming inseparable elements of everyday life. We can assume that media-related options and decisions have become reified in a stable pattern of daily cultural practices – the people and technologies that an individual interacts with, the activities they spend time on, and where that time is spent – that have turned into routines. Statistics and studies on the viability of new communication technologies (Baym et al. 2004; Flanagin 2005; Ishii 2006; Kim et al.2007; Thulin & Vilhelmson 2007) clearly show that the number of people with access to several ICTs has risen noticeably throughout the world.

Third, the term active also refers to an area that has been strongly emphasised in the context of the COST action 298 programme (2005, 8-9) but somewhat neglected in the uses and gratification perspective – the area of social consequences. This notion of active is closer to the sociological understanding of an active individual as it relates to individual intervention in the social world and changing the existing societal patterns and conditions of living (e.g., Touraine 1995). In this sense, active refers more to the consequences of some use than to the process of using a communication device. Many studies investigate the interconnection between the use of ICTs and social consequences, especially on the level of concepts like social capital (Best & Krueger 2006; Ellison et al. 2007; Kavanaugh & Patterson 2002), social cohesion (Boneva & Kraut 2002; Ling 2007) and social networks (Haythornthwaite 2002; Licoppe & Smoreda 2005; Kim et al. 2007). This is not surprising as ICTs have flooded the terrain of everyday life communication and started to play their role in such vital social processes as maintaining and establishing social relations, cultural patterns, identities and norms.

The above discussion sheds light on one, bottom-up part of the structuration process that concerns the use of interpersonal communication devices. To sum up, individuals find more or less creative ways of using interactive communication devices to intervene in the social conditions of their lives. Some of these social practices can consolidate and extend into a wider societal and cultural sphere where they represent normative and intersubjective frameworks upon which people draw while seeking to interpret and/or use these technologies. The structuration process also includes a top-down part which refers to the social embeddedness of media use, where social context, socio-cultural representations and technological characteristics set the perception limits and boundaries of the 'normal' use of a communication device. This part will be considered in the following section where we propose that an active user can only be comprehensively understood in the context of their social embeddedness.

The social embeddedness of active users

The social embeddedness of an active user has many different layers but we will only mention two of those we believe should be considered in the context of our empirical study. First, as Johnstone (1974) already claimed, people do not experience media as anonymous and isolated individuals but as members of social groups and also participants in the social and cultural milieu. The use and choice of media is thus related to the idiosyncrasies and intentions of a single user only within certain limits since it always reflects the relationship of communication partners as well as certain role behaviour patterns. Most notably, the practice of media usage is always a shared experience[2]; technologies for interpersonal communication can only be used together with other communication partners, and not everything that is compatible will be supported by others. The use of a communication device from this perspective accounts for the intersubjective dimensions or shared rules underlying the cultural practices of media usage. Various authors have already grasped this idea when asserting that the uses of communication devices more or less follow the 'normative images' (Lichtenstein & Rosenfeld 1984) or 'functional images' (Flanagin & Metzger 2001; Höflich & Gebhardt 2005) of media, which are collectively held notions of how communication devices should be used that stem from socio-cultural representations of the technology. We should then pursue Cockburn's (1992) suggestion that the adoption and usage of ICTs is socially conditioned as technology is deployed and used in environments with different social and cultural milieu which involve an array of diversified social relations.

Second, social embeddedness not only entails an immediate or wider sociocultural context of media use but also a whole socio-technical system (Kling et al. 2005) composed of people, human activities, social practices and contexts as well as technological artefacts, tools, devices and competencies for using them. In the modern technologically saturated environment we have to consider the fact already mentioned above – that the use of any particular communication device can only be comprehensively understood after considering (all) the other technological devices that were not used in a particular activity but could have been. The variety of ways in which various 'old' and 'new' media accommodate each other and co-exist in symbiotic forms (e.g. Bausinger 1984; Höflich & Gebhardt 2005) needs to be considered in any empirical study that aims to deal with the contemporary active user and attempts to paint their communicative portrait(s).

---

2   For an insightful discussion of how different types of technologically (electronically) extended human interaction are perceived as a shared experience through which communicators can be bonded to each other in the mediated environment, see Thompson (1995, 82-85).

The social embeddedness of media use has been most empirically researched from the perspectives of gender and age. Already in the original collection of articles on the uses and gratifications approach (Blumler & Katz 1974; Johnstone 1974) it was found that gratifications obtained from media can vary significantly between males and females as well as across different age cohorts. Later, Fischer (1992) provided extensive evidence that women have an 'affinity for the fixed phone' and he searched for the reasons for this in the social roles females play. These results were confirmed several times (Smoreda & Licoppe 2000; Fortunati & Manganelli 1998; Rakow 1992). Research on mobile phones and the Internet has provided rich, but generally similar conclusions. For example, Wei and Lo (2006) discovered that among Taiwanese students girls tended to use the mobile phone for expression and affection and to take advantage of the mobility of wireless technology, whereas boys appeared to use the mobile phone to seek or retrieve information. As regards the appropriation of short text messages, Ling (2004) pointed out how males use texting as a key tool for organising their daily meetings and activities, whilst females send longer and more complex messages expressing more emotions. The gendering of Internet use has comparable characteristics (Hoffman et al. 1996; Jackson et al. 2001). In a cross-cultural collection of scholarly research on the place of the Internet in everyday life (Wellman & Haythornthwaite 2002) it was argued that the diversity of symbolic realties and demographic factors, including education, income, social status and ethnicity, can mediate the social knowledge and cultural resources which set up people's digital lives and online social interactions. Likewise, substantial differences regarding the socio-cultural background and demographic-specific features of users have also been found while investigating various facets of mobile communication modalities (e.g. Glotz et al. 2005; Katz & Aakhus 2002; Ling & Pedersen 2005).

Research questions

Reflecting on the above discussion we can now offer a tentative definition of an active user which will guide our research questions: *An active user is an individual who has many devices available for interpersonal communication and is regularly involved in a decision-making routine in which they select devices in accordance with their socially conditioned perceptions, needs and beliefs regarding the interactional capabilities of these devices, and simultaneously face specific consequences in their experience of the socio-cultural milieu due to their active appropriation of technologies.*

An important goal is thus not only to understand how the available technological features of different communication devices have been appropriated by users, but also to address the question of how configurations of (un)mediated, ubiquitous, wireless and wired communication relationships are interrelated with users' socio-cultural features that go beyond gender- and age-based differences and are concerned with the entirety of factors that make up the whole socio-cultural milieu of technology use. In short, on the empirical level we want to investigate whether people cluster in distinct groups according to the purposes of their use of various communication devices. If so, we wish to explore the social embeddedness of these clusters and the social consequences of the patterns of use of communication devices. This leads to the three following research questions (RQ):

RQ1: Do people who have access to commonly used interpersonal communication channels (i.e., face-to-face, mobile phone voice call, SMS/MMS, fixed phone, and the Internet) cluster together in distinct groups according to their shared ways of achieving communication goals via various communication channels?

RQ2: If different clusters of active users are found, do these groups have specific socio-technical embeddedness in terms of their socio-demographic structure, detailed aspects of their technology use, and technological competencies?

RQ3: If different clusters of active users are found, do these groups experience specific social consequences in terms of social networks and social participation due to their use of various communication devices?

Research framework

To gain insights into empirical regularities on the level of social interactions over various communication channels, their social embeddedness and social consequences, we needed to closely follow the rules of quantitative methodology (Neumann 1997). First we conceptualised and operationalised all the necessary elements of research questions, framed a relevant random and representative national sample and then collected data via a survey questionnaire.

Measures

The communication goals people achieve with the use of various communication channels were conceptualised and measured with the help of some relevant studies from the uses and gratification tradition. This seems to be a justifiable step since in uses and gratification studies we can find a plethora of creative uses that communication devices are put to. The goal of our study was not to discover innovative uses that individuals put their communication devices to, but to measure to what extent they use the devices they possess for certain activities that were derived from existing uses and gratification studies. We decided to take the well-established purposes discovered in use of the Internet (Cummings et al. 2002; Flanagin 2005; Flanagin & Metzger 2001; Leung 2001; Papacharissi & Rubin 2000) – as a technology with many interpersonal interaction affordances – but which are, at the same time, relevant across all channels. The following concepts were included: work-related use for accomplishing organisational tasks at work or school, use for socialising, and expressive use[3]. Moreover, as recent uses and gratifications studies (Wei & Lo 2006; Leung & Wei 2000) have identified the prevalence of mobile phone use for logistical purposes (e.g. firming up the place and time for a meeting or asking a family member to stop by the store on their way home), which is referred to as micro-coordination (Ling & Yttri 2002), the respondents were also asked to report their usage of all communication channels for micro-coordinative purposes.

For example, the measurement instrument for four different mobile phone uses was the following:

a. Work-related use: 'How often do you use your mobile phone to talk about work, business and school matters (e.g., to arrange work meetings, to co-ordinate work/research/school projects, to send and retrieve news, to communicate with customers/schoolmates)?'[4]
b. Micro-coordinative use: 'How often do you use your mobile phone to talk about practical matters such as deciding on a place or time to meet, determining transportation to a given location, locating someone else in a busy park, or trying to co-ordinate arriving at a location at the same time?'
c. Use for socialising: 'How often do you use your mobile phone to chat, socialise and exchange messages that are a resource of companionship and social support (e.g., to keep in touch with family, friends or relatives, to keep up, support or revive personal relationships)?'
d. Expressive use: 'How often do you use your mobile phone to talk about personal-intimate matters that, for example, include the sharing of your personal emotions, desires or feelings?'

---

3 In adopting the term expressive use we are referring to the notion of dramaturgical action outlined by Habermas (1984) in his four-fold typology of social action. For Habermas, dramaturgical action stems from the individual's own subjective world, defined as the totality of subjective experiences, including *feelings*, *desires*, *needs*, to which the individual has, in relation to others, privileged access and about which he can deliberatively decide whether they will be *expressed* in the external (social) world.
4 For each statement the respondents answered on a five-point scale, where 1 = 'never' to 5 = 'daily'.

These statements were then repeated in the separated questionnaire modules for face-to-face communication and all the other mentioned communication technologies.

The social embeddedness of individuals' communication device usage was grasped by several socio-demographic characteristics (gender, age, education, labour status, family status, type of locality), technological environment (Internet use, broadband access in the household) and a computer literacy index[5].

The level of social consequences was comprehended with the size of the social support network[6] of an individual and participation in social events[7] as two quite common dimensions of social capital (Hall 1999; Putnam 2000).

Data collection and sample

The research reported here is built on a larger IKT-GOS 2005 survey which formed part of the Slovenian implementation of the Eurostat survey on information-communication technology. The IKT-GOS 2005 survey was thus conducted in the framework of the Eurostat guidelines for the 2005 European Union survey[8] and in line with the standards of the Statistical Office of the Republic of Slovenia. The survey's purpose was to measure the usage of personal computers, mobile phones and other information-communication technologies. The questionnaire was divided into two parts. In addition to the harmonised Eurostat part of the questionnaire, which was conducted in all 25 European Union member states, there were three

---

5   The computer literacy index was calculated by summing up the six item scores that measured the respondent's knowledge and ability to use computers and technology efficiently, including using a mouse to open programmes, copying or moving a file or folder, using copy or cut and paste tools, using basic arithmetic formulas in a spreadsheet, compressing files, and programming.
6   Specifically, we deal with ego-centred networks which consist of a focal actor (ego), a set of people who have ties to this actor (alters), and measurements of the ties between the actor and these other people. The questionnaire included a standard name-generator question on the provision of emotional social support for each respondent. The exact translated wording was as follows: 'Sometimes people discuss important personal matters with other people, for instance, when they argue with someone, have problems at work, and similar. Who do you discuss important personal matters with?' Respondents could name at most 12 intimate alters. The size of their network was calculated after name interpreters were administered and a list of alters was collected for each respondent.
7   Social participation was computed as an index of several indicators measuring the frequency of various social activities: visiting friends, family, participation in associations.
8   The raw data file is available at Eurostat's home page: http://epp.eurostat.cec.eu.int, Themes Science and Technology, Data Information Society Statistics.

20-minute modules that focused on the social aspects of the fixed telephone, mobile phone and the Internet.

The units were persons aged 10 to 74 and their households and the basis for the sampling frame was the Central Population Register (CRP). The face-to-face survey was carried out in April and May 2005. In the initial sample size of 2,000 units there were 1,827 eligible units and 1,422 people took part in the survey. The overall response rate of the survey was 77.8% (the number of completed interviews among all eligible units in the initial sample), which is a standard response rate in Slovenia when conducting face-to-face surveys on representative household samples.

Since only half of the interviewees who took part in the survey were supposed to answer all three modules in the second part of the questionnaire the final sample was 651 and this is treated as a representative sample of the general population of Slovenian adults. The socio-demographic structure is in line with the 2002 Slovenian census (Statistical Office of the Republic of Slovenia 2005). The sample consisted of 51% males and 49% females distributed across the following age ranges[9]: 10-25 (22%), 26-45 (31%) and 46-75 (47%), and with a mean age of 42.1 years (SD = 17.9). Of the 651 respondents in the sample, 16% had some university education, 45% of them were employed, 20% attended school (primary, secondary, university), almost one-half (49%) were married, and 35% lived in urban areas (towns with at least 10,000 inhabitants).

Out of the 651 respondents, 337 (52%) had used the Internet in the last three months, 556 (85%) were mobile phone users, 529 (81%) had already sent and received short text messages, and 582 (89%) had access to a fixed telephone in their household. However, only 299 (46%) of the 651 respondents reported using all four communication technologies at least occasionally, whereas 352 (54%) of the respondents gave an account of never using at least one of the four communication technologies. As we aimed to provide a comprehensive insight into the communication patterns of active users who are fully embedded in the broadband society, the remainder of our analyses are only based on data from those respondents who used all five communication channels at least occasionally.

---

9   Considering that teenagers are among the most early, intensive and creative adopters of ICTs and that recently carried out research has frequently focused on teenagers' use of Internet-based and mobile media (e.g. Lenhart et al. 2007; Ling & Yttri 2002; Thulin & Vilhelmson 2007), a subpopulation of teenagers aged 10-15 was enrolled in the study sample. Mindful of the methodological problems related to children's comprehension of questions concerning media use, an additional pivot study was conducted in order to identify possible difficulties of comprehension in the questionnaire. Since there were no problems reported with the factual questions used in this study, the results for the sub-sample of the teen population aged 10-15 are presented in this paper.

Results

Clusters of active users with similar communication patterns

In order to discover groups of people with similar and distinct patterns regarding their use of various communication channels, a cluster analysis[10] was performed on a sub-sample of 299 respondents using all five communication channels at least occasionally[11]. A standard three-step approach (Ferligoj 1989; Dillon & Goldstein 1984) was used to determine the number of clusters and individual membership in them. In the first step, the standardised variables that measured social interaction in all five communication channels were analysed by a hierarchical cluster procedure, which begins with Euclidian distances as the similarity measure and uses Ward's method of cluster identification. After considering a dendrogram that indicates the degree of similarity between different clusters and their theoretical relevance, a four-cluster solution appeared to be the most appropriate. Therefore, in the second step a K-means cluster analysis was carried out with the input of four groups to optimise the cluster membership and determine the cluster centroids. Finally, the cluster membership of each unit was saved as a categorical variable and then used in further analysis.

The procedure resulted in four distinct clusters with recognisable patterns of the use of various communication devices and we accordingly labelled them: techno-ascetics, cyber-communicators, work-collaborators, and mobile-traditionalists. It should be noted that the choice of names for clusters is rather arbitrary, but generally reflects the distinct patterns of technology use and does not imply any particular attitude toward technologies. In Table 1 the purposes of use of each of the five communication channels are broken down by membership in clusters.

Techno-ascetics is the largest group and comprises 37.8% of the respondents with access to all five communication channels. However, although they possess all modern information and communication gadgetry they are quite reserved in their use. Compared to all the other groups, the techno-ascetics are the least intense users of all five communication channels across all four communication goals. Besides that, they show a consistently below-average use of communication technologies and face-to-face channels for work, school or business related matters as well as for sharing messages that have a relational or expressive nature. Although the techno-ascetics use mobile phone voice calls and face-to-face conversations for micro-coordination (i.e., managing everyday practical issues) the most often,

---

10 Because the study aimed to identify similarities among respondents along their uses of communication technologies, cluster analysis was the preferred analytical strategy (see Ferligoj 1989; Lorr 1983; Perse & Courtright 1993).
11 Hereafter referred to as respondents with access to all five communication channels.

they are not nearly as intense in these technologically mediated communicative practices as the members of the other clusters. In other words, members of this group share their vague interest in the appropriation of devices for interpersonal communication.

Cyber-communicators is the second smallest group – 18.4% of the respondents with access to all communication channels – yet the most active group of users of ICTs. Compared to the techno-ascetics, members of this group are far more intense in their use of unmediated and mediated forms of communication channels and it seems that they fully integrate and take advantage of the interactive affordances of various communication devices in everyday life activities. More precisely, they exploit mobile phone voice calls, texting and the Internet on a daily basis for both work and socially. Although they use mobile phones for micro-coordination and socialising less often, what separates the cyber-communicators from the other three groups is their considerably above-average use of the Internet. Moreover, they are the only group that goes online on a daily basis not only for work matters but also to use Internet-based interactive services. In a nutshell, this group comprises people who find all the new technologies to be suitable devices for a variety of communication goals, but they are very modest in their use of 'old', space-determined technologies.

The third user type is *work-collaborators*. They are the second largest group of respondents (25.8 %) with the most specialised user profile among the four groups. The degree to which new technologies have become integral to the work-collaborators' everyday lives is highlighted by the gap between them and the other groups in their use of communication channels for purposes related to work. They tend to have a utilitarian, work-oriented approach to their use of all communication channels and, with the exception of the techno-ascetics, are much less likely than the other groups to use old and new communication technologies for micro-coordination, personal matters or socialising. Even though they have full access to the Internet, mobile and fixed phones they mainly exploit them as work utilities, while leaving face-to-face conversations with the primary role of conveying messages for everyday co-ordination and personal sharing. The work-collaborators are thus relatively inert in their exploitation of the interactional affordances of communication devices and limit their interpretative flexibility to the coordination of work related activities and relationships.

The smallest group, called *mobile-traditionalists*, is made up of 18.1% of the respondents with access to all five communication channels. They have moved rapidly to integrate the mobile phone and texting into their lives and especially use them as a tool to stay in touch with their friends and family. Interestingly, they also show the same level of activity with more 'traditional' interpersonal communication technologies, namely the fixed phone. Like the cyber-communicators, the mobile-traditionalists frequently participate in face-to-face conversations, especially in those that are relationally and expressively motivated. But they stand apart from cyber-communicators in their reduced online involvement and more intensive use of the fixed telephone for all four purposes.

Indicators	Techno-ascetics		Cyber-communicators		Work-collaborators		Mobile-traditionalists		Total
mobile – work	---	2.37	+++	4.05	+++	4.14		3.48	3.34
mobile – micro-coordination	-	3.65	++	4.73		3.77	++	4.81	4.09
mobile – socialising	-	2.86	++	4.44	---	2.49	+++	4.48	3.35
mobile – expressive	--	1.64	+++	3.20	---	1.44	+++	3.13	2.14
SMS/MMS – work	--	1.45	+++	2.96		1.94	++	2.46	2.04
SMS/MMS – micro-coordination	-	2.38	+++	3.89	--	2.03	+++	3.54	2.78
SMS/MMS – socialising	--	2.07	+++	4.04	---	1.66	+++	3.35	2.56
SMS/MMS – expressive	-	1.29	+++	2.91	---	1.12	++	2.26	1.72
telephone – work	---	1.80	-	2.75	+++	4.35	++	3.74	2.98
telephone – micro-coordination	--	2.18		2.78		3.05	+++	4.30	2.90
telephone – socialising	--	1.93	-	2.31	-	2.21	+++	4.31	2.50
telephone – expressive	-	1.33		1.56	-	1.35	+++	3.04	1.69
f-t-f – work	---	3.12	++	4.64	++	4.75	++	4.63	4.09
f-t-f – micro-coordination	-	3.84	++	4.69	+	4.57	++	4.72	4.34
f-t-f – socialising	--	3.77	++	4.78		4.25	++	4.74	4.25
f-t-f – expressive	--	2.44	++	3.76	-	2.86	+++	3.83	3.04
internet – work	---	1.39	+++	3.67	+++	3.58		2.67	2.61
internet – micro-coordination	-	1.60	+++	3.53		2.36	+	2.61	2.33
internet – socialising	--	1.73	+++	3.56	-	1.79	++	2.89	2.29

internet – expressive	-	1.11	+++ 2.24	1.16	1.46	1.39
Total (N)	113	55	77	54	299	
%	37.8	18.4	25.8	18.1	100	

Note. Differences in the average between the cluster centroids and the total averages are marked with + or – in such a way that +++ indicates differences larger than 0.75, ++ indicates differences on the interval 0.51 – 0.75, while + indicates differences on the interval 0.25 – 0.50. The system of – is analogous to +, but indicates negative differences.

Table 1: A typology of respondents by uses of five communication channels for four purposes

Similarly to the work-collaborators, the mobile-traditionalists also arrange their work/school tasks through mobile phones and fixed telephones on a daily basis. However, besides using voice calls they are more likely to exchange short text messages. The mobile-traditionalists are less likely to go online to settle work- or school-related matters than the work-collaborators or the cyber-communicators. In short, the mobile-traditionalists are quite active appropriators of mobile phones in all their affordances yet they do not take full advantage of the available interactional possibilities of the Internet and instead stick to the 'good old' fixed telephone.

The socio-cultural embeddedness of groups

Cramer's V index (Argesti 2002) was used as a measure of association that is applicable to a contingency table of any dimensions in order to quantify the strength of the relations between the structural variables and cluster membership. The results presented in Table 2 suggest there are significant differences between the members of the four clusters according to their gender, age, education as well as their labour market status, family status and computer literacy. More precisely, the techno-ascetics are mostly male (58%), younger respondents – just under half of them (46%) are below the age of 25 versus 39% among all the respondents. Among the techno-ascetics there are fewer (45%) employed respondents (against the average of 55%) and those who have graduated from post-secondary or higher education programmes.

As we mentioned above, the most innovative and enthusiastic users of the new communication technologies are the cyber-communicators. The composition of this group is heavily weighted towards school-age youth, with the majority (58%) being in the 10-25 age range, as well as single people. Since 56% of the cyber-communicators are still attending school, 33% of them have a lower education (against the average of 24%). While the cyber-communicators are the most intensive users of online services for interpersonal communication and enjoy a significantly higher level of computer literacy than the techno-ascetics, they do not differ markedly from the other clusters in terms of their Internet use at home and broadband access in the household.

The work-collaborators form the oldest group – 47% of its members are aged from 45 to 75 years – and it has the highest share of working and married respondents. Most of them (66%) are men (against the average of 53%), employed (81%) and well educated since four in ten (42%) have at least a university-level education. The Internet-use rate of this group is slightly below the average, while group members' access to broadband at home is somewhat above-average.

	Techno-ascetics	Cyber-communicators	Work-collaborators	Mobile-tradionalists	Total	Cramer's V
Gender						
Males	58	51	66	22	53	0.302*
Females	42	49	34	78	47	
Age						
10 - 25 years	46	58	16	37	39	0.280*
26 - 45 years	30	38	38	46	36	
46 - 75 years	24	4	47	17	25	
Education						
Lower	27	33	12	28	24	0.208*
Middle	58	45	45	37	48	
Higher	15	22	43	35	27	
Labour market status						
School-age youth	37	53	14	39	34	0.252*
Worker, farmer	45	36	81	56	55	
Retired, homemaker, unemployed, disabled	18	11	5	6	11	
Family status						
Married	32	13	58	33	35	0.230*
With partner	15	22	13	15	16	
Single	53	65	29	52	49	

Area						
Rural	64	64	55	46	58	0.137
Urban	36	36	45	54	42	
Use the Internet at home?						
No	25	20	30	22	25	0.080
Yes	75	80	70	78	75	
Broadband access in the household?[a]						
No	60	55	48	43	53	0.130
Yes	40	45	52	57	47	
Computer literacy[b]						
	4.2a	4.7a	4.4	4.4	4.4	
Total						
N	113	55	77	54	299	
%	38	18	26	18	100	

Note. The values represent mean percentages. n = 299. [a]n = 250. *p < .01. [b]The values represent the means of the computer literacy index, that ranged from 0 to 6, with higher values indicating greater literacy. The means of computer literacy that share the same subscripts differ significantly at p < 0.05 by Bonferroni post-hoc pairwise comparison tests.

Table 2: The socio-cultural milieu and demographic characteristics of the four groups

The mobile-traditionalists differ markedly from the other groups since this is the only cluster where women make up the majority (78%) of the group. Moreover, almost half of the mobile-traditionalists (46%) are middle aged, whereas more than one-third of them (35%) ended their schooling with at least a bachelor's degree. Although there are no significant differences with the other groups in terms of their Internet use and broadband access, home Internet use is high for this group (78%) and six in ten (57%) have broadband access at home.

Social networks and social participation

To estimate the influence of membership in clusters on the size of the supportive network and intensity of social participation, it is necessary to control the relationship between the use of technologies and social effects for relevant socio-demographic variables which might potentially initiate differences between the clusters (cf. Hlebec et al. 2006). For this goal we ran a Multiple Classification Analysis ('MCA'), which is a suitable method for situations involving a number of categorical independent variables and one at least interval-dependent variable (Andrews et al. 1969). MCA usually produces two tables of results – in Table 3 there are unadjusted and adjusted (controlling for the impact of socio-demographic variables) means for the four clusters. Table 4 shows the relative strength of the influence of the cluster variable on the social supportive network size and intensity of social participation controlled for socio-demographic characteristics.

The four clusters express significantly different average means of the size of the supportive network. The cyber-communicators have the largest supportive network (4.58), followed by the mobile-traditionalists (4.17), work-collaborators (3.78) and techno-ascetics (3.13), who have a supportive network that is on average more than one person smaller than that of the cyber-communicators. It is important to acknowledge that these differences are already controlled (adjusted) for commonly used socio-demographic variables, which indicate that the communication styles these groups engage in have relevant effects on their supportive network independent of the age, education and gender structure of the group. As shown in Table 4 the values of betas[12] confirm this finding as the relative influence of cluster membership (beta = 0.27) is the largest in comparison with the other independent variables included in the analysis.

	Network Size	Social Participation
Techno-ascetics	3.13	2.60a
Cyber-communicators	4.58a	2.69ab
Work-collaborators	3.78b	2.58ab
Mobile-traditionalists	4.17ab	2.79b
Sig. (F-test)	7.69*	2,41*

Note. n = 299. Means in the same column that do not share subscripts differ at $p < .05$.
*$p < .10$

Table 3: Means of the size of the supportive network and intensity of social participation, adjusted for socio-demographic variables

---

[12] Betas obtained with MCA can have a similar interpretation as regression beta (they indicate the association between dependent and independent variables that would occur if all independent variables were held constant), but they do not express the direction of the influence.

	Network Size		Social participation	
	Eta	Beta	Eta	Beta
Clusters	0.27	0.27	0.16	0.11
Age	0.28	0.18	0.17	0.17
Education	0.25	0.16	0.18	0.19
Gender	0.05	0.04	0.11	0.05
Area	0.11	0.12	0.12	0.11
R^2	0.17		0.10	

Note. n = 299.

Table 4: Uncontrolled (Eta) and controlled (Beta) influence of socio-demographic variables on the size of the social support network and intensity of social participation

The intensity of social participation is, on the other hand, not significantly influenced by cluster membership, although some observable differences exist. The mobile-traditionalists are the most intensive when it comes to participating at social events, meeting friends and acquaintances (2.79), followed by the cyber-communicators (2.69), techno-ascetics (2.60) and work-collaborators (2.58). However, these differences are so small that we cannot generalise them to the population. Social participation is more influenced by education (beta = 0.19) and age (beta = 0.17), while the effect of cluster membership shrinks after controlling for socio-demographic characteristics (beta = 0.11). All the independent variables together explain a relatively low, but statistically significant, percentage of the variability of both dependent variables. Namely, cluster, gender, age, education and geographical area, together explain 17% of the variability of size of the supportive network and 10% of the variability of social participation.

Discussion and conclusion

The primary intention of this paper was to provide a comprehensive empirical insight into the socio-technical realities of the users of communication devices by building on a concept of active use as a structuration process which involves a complex interrelationship between skilful, creative uses of various communication devices, their social embeddedness and resulting social consequences. Our results show that Slovenian users of interpersonal communication technologies, who are fully equipped with new communication technologies, react quite differently to the appropriation of these technologies and this appropriation is socially conditioned and carries certain consequences. Having access to the most popular state-of-art ICTs with various interactional affordances does not automatically lead to an open, creative and experimental relationship with them. Hence, we suggest that from ubiquitous connectivity and connected co-presence through the interweaving forms of mediated communication not one but four communicative portraits of active users have emerged.

Members of the largest cluster of users with a similar appropriation of communication devices, we named them techno-ascetics, in comparison with the other three groups had a rather bland response to and interpretation of the flexibility of the analysed technologies. Accordingly, despite having access to all communication technologies they narrow down their usage of ICTs, with the exception of the mobile phone which they appropriate in line with their dominant representation as a useful (micro)coordinating, security-assuring tool. On the other hand, the mobile-traditionalist and cyber-communicator groups take full advantage of (some) ICTs in the wide spectrum of the purposes they can help them to achieve. Their media use is a dynamic interchange of different communication channels, unburdened by their predefined functions, and involves more of an active, ever-changing arrangement and conscious awareness and selection of affordances in various communication settings. Interestingly, the mobile-traditionalists are a little more reserved with the affordances of the Internet but completely committed to the 'traditional' telephone, while just the contrary holds true for the cyber-communicators. The work-collaborators is a group of users who are by their inactivity quite similar to the techno-ascetics since they do not take advantage of the wide range of interactive affordances of various communication devices. However, their relation to technologies can be described as 'sober' in the sense that they possess them out of need, for system-defined functions and security reasons, yet they do not see or use them as a socialising or expressing tool – they prefer to perform the latter communicative functions in face-to-face settings.

Further, the results speak quite clearly of the complex relationship between social embeddedness, activeness of appropriation and use of available communication channels and social consequences. The mode of media relation, choice and use is clearly socially conditioned and not totally idiosyncratic, in line with the transient, immediate purposes of each individual. It is true, on one hand, that communication practices are not static as Höflich and Gebhardt (2005, 22-24) claim, yet we suggest that they are not completely free-floating but eventually consolidate themselves around several socio-cultural anchors as a result of a dynamic structuration process between individual processes of learning, experiencing, changing and experimenting and structural processes of setting normative and technological limits. This does not imply that communication practices are becoming completely fixed but they are instead stabilising themselves for a certain time in one's lifespan within a set of specific time-space-technology arrangements. The work-collaborators, for instance, have achieved a 'sober', utilitarian relationship towards new communication devices since they are situated in a more stable social and material environment (older, employed, married) and do not feel the need to transcend the purely instrumental purposes defined by the needs of work tasks. The cyber-communicators, on the other hand, represent a younger, curious, 'computer literate' population in an intensive phase of identity searching and social affirmation. Their appropriation of devices is clearly a reflection of their institutional role in the family, within which they are yearning to develop contact with their peers and emancipate themselves from their parents' control (Ling & Yttri 2006; Rubin 1985). Their active use of communication devices and discovery of the many interactional affordances offered by them rewards cyber-communicators with larger support networks which are very important in contemporary post-modern societies that are experiencing the demise of the welfare-state (Dremelj 2005). Likewise, the supportive networks of the mobile-traditionalists are larger due to their creative engagement with a plethora of communication devices, while the other two groups are significantly weaker in this important dimension of social capital.

Further, when viewed from the perspective of recent studies which suggest that mobile phone voice calls and texting are narrowing-down media (for communicating with people with strong ties), whilst Internet-based communication services tend to be used as expanding media (Ishii 2006; Kim et al. 2007; Thulin & Vilhelmson 2007), the difference in interaction patterns and network size between the cyber-communicators and the mobile-traditionalists can be translated into differences in the structure of their social capital. Expressed in Putnamian terms, the cyber-communicators, whose increased use of mobiles has gone hand-in-hand with them spending more time on computer-mediated communication, may experience higher levels of bridging social capital. Conversely, the mobile-traditionalists, whose expressively motivated mobile and fixed phone use is most likely oriented to strengthening social ties within existing social networks, as the size of their social supportive network is smaller than that of the cyber-communicators, are expected to accumulate and hold a higher amount of bonding social capital.

Although more research is needed to map the nature of the relationship between the notions of an active user and social capital, the results of our application suggest that the proposed active user concept may provide a useful starting-point for investigating other micro and macro social phenomena which, like social capital, are recurring themes in the contemporary social sciences.

References

Andrews F., Morgan J., Sonquist J. Multiple Classification Analysis. Ann Arbor, MI: Institute for Social Research (1969)

Argesti A. Categorical data analysis. Hoboken, NJ: John Wiley & Sons (2002)

Barak A. 'Sexual harassment on the Internet' Social Science Computer Review 23: 1 (2005) pp. 77-92

Bausinger H. 'Media, technology and daily life' Media, Culture and Society 6 (1984) pp. 343-351

Baym N., Zhang Y. B., Lin M. C. 'Social interactions across the media: Interpersonal communication on the internet, telephone and face-to-face' New Media & Society 6 (2004) pp. 299-318

Best S. J., Krueger B. S. 'Online interactions and social capital: Distinguishing between new and existing ties' Social Science Computer Review 24 (2006) pp. 395-410

Blumler J. G., Katz E. eds. The uses of mass communications: Current perspectives in gratifications research. Beverly Hills: Sage (1974)

Boneva B., Kraut R. 'Email, gender, and personal relationships' eds. Wellman B., Haythornthwaite C. The internet in everyday life. Malden: Blackwell Publishing (2002)

Burnett G., Buerkle H. 'Information Exchange in Virtual communities: A Comparative Study' Journal of Computer-Mediated Communication 9 URL: http://jcmc.indiana.edu/vol9/issue2/burnett.html (2004) (accessed March 2008)

Cockburn C. 'The circuit of technology: Gender, identity and power' eds. Silverstone R., Hirsch E. Consuming Technologies: Media and Information in Domestic Spaces. London: Routledge (1992)

COST298 COST action 298: Participation in the broadband society. Memorandum of Understanding for the implementation of a European concerted research action. Rome: Author (2005)

Cummings J. N., Butler B. S., Kraut R. 'The quality of online social relationships' Communications of the ACM 45 (2002) pp. 103-108

Dillon W. R., Goldstein M. Multivariate Analysis: Methods and Applications. New York: John Wiley & Sons (1984)

Dremelj P. 'Family and kin ties as sources of individuals' social support' 'Rethinking inequalities', Proceedings of the 7th European Sociological Association Conference. Torun, Poland (2005)

Ellison N., Steinfield C., Lampe C. 'The benefits of Facebook 'friends': Social capital and college students' use of online social network sites' Journal of Computer-Mediated Communication 12 (2007) pp. 1143-1168

Ferligoj A. Razvrščanje v skupine [Clustering] Ljubljana: FSPN (1989)

Fischer C. S. America calling: A social history of the telephone to 1940. Berkeley: University of California Press (1992)

Flanagin A. J. 'IM online: Instant messaging use among college students' Communication Research Reports 22 (2005) pp. 175-187

Flanagin A. J., Metzger M. 'Internet use in the contemporary media environment' Human Communication Research 27 (2001) pp. 153-181

Fortunati L., Manganelli A. M. 'La comunicazione tecnologica: Comportamenti, opinioni, ed emozioni degli Europei' [The technological mediated communication: behaviors, opinions, and emotions of Europeans] ed. Fortunati L. Telecomunicando in Europa. Milano: Agneli (1998)

Giddens A. The Constitution of Society: Outline of the theory of structuration. Cambridge: Polity (1984)

Giddens A. The consequences of modernity. Stanford: Stanford University Press (1990)

Glotz P., Bertschi S., Locke C. eds. Thumb culture: The meaning of mobile phones for society. Bielefeld: Transcript Verlag (2005)

Goggin G. The cell phone culture: Mobile technology in everyday life. London: Routledge (2006)

Habermas J. The theory of communicative action: Reason and the rationalization of society Vol. 1. London: Heinemann (1984)

Haddon L. 'Domestication and mobile telephony' ed. J.E. Katz: Machines that Become Us. New Brunswick, NJ: Transaction (2003)

Hall P. 'Social Capital in Britain' British Journal of Political Science 29 (1999) pp. 417-461

Haythornthwaite C. 'Strong, weak and latent ties and the impact of new media' The Information Society 18 (2002) pp. 385-401

Hlebec V., Lozar-Manfreda K., Vehovar V. 'The Social Support Networks of Internet Users' New Media & Society 8 (2006) pp. 9-32

Hoffman D. L., Kalsbeek W. D., Novak T. P. 'Internet and web use in the U.S.' Communications 39 (1996) pp. 36-46

Höflich J. R., Gebhardt J. 'Changing cultures of written communication: letter – e-mail – SMS' eds. Harper R., Palen L., Taylor A. The Inside Text: Social, cultural and design perspectives on SMS. Norwell: Springer (2005)

Ishii K. 'Implication of mobility: The uses of personal communication media in everyday life' Journal of Communication 56 (2006) pp. 346-365

Jackson L. A., Ervin K. S., Gardner P. D., Smith N. 'Gender and the internet: women communicating and men searching' Sex Roles 4 (2001) pp. 363-79

Johnstone J. W. C. 'Social integration and mass media use among adolescents: A case study' eds. Blumler J. G., Katz E. The Uses of Mass Communication: Current perspectives on gratifications research. Beverly Hills: Sage (1974)

Katz E., Gurevitch M., Hadassah H. 'On the uses of the mass media for important things' American Sociological Review 38 (1973) pp. 164-181

Katz J. E., Aspden P. 'Motivations for and barriers to internet usage: Results of a national public opinion survey' Internet Research: Electronic Networking Applications and Policy 7 (1997) pp. 170-188

Katz J. E., Aakhus M. eds. Perpetual Contact: Mobile communication, private talk, public performance. Cambridge: Cambridge University Press (2002)

Kavanaugh A. L., Patterson, S. J. 'The impact of community computer networks on social capital and community involvement in Blacksburg' eds. Wellman B., Haythornthwaite C. The Internet in Everyday Life. Malden: Blackwell Publishing (2002)

Kim H., Kim G. J., Park H. W., Rice R. E. 'Configurations of relationships in different media: FtF, email, instant messenger, mobile phone, and SMS' Journal of Computer-Mediated Communication 12 (2007) pp. 1183-1207

Kling R., Rosenbaum H., Sawyer S. Understanding and Communicating Social Informatics: A Framework for Studying and Teaching the Human Contexts of Information and Communications Technologies. Medford, NJ: Information Today Inc. (2005)

Lenhart A., Madden M., Rankin-Macgill A., Smith A. 'Teens and social media: The use of social media gains a greater foothold in teen life as they embrace the conversational nature of interactive online media' Washington, DC: Pew Internet & American Life Project URL: http://www.pewinternet.org (2007) (accessed March 2008)

Leung L. 'College students' motives for chatting on ICQ' New Media & Society 3 (2001) pp. 483-500

Leung L., Wei R. 'More than just talk on the move: Uses and gratifications of the cellular phone' J&MC Quarterly 77 (2000) pp. 308-320

Lichtenstein A., Rosenfeld L. B. 'Normative expectations and individual decisions concerning media gratification choices' Communication Research 11 (1984) pp. 393-413

Licoppe C., Smoreda Z. 'Are social networks technologically embedded? How networks are changing today with changes in communication technology' Social Networks 27 (2005) pp. 317-335

Ling R. Mobile connection: The cell phone's impact on society. New York: Morgan and Kaufmann Publishers (2004)

Ling R. 'Mobile communication and the generation of social cohesion' ed. Nyiri K. Towards a Philosophy of Telecommunications Convergence. Budapest: The Hungarian Academy of Sciences (2007)

Ling R., Campbell S. W. eds. The Reconstruction of Space and Time: Mobile Communication Practices. New Brunswick, N.J.: Transaction Publishers (2008)

Ling R., Pedersen P. eds. Mobile Communications: Re-negotiation of the social sphere. London: Springer (2005)

Ling R., Yttri B. 'Hyper-coordination via mobile phones in Norway' eds. Katz J., Aakhus M. Perpetual Contact: Mobile communication, private talk, public performance. Cambridge: Cambridge University Press (2002)

Ling R., Yttri B. 'Control, emancipation, and status: The mobile phone in teens' parental and peer relationships' eds. Kraut R., Brynin M., Kiesler S.: Computers, Phones, and the Internet: Domesticating information technology. Oxford: Oxford University Press (2006)

Lorr M. Cluster Analysis for Social Scientists: Techniques for analyzing and simplifying complex blocks of data. San Francisco: Jossey-Bass Publishers (1983)

Neumann W. L. Social research methods: qualitative and quantitative approaches (3rd ed.). Boston: Allyn and Bacon (1997)

Noble G. 'Discriminating between the intrinsic and instrumental domestic telephone user' Australian Journal of Communications 15 (1987) pp. 63-85

Papacharissi Z. 'The real-virtual dichotomy in online interaction: New media uses and consequences revisited' ed. Kalbfleisch P. J. Communication Yearbook 29. Mahwah: Lawrence Erlbaum Associates (2005) pp. 215-237

Papacharissi Z., Rubin A. M. 'Predictors of internet use' Journal of Broadcasting & Electronic Media 44 (2000) pp. 175-196

Perse E. M., Courtright J. A. 'Normative images of communication media: mass and interpersonal channels in the new media environment' Human Communication Research 19 (1993) pp. 485-503

Pool de Sola I. The Social Impact of the Telephone. Cambridge: MIT Press (1977)

Putnam R. Bowling Alone – The Collapse and Revival of American Community. New York: Simon & Schuster (2000)

Rakow L. Gender on the line. Urbana: University of Illinois Press (1992)

Rettie R. 'Interactional Divergence notwithstanding Technological Convergence' ed. Nyiri K. Towards a Philosophy of Telecommunications Convergence. Budapest: The Hungarian Academy of Sciences (2007)

Rubin L. Just Friends. The role of friendship in our lives. New York: Harper & Row (1985)

Ruggiero T. E. 'Uses and gratifications theory in the 21st century' Mass Communication & Society 3 (2000) pp. 3-37

Smoreda Z., Licoppe C. 'Gender Specific Use of the Domestic Telephone' Social Psychology Quarterly 63 (2000) pp. 238-52

Statistical Office of the Republic of Slovenia. Slovenian Census (2002) URL: http://www.stat.si (2005) (accessed December 2005)

Stillman L. J. H. Understandings of Technology in Community-based Organisations: A structurational analysis. Unpublished doctoral dissertation. Monash University: Prato (2006)

Thompson J. B. The media and modernity: A social theory of media. Stanford, CA: Stanford University Press (1995)

Thulin E., Vilhelmson B. 'Mobiles everywhere: Youth, the mobile phone, and changes in everyday practice' Young Nordic Journal of Youth Research 15 (2007) pp. 235-253

Touraine A. Critique of modernity. Cornwall: Blackwell (1995)

Trevino L.K., Webster J., Stein, E.W. 'Making Connections: complementary influences on communication media choices, attitudes, and use' Organization Science 11 (2000) pp. 163-182

Wei R., Lo V. H. 'Staying Connected while on the Move: Cell phone use and social connectedness' New Media & Society 8 (2006) pp. 53-72

Wellman B., Haythornthwaite C. eds. The Internet in Everyday Life. Malden, MA: Blackwell Publishing (2002)

Hajo Greif, Oana Mitrea and Matthias Werner

Usability vs. Functionality? Mobile Broadband Technologies and User Agency[1]

Arguable Definitions

One of the authors of this paper once witnessed two philosopher colleagues engaging in a heated and seemingly irresolvable debate about the true path to a truly democratic computer technology. Such a technology would not only enable users to participate *in* it, that is, allowing for the largest possible variety of uses by the largest possible share of the general population, but also *through* it, that is, making the use of computers an exercise in democracy beyond the issues of access to and usage of technology, namely as a model for and a medium of political and social participation in general. The argument revolved around the following question: In order to achieve this goal, should the mode of interaction with computers, and thus the interface design, follow the norm of designing a technology so as to allow direct contributions to system and application development by its users in the first place, or should it adhere to the norm of creating an easily accessible, readily and intuitively usable user interface and application design?

However simplified the questions and positions in this debate are restated here, what emerged from that debate were different underlying assumptions that seem to resonate with ongoing debates about the social aspects of computing: Should the first principle of design be usability – the possibility of using a system towards a given purpose with as little effort, as much efficiency and perhaps even as much pleasure as possible – or should it be functionality, namely the availability of a wide variety of functions in a system and of the means of controlling them?

In those debates, functionality and usability are seen as two aspects of any user-oriented technology that, although being different aspects, they both have to be properly accounted for in design processes (Goodwin 1987; Davis 1989; Shackel 1991; McNamara & Kirakowski 2005). The questions are, first, whether these aspects imply trade-offs in design practice or whether they need to be in-

---

1   This chapter discusses the conceptual foundations and empirical findings of a research project conducted by the authors of this paper. It is not intended to be a conclusive presentation of the project's results. The project was funded by the provincial government of Styria, Austria, Department of Science and Research.

terpreted as complementary and mutually supporting.[2] Depending on the answer to this question, it may be asked, secondly, whether usability and functionality are on an equal footing or whether one of them may have, generally or in certain circumstances, preference over the other. Clearly, the meanings given to the terms 'usability' and 'functionality' bear on the answer one will consider appropriate to these questions.

Standard definitions are available, at least for the concept of functionality: This concept refers to a set of functions offered by, or associated with, a technological system – the capabilities it has as mapped onto the purposes to which it should be used. Put plainly and simply, a functional system is one that has the capacity of serving a certain set of purposes. In the case of computers, functionality is a matter of the tasks that can be fulfilled by a certain program, or with a certain configuration of software and hardware, and of how they can be fulfilled.

Things seem a little less clear for usability given the many competing definitions in the literature. In a first approximation, the term refers to the property of a system of being capable of being used towards its given purpose – as would fit the word's etymology. It addresses the properties of the system in relation to the usage conditions surrounding the system that allow the users, given their level of technical expertise, and given their specific purposes, to actually use the functions offered by that system. In the case of computers, usability particularly matters for issues of interface design: How are the functions of the system made known and displayed to the user? What conditions would impede or facilitate the perception and use of those functions?

However, in the *analysis* of this issue a variety of different definitions and interpretations emerge: Usability may refer to the effectiveness and efficiency with which a system can be used – the traditional definition which is partly preserved in the ISO and IEEE standards – or to the usefulness of a system as perceived by the users in conjunction with their degree of confidence and satisfaction in using it, jointly accounting for the system's acceptance by users (Davis 1989), or even to the quality of the user's subjective experience as such (Thomas & Macredie 2002; McNamara & Kirakowski 2005). Thus, usability may be a category allowing for quantifiable measurements (what are the costs of error detection and correction, and of learning commands and procedures required for proper usage of a system?), it may be a domain of statistical generalisations over users' subjective behaviours towards a model of acceptance of some technology, it may be a category exclusively reserved for the non-quantifiable, intrinsic and essentially subjective aspects

---

2   Goodwin (1987) strongly argues for complementarity, as do McNamara and Kirakowski (2005) who further differentiate the user-related aspects into usability proper and user experience, while Jordan (2002) favours a hierarchical view.

of using a technology (do users feel safe and comfortable when using a system?), or it may be a mixture of any of these approaches (Gould 1988; Nielsen 1993).

Another question of at least equal importance is whether one perceives usability as a property of a system taken by itself, or as a quality of the interaction between the system and the user, thus shifting the focus towards the particular contexts, predispositions and environments of use. The latter position has gained much credit since the 1990s, especially for the fact that the contexts of usage of computers, starting from a comparably uniform workplace setting, have diversified significantly to generate not only a wider variety of devices and applications but also many different locales and modes of interaction.

User Agency

It cannot be our purpose here to provide *the* correct definition of usability. In fact, there may not even be one definition that fits all purposes. Broadly speaking, the choice is a matter of one's interests (research or other) and of the kinds of systems in question:

I. Effectiveness and efficiency are criteria that are operable in the investigation of work environments, and usability is best defined in these terms when looking at work-oriented applications, viewed from the perspective of optimising procedures towards given tasks.
II. Subjective well-being, on the other hand, becomes an issue if one takes the entire work situation into account, seeking to improve it beyond the level of task fulfilment, namely towards task *definition*. The aim is to empower users to define not only *how* to do their work, but also *what* they can do.[3]
III. If attention is focused on consumer-oriented applications, where usage moves beyond work environments, so that measurable, standardised criteria of efficiency and work satisfaction are not applicable, the aspect of 'user experience', becomes a key topic in designing and evaluating applications from the perspective of manufacturers and service providers.

Following these observations, the right balance between usability and functionality is also an empirical issue. Like the definition itself, this balance depends, firstly, on the given context and, secondly, on the concepts of user agency em-

---

3 This was one of the main motives behind the Participatory Design movement of the 1980s (Bjerknes et al. 1987).

ployed in each case. These concepts seem to diverge among the three examples outlined above.

If actions are behaviours of a person that occur purposefully and voluntarily, that is, if they are directed towards a goal and if they are produced by that person in accordance with, or at least not in contradiction with that person's own beliefs and desires, then a person's or a collective's agency amounts to the ability to determine their own courses of action, in deciding both what to do and how to do it. This ability depends on the possibility, first, of determining one's purposes, that is, the goals of, and reasons for, acting in a certain way, and, second, on being in command of the appropriate means of fulfilling those purposes. Of course, this is an abstract definition of the concept of agency and not an empirical description of how actions work. All sorts of constraints apply along with imperfections and mistakes in conceiving one's purposes and the appropriate means occur – without necessarily disqualifying some behaviour as an action.[4]

The two mentioned conditions – determining both one's purposes and one's means towards them are, in turn, dependent on and vary with the specific environment in which a course of action is placed, where the 'environment' is to be understood not as the surroundings in general, but as a specific set of conditions one encounters in one's surroundings that affect the initial possibility, execution and outcome of one's actions. It may be a different environment for different individuals or even for the same individual at different times. This environment consists of other people, institutions, natural conditions, infrastructures and artefacts that enable or constrain certain actions to which purposes and actions are directed and which may also function as means for those actions.

If technologies are thus part of one's courses of action and if they are supposed to support users' agency, the expectation is that in the given context they enable, rather than constrain, the definition of new purposes and that they are suitable and available as a means of attaining the so-defined purposes. Among the above examples, the assumptions about the sources of the purposes and the weight given to the means for those purposes are at variance: User agency may be understood as being equipped with the best pre-fabricated set of means available to meet pre-arranged purposes that one may only partly have chosen oneself, as in (I); or as having the fullest control possible over the means and purposes of one's action, implying participation in both the definition of purposes and the design of the means, as in (II); or it may mean the ability to freely choose from a pre-fabricated set of means to meet pre-arranged purposes that one has consciously selected, as in (III).

---

4   The philosopher's answer to this problem is that a behaviour is an action if there is at least one description that its author would give under which it appears as occurring purposefully and voluntarily: Davidson (1980).

Given our above definition of user agency, (II) seems preferable, although this approach has its own difficulties.

Our suggestion is that practical definitions of user agency like these are the level on which the disagreement between our philosophers, and the competing definitions of what usability and its relation to functionality is, are best analysed and probably also resolved. Such practical definitions have formed part of the historical development of personal computing and may be instructive for the analysis of current developments whereby computers have not only become a consumer commodity but also immensely diversified in form, function, size and mobility. Among this range of products, we will focus on mobile broadband devices and applications since this is where the most significant innovations in consumer-oriented digital devices seem to happen and since a variety of design concepts is detectable there, with different preconceptions of, and implications for, user agency.

The Universal Machine and Later

The development of the personal computer in the 1970s was driven by grassroots-technology activists whose main normative concern was to wrest computing from the hands of the centralised, bureaucratic, hierarchical institutions that hosted mainframe computers and to open up the possibility of computers being primarily programmed and used by individuals.[5] Apart from this normative goal, the practical interest of these users-as-developers focused on the technology as such, namely on constructing a stand-alone computer from widely available and affordable resources, and on exploring, adapting and controlling its functionality. The drawbacks in performance and usability were not much of an issue to the people who bought (and manually mounted and set up) an Altair computer – whose input device initially consisted of an array of switches with which to enter binary code (one for each bit of one byte, and one for 'enter'). Inventing programming languages to automate such tedious routines was the main usability-related goal.

The first ventures in the direction of task-oriented applications for non-technically-minded users were not overwhelmingly successful as, for want of user-oriented design strategies and experience, those systems did prove not to be very reliable and usable. A significant population of application users only emerged when the field was developed by the Do-It-Yourself practitioners to the point where computer and business machine manufacturers began to see some commercial potential.

---

5 We are taking the following historical observations from Haddon (1988) and from the chapter on personal computers in Weyer et al. (1997).

The manufacturers' target groups were, firstly, people in business and administration who had previously been users of business machines. Their interest was to shift specific work-intensive tasks to the machines: doing calculations, producing, designing and archiving documents, or creating databases. Early PC systems, applications and programs were tailor-made to the client's needs instead of offering universally applicable solutions. However, the latter became important for a second group, namely home computing enthusiasts who used their computers for education and leisure purposes. A wider variety of less powerful functions was offered to them (games, word-processing, BASIC programming), which still suited their more playful and less specific purposes well enough. The home computing market blended into the personal computing market in the early 1990s when personal computers became standardised enough to be offered as affordable off-the-shelf solutions to home users.

Although it may seem that the entire landscape of the computing world has dramatically changed in the meantime, each of the aforementioned groups – technology enthusiasts, expert and general users – each with their own modes of usage, has found its niche in present-day computing practice. Technology as a purpose in itself or as a genuine means of social participation is still endorsed by a highly active and interconnected minority – the Open Source movement, for example. At the same time, there is a market for highly specific, advanced applications for specialised, mostly professional purposes where functionality is the main issue and usability amounts to questions of effectiveness and efficiency of use. Meanwhile, the majority is made up of a broad range of applications for a broad variety of everyday purposes of general consumers for whom convenience and ease of use seem to be the main concern.

The heterogeneity of users and uses suggests that neither a fixed position on an imaginary scale between usability and functionality (if we treat these aspects as competing, implying trade-offs), nor a perfect blending of the two (if we treat them as complementary and synergetic) may hold the ultimate answer. The way users are best enabled to define their purposes and to choose the means towards these purposes, as well as the extent to which users are thus enabled, depends firstly on the matching between available designs and the options for (inter-)acting they offer to their users. Secondly, it depends on the users' knowledge, interests and social roles that guide them in their selection and appropriation of what is offered.

In spite of this heterogeneity and although the design concept of personal computers may have its shortcomings, personal computing is now well-established and standardised, having achieved what is called 'closure' in Science and Technology

Studies:[6] The traces of the tortuous and often contested route of development have given way to a considerably unified concept that appears as if it had been the *telos* of a straightforward, linear development all along. However, the uses and design of the contemporary personal computer were not clearly visible at all in the early 1970s. Many initially equiprobable alternative directions of development did not ultimately materialise and many innovative, by now firmly established design options such as the mouse-controlled graphical user interface did not succeed when first introduced, due to institutional and/or technological impediments. Nonetheless, what has ultimately been retained throughout the development of the personal computer are the guiding goals of individual use and of maximum functional versatility. In conjunction, they aim at the ideal of a 'universal machine' – which is meant to be a very specific machine well-adapted to each individual user.

Looking back at the origins of computing, the universal machine was the guiding principle behind the development of computing as such. A universal machine is a machine that can be made to meet any variety of tasks involved in information-processing. Although the concept itself as developed by Turing (1936) was highly abstract and not intended to deliver a blueprint for real-world machines, it exerted a strong influence on computer science and the science-led development of computer technology. Computers were in principle meant to be an indefinitely flexible match to the cognitive and intellectual versatility of people, augmenting their memory, their calculating capacities, and their orientation among available information in any direction desired. The hardware-software distinction may be cited as the technical incarnation of this principle: To change the task the machine was to fulfil, one did not have to re-wire it, but (ideally) only to input semantically and syntactically correct instructions.

Limited Designs

Unlike computers, telephones were generally not meant to be universal machines. Although their purposes have changed over time – losing their once-prominent role as a medium of broadcasting messages and music, instead becoming the privileged medium of interpersonal communication over distances – these purposes always remained of limited scope. Second-generation mobile phones were immensely successful as more versatile telephones, offering text messaging and organiser functions while effectively becoming portable communication centres for individuals. Yet universality was still not the aim. Now that mobile phones have become, at least

---

6   The concept of closure was introduced by Pinch and Bijker (1987); also see Weyer et al. (1997).

to some extent, for certain groups in certain cultures the 'first truly personal computer' (Jarvenpaa & Lang 2005), things seem less clear. Are these devices meant to be further enhanced, more versatile telephones, yet without any further aspirations, or are they meant to converge towards the 'universal machine' paradigm?

In order to address this question, we would like to return to the norms of usability and functionality discussed above by introducing a twofold distinction between different norms in design:

(α)   maximum control ↔ maximum ease of use; and
(β)   maximum functional versatility ↔ maximum functional specialisation.

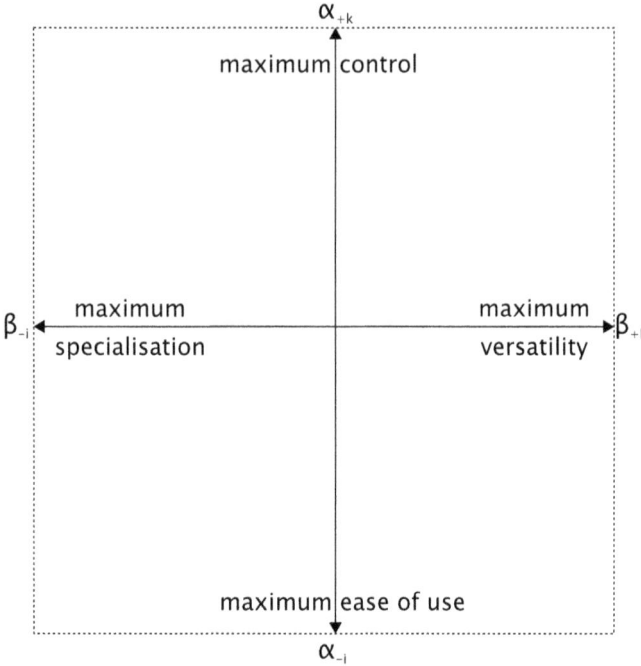

Figure 1: Coordinates of functionality and usability

These distinctions are meant to be gradual rather than strictly disjunctive. Consistently following either of these norms may need but not imply deficiencies with regard to the norm at the other end of each scale. More control over the functionality of a device often implies more parameters to set, more commands to enter, and thus less ease of use. Conversely, ease of use is often achieved at the cost of fewer control and configuration options. In an analogous fashion, more functional versatility often implies less performance for each function, and vice versa.

One can now combine the 'usability' scale (α) with the 'functionality' scale (β) to see how they match. While the norm of ease of use will go with both functional versatility and functional specialisation, the norm of control will be more sensibly connected with functional versatility as the latter creates a stronger need for control options compared to a device with only one or a few functions, which will normally be easier kept in view by the user, even without special provisions. Both control and versatility are characteristics of the personal computer design concept. On these conceptual grounds, we tentatively identified three design concepts regarding our case in question, namely, Third-Generation (3G) mobile phones, with their web-oriented applications and broadband capabilities:

(A) A mobile telephone with some extra, mostly multimedia functions that take advantage of the available bandwidth: Internet applications, mobile television, music, games. The design focuses on the integration of a broad variety of functions, not on their specialisation, and focuses on usefulness and convenient access in the conditions of mobility and limited size. Under the rubric of the 'Swiss army knife', this design concept is critically reflected upon by Satyanarayanan (2005).

(B) A new and unique kind of mobile communication device with a very specialised and intuitively accessible interface along with a specific selection of functions that are tailored to the mobile user's needs (e.g. location-based services, navigation, mobile entertainment). Being less versatile but more adapted to specific needs, these devices can be subsumed under the 'information appliance' design concept as introduced by Norman (1998) and Bergman (2000).

(C) A form of scaled-down mobile computer centred around organiser and office functions; the design logic and configuration options of the personal computer's interface and applications are retained where possible and adapted to new usage contexts. Here, for the sake of versatility the norm of functionality is put first; the users are meant to select and configure the desired functions by themselves.This preliminary classification is not meant to map onto given design concepts in a clear-cut and unequivocal way, but it may help identify the different currents in design practice. Whether these tentatively identifiable directions will mature into properly defined standard designs and whether or not one of them will prevail over the others is less than clear at the current stage. In fact, there is a significant lack of definition as to what actually *are* the characteristic features of a 3G phone, besides broadband capabilities.

Still, one seemingly common characteristic of mobile broadband devices is that they borrow much of the symbolic code and layout of the PC's graphical user interface (desktop metaphor, windows, icons, menus) in order to give them a recognisable face. Even key features of the functional architecture of PCs are retained in smartphones and their kin while, at the same time, the latter are no match to the functional versatility and power of PCs. Their limitations are due, at least partly, to technical constraints such as storage capacity, battery power and the size and quality of displays. The problem for design lies in the selection of a strategy for coping with these limitations. One could either accept them and still seek to keep the system as usable as possible (as in A), try to overcome them by adapting the 'universal machine' concept of the personal computer to the new circumstances (as in C), or one could seek to abandon the paradigm of the personal computer altogether and try something new (as in B).

The information appliance design concept is based on the assumption that the personal computer does not provide a useful model for contemporary mobile communication and computing (Norman 1998; Bergman 2000). Personal computers require considerable attention and a certain degree of knowledge for proper usage, while they also require the adaptation of the user's behaviour to their operational routines and limitations which they possess precisely because they provide, it is claimed, 'excess functionality' (Norman 1998, 60 and Ch. 4), as the flipside of the coin of universality.

The idea of the universal machine is being replaced by a concept of networked, small, single-purpose or limited-purpose machines: 'An information appliance is designed to perform a specific activity, such as music, photography, or writing. A distinguishing feature of information appliances is the ability to share information among themselves' (ibid., 53). Additional tasks ask for additional devices, all of which are supposed to communicate among themselves without first requiring tedious installation and configuration procedures. In this fashion, information appliances, it is promised, should not only be maximally usable but pleasurable and functionally self-evident to average consumers who are the primarily envisioned customers with highly individualised uses that should not require any kind of formal training.

The acknowledged cost is that the devices' functions are fixed and expressly limited. They may not allow for extensions and upgrades and significantly fall behind personal computers in terms of configuration options (modifying the operating system, installing additional applications, (re)-programming the source code). Generally speaking, options for the user to 'look under the bonnet' of the device are largely absent. While, with the 'Swiss army knife' approach (A) these limitations appear as an inevitable sacrifice, they are turned into some kind of virtue for information appliances.

However, whether trading in control and configuration options for ease of use, as in (A) and (B), will provide the key to success for mobile broadband seems questionable from both empirical and conceptual perspectives.

The Empirical Case

An Austria-wide online survey (n=632) on the usage of 3G and GSM mobile telephony was developed by the *evolaris research lab* of Graz, Austria, together with the authors.[7] It was conducted by *evolaris* in September 2007. An 18% (n=115) sub-sample of the respondents was comprised of 3G users, which roughly accords with recent market statistics (15.8% in Austria for 2006, according to *Mobile Communications* 450, 24 July 2007). The guiding questions of the study were:

(i) What are the patterns of dissemination of 3G mobile devices along demographic lines, and among different types of users?
(ii) What are the patterns of the adoption of functions typical for 3G mobile telephony among different types of users?
(iii) Where and how do the patterns of dissemination under (i) and of adoption under (ii) diverge?
(iv) What is the role of perceptions of the design norms of functionality and usability in the usage/non-usage of 3G phones and their functions?
In one part of the survey, we tested the design concepts (A-C) introduced above, and the underlying notions of functionality and usability, by asking respondents what qualities they expect from a mobile phone, with particular focus on multimedia and web-based services. The concepts were not explicated in the questionnaire and the questions were posed in random order, with multiple replies being possible. The qualities inquired were:

(A1) versatility – the availability of many different functions in one device;
(A2) integration – the availability of functions that prove useful in a variety of practical contexts;
(A3) generality – an emphasis on a wide functional scope, even at the cost of lower performance for each function;
(A4) convenience – the availability of plug-and-play functionality at the cost of configuration options;
(A5) ease of use – the availability of simple usage routines at the cost of functional versatility;

---

7 For a detailed report, see Greif et al. (2008).

(A6) specialisation – excellence in a certain set of specific functions at the cost of generality;
(A7) control – the availability of elaborated configuration options at the cost of having to invest some effort;
(A8) customisation – the possibility of obtaining functions tailored to the user's needs; and
(A9) participation – the presence of options for contributing to the design of new functions.

Clusters of users could be identified among the respondents whose preferences map onto the usability/functionality co-ordinates (α/β) introduced above, and thus onto variations of the three design types (A-C). Although this mapping is imperfect, the concepts were largely recognised by the respondents (with 21% to 24% exclusive matches for each concept) and, where combinations of those concepts were picked, these proved to be instructive. The resulting clusters were:

($\alpha+/\beta+$) users with a desire for controllable functionality, that is, with a preference for the integration of many versatile functions accompanied by means of control, customisation and participation (28% of all respondents); this preference has the closest match with type (C);

($\alpha-/\beta+$) users with a desire for convenient functionality, that is, with a preference for the integration of a wide variety of useful functions, yet without a need for control and customisation options (28% of all respondents); this preference has the closest match with type (A);

($\alpha-/\beta_0$) users with a desire for simplicity, that is, with a strong preference for ease of use, with no particular other desires for either versatility or specialisation (44% of all respondents); this preference partly matches type (B), *however without its inherent aspect of specialisation.*

The distribution of these types among the 3G/GSM user sub-samples was markedly differential: Type ($\alpha+/\beta+$) mainly comprised 3G users (51% vs. 24% among GSM users), while type ($\alpha-/\beta+$) appeared quite evenly distributed (28% each), and type ($\alpha-/\beta_0$) was characteristic of GSM users (at 48%, vs. 22% among 3G users).

If we look at the demographic profiles of the users in their mapping on the different clusters, GSM users among cluster ($\alpha+/\beta+$) tended to be male, higher educated, and professionally higher-ranking than GSM users among the members of cluster ($\alpha-/\beta_0$). Above all, they were also significantly more likely to be technically minded, that is, they were more willing and prepared to invest time and effort in exploring different functions. Moreover, given that the preference for control, at 57%, ranks second highest among 3G users (after versatility and before integration and customisation) and given that, with the preference for control, the cost of having to invest some effort is explicitly acknowledged, a willingness and even a perceived need to 'look under the bonnet' can be identified among this group and particularly among its (α+/β+) subset.[8] Doing so appears more as part of their user experience than as a need to be accepted.

In contrast, most non-users of 3G phones prefer simplicity and ease of use (model B) and are not very much attracted by the other concepts (A and C). However, functional versatility and the possibility of customisation, ranking second (43%) and third (38%) among their preferences, are also important for them, but not to the same extent as with the 3G users. Moreover, the non-usage of 3G phones does correlate with a comparably low interest in integration, specialisation, control and participation.

If these observations are valid, and given the perceived needs for simplicity and ease of use among GSM users, and especially the $(\alpha\text{-}/\beta_0)$ majority of them, it would be intuitive to assume that 3G devices offering such simplicity and ease of use will facilitate them upgrading from GSM. Here, the Swiss army knife and the information appliance would seem to have their proper place. However, first, although being more important to GSM users in general than to 3G users usability still does not appear to be the most pressing concern for them inasmuch as the majority of either group feels confident about mastering most or all functions of their devices.[9] Second, 41% of all GSM users state that they perceive no need for upgrading and, among their $(\alpha\text{-}/\beta_0)$ subset, a particularly low usage of those advanced functions that are already available to them can be detected.

Thus, we were able to identify different clusters of users with significantly different preferences for the functionality and/or usability of their devices that are differentially distributed over 3G/GSM usage. Especially among people who have already adopted 3G technology, versatility, control, integration, customisation and participation are highly valued. The assumption that maximally usable devices and applications *per se* will be sufficient for the widespread adoption of mobile broadband does not seem warranted.

---

8   More surprising was the finding that professional users are *not* more likely to be located in the (a+/b+) cluster than elsewhere. This observation somewhat contrasts with the findings in Jarvenpaa & Lang (2005); Juntumaa & Tuunainen (2006).
9   A larger portion of 3G users, despite any alleged over-complexity and excess functionality of their devices, seems to be fully confident than GSM users, of which, however, still a majority seems to be fully confident as well (71% vs. 51%), while only very few users from either group admit that they find the use of their device (2% vs. 3%) or certain functions and applications thereof (3% vs. 7%) difficult.

In the face of the under-utilisation of 3G services and bandwidth,[10] the apprehension of high costs (Lehmann et al. 2004) is given as a reason alongside the oft-cited, but apparently only partly applicable argument of poor usability. However, this assumption is also not fully supported by the results of our survey. In fact, only 19% of the non-users were found to support the cost argument while, besides the non-perception of a need by 41%, ignorance of the concept of 3G technology is admitted by 43%.

Moreover, non-perception of a need for certain functions also seems to be the main reason for the non-usage of available functions by 3G users. Although we could not inquire directly into the nature of this perceived lack of need in our survey, at least one finding suggests that the quality and/or adequacy of the content provided does play a role. For location-based services, the most significant divergence in adoption between 3G and GSM users can be found. Given that location-based services are the most mobility-specific service and given, as a comparison, the advanced development of mobile broadband in Japan, with its very broad and successful variety of location-based services (Billich 2007), the provision of well-adapted content is likely to make those services the candidate for becoming the mark of distinction for 3G technology.

Another part of the explanation for the non-use of available services by many 3G users again relates to the question of design concepts: As what kinds of devices are 3G phones perceived to be in the first place? Sugai (2007) argues for the inertia of pre-existing usage habits. Even if the motivation to upgrade to a 3G phone is due to the devices' capabilities and their new *possible* uses, at least initially de-facto usage behaviour largely continues along 'traditional' lines, leaving the new devices to be perceived above all as telephones. This perception may change over time but it is only doing so slowly.

In our own study, one finding that may help corroborate this claim is that even the majority of those 3G users who assert that they know, and know how to use, most of their devices' functions, do not use many of the advanced functions that are provided to them. The use of these functions and the awareness of their presence do not co-vary with their availability. Instead, they partly co-vary with users

---

10 With 47% (74% among 3G vs. 41% among GSM users) and 30% (68%/21%) respectively, mobile Internet and email are the most-used of those advanced mobile services that are meant to break the ground for 3G technology. The least-used applications, however, are, first, music downloads, being used by 29% of all users (41%/25%), being used frequently only by 7% (15%/5%), and never being used by 55% (58%/54%), while that service is not available to 17% (1%/19%). Second, location-based services are used by 15% of all users (41%/10%), with 4% (20%/1%) frequent and 33% (32%/33%) non-users, while these services are not available to 52% (28%/57%). Mobile TV ranks last with an overall usage of 18% (34%/14%), with 3% (7%/2%) for frequent use, 33% (43%/31%) for non-use, and 49% (23%/56%) for non-availability.

being or not being technically minded, that is, with their willingness to explore new functions. It is not unlikely that the actual way in which these users adapt those functions to their wishes – to the extent they do so – will be the first decisive step towards the more widespread adoption of 3G functions.

The Conceptual Case

Against the background of the above findings, we would see the claim as being warranted that trying to pre-define possible uses in design, as implied by the 'information appliance' design concept in particular, does not only appear to be an empirically unsuitable strategy. It may also be conceptually flawed:

First, the history of technology provides evidence that trying to anticipate or even enforce the closure of a technological design is unlikely to be successful since closure is the result of social processes and individual appropriations of a technology that are notoriously elusive of prediction (Pinch & Bijker 1987).

Second, users are not a monolithic entity. Envisioning them as standardised buyers of standardised products has its limits, while further assuming that their desires are above all of a relatively simple and uniform nature, limiting their interests to plug-and-play convenience, is misleading.[11]

Third, as discussed in Section 2 above, what functionality and usability are to different users cannot be determined in advance. The meanings of these notions depend on the interaction between the systems, their users, and the contexts of use, all of which are highly variable and specific – especially in the case of mobile devices since usage conditions vary with changing locales.

The uses and adoptions of a technology frequently diverge from the uses originally intended, and they do so in different directions according to different users' needs, and according to different environments of use. There are many examples with the best known certainly being users' adoption of the SMS function of mobile phones, which they transformed from a service message broadcast medium into a medium and style of instant communication between individuals. The widespread non-adoption of some of the core functions of mobile broadband may also serve as, albeit negative, evidence. It seems that a concept of user agency as the conscious selection of pre-fabricated means for pre-arranged ends (see point III in Section 2 above), as it is part of commercially-oriented design strategies, does not

---

11 With 14% (3% among 3G, 16% among GSM users), convenience in this sense was the second-least desired quality (after generality) among the respondents of our survey.

match the actual practices of use:[12] Not only are the means of action modified in use, often in innovative ways, but the purposes are also re-invented.

Observations like these may be generalised to the level of a conceptual argument about the origin of functions as has been proposed by etiological theories of function:[13] Any thing or property may become subject to processes of the selection of its effects. If these effects contribute to the continued existence and/or reproduction of that thing or property, they become its functions. Accordingly, the function of anything that people use is the result of the history of uses to which that thing has been put in the past, and of the effects that it displayed on those occasions. Thus, a thing's function is not something that can be determined in advance on the level of design purposes.

Trying to determine what users want and what the uses shall be may prove to be a vain effort for yet another reason – the users' agency may be limited by all sorts of constraints, but it is a highly flexible, adaptable, and often unpredictable trait of human beings. People select the purposes and means of their actions amidst the enabling and limiting conditions they encounter in the environment in which they act. Technical artefacts and infrastructures form part of that environment and are thus part of the enabling and limiting conditions in which actions take place. The selection of purposes and means, even if it may not follow the paradigm of 'optimising agents', occurs in response to those conditions, with the aim of enabling beneficial courses of action. What these beneficial courses of action are varies with conditions in the environment along with the knowledge, interests and means available to the agents. Moreover, the fact that the question of user agency concerns technologies does not imply that it is restricted to technology, that is, to issues of functionality, usability or technical knowledge. The ability to use technologies is one contribution to, and sometimes a precondition of, general agency in a social environment.

Therefore, a seemingly paradoxical picture emerges whereby, on one hand, some technologies may not be designed for any sort of emancipative purpose but can be found to enable their users to undertake forms of interaction and social participation hitherto unknown. In certain respects, this can be said of the mobile

---

12 In some cases, providers have recognised the importance of a more open approach to design; see Fortunati (2006).
13 These theories in the philosophy of science have been developed by Wright (1973); Neander (1991a, 1991b); Millikan (1984). Interestingly, these theories mainly aim at the functions of biological traits using arguments from the theory of evolution, while assuming their general applicability to, among other things, technical artefacts. The tendency to view functions of artefacts from the design perspective tends to obscure this possible explanation.

phone.[14] On the other hand, we may find technologies whose originally intended purpose was social empowerment but whose modes of use may be found to be difficult and exclusionary by many. This seems to be the case of personal computers. However, the principled openness of the design of personal computers and the different levels on which they, ideally at least, allow themselves to be interacted with, from command-line control to self-configuring applications, leave much potential for adapting their functions to meet, and ideally also to define, one's own specific purposes.

It may seem ironic that this is precisely the one aspect that is often sought to be designed away from mobile broadband devices in design concepts that pit usability against functionality in the name of the user who may end up with less of a choice as to which functions to use and which ones to omit. It may be too early to say what users will make of this attempt, but if mobile broadband technologies really prevail their uses and functions, once selected, are likely to turn out to be something quite different from what they were intended to be. Keeping the doors of design open to a greater variety of adoptions by a variety of different users and thus to let them define by themselves what is functional and usable for them may not only improve the chances of success of mobile broadband.[15] It may also improve their agency as social beings.

References

Bergman E. E. ed. Information Appliances and Beyond. San Mateo: Morgan Kaufmann (2000)

Billich C. 'Mobile Japan 2007' Lecture. Vienna: Mobile Marketing Association (9 May 2007)

Bjerknes G., Pelle E., Kyng M. eds. Computers and Democracy. A Scandinavian Challenge. Aldershot: Avebury (1987)

Davidson D. Essays on Actions and Events. Oxford: Oxford University Press (1980)

---

14 For a comprehensive survey, see Katz & Aakhus (2002).
15 Interesting examples are, first, the open-source, Linux-based development of the so-called GPE environment for palmtops and smartphones that allows for the development and implementation of a variety of applications by users themselves; and, second, the Open Moko project (www.openmoko.com) which directly aims at an open design of smartphones, on both the software and hardware levels. Whether Google's much-advertised Android mobile operating system will join this list has to be evidenced by experience.

Davis F. D. 'Perceived Usefulness, Perceived Ease of Use, and User Acceptance of Information Technology' MIS Quarterly 13(3) (1989) pp. 319-40

Fortunati L. 'Understanding Mobile Phone Design' ed. Pertierra R.: The Social Construction and Usage of Communication Technologies: European and Asian Experiences. Singapore: Singapore University Press (2006)

Goodwin N. C. 'Functionality and Usability' Communications of the ACM 30(3) (1987) pp. 229-33

Gould John D. 'How to Design Usable Systems' ed. Helander M.M.: Handbook of Human-Computer Interaction. North Holland: Elsevier (1988)

Greif H., Mitrea O., Werner M. Mobile Broadband: Design, Applications, and User Experience Report. Graz: IFZ (2008)

Haddon L. 'The Home Computer: The Making of a Consumer Electronic' Science As Culture 2 (1988) pp. 7-51

Jarvenpaa S. L., Lang K. R. 'Managing the Paradoxes of Mobile Technology' Information Systems Management 22(4) (2005) pp. 7-23

Jordan P. W. Designing Pleasurable Products: An Introduction to the New Human Factors. London: Taylor & Francis (2002)

Juntumaa, M., Tuunainen V. K. 'PIM Applications: An Explorative Study on Benefits and Barriers' Bled, Slovenia: 19th Bled eConference (5-7 June 2006)

Katz J. E., Aakhus M. A. eds. Perpetual Contact: Mobile Communication, Private Talk, Public Performance. Cambridge: Cambridge University Press (2002)

Lehmann H., Kuhn J., Lehner F. 'The Future of Mobile Technology: Findings from a European Delphi Study' Proceedings of the 37th Hawaii International Conference on System Sciences IEEE (2004)

McNamara N., Kirakowski J. 'Defining Usability: Quality of Use or Quality of Experience?' Limerick, Ireland: IEEE International Professional Communication Conference (2005)

Millikan R. G. Language, Thought and Other Biological Categories. Cambridge: MIT Press (1984)

Neander K. 'Functions as Selected Effects: The Conceptual Analysts Defence' Philosophy of Science 58(2) (1991a) pp. 169-84

Neander K. 'The Teleological Notion of 'Function'' The Australasian Journal of Philosophy 69(4) (1991b) pp. 454-68

Nielsen J. Usability Engineering. London: Academic Press (1993)

Norman D. A. The Invisible Computer. Cambridge: MIT Press (1998)

Pinch T. J., Bijker W. E. 'The Social Construction of Facts and Artifacts: or how the sociology of science and the sociology of technology might benefit each other' eds. Bijker W. E., Hughes T. P., Pinch T. The Social Construction of Technological Systems. Cambridge: The MIT Press (1987)

Satyanarayanan M. 'Swiss Army Knife or Wallet?' IEEE Pervasive Computing 4(2) (2005) pp. 2-3

Shackel B. 'Usability: Context, Framework, Definition, Design and Evaluation' eds. Shackel B., Richardson S.: Human Factors for Informatics Usability. Cambridge: Cambridge University Press (1991)

Sugai P. 'Exploring the Impact of Handset Upgrade on Mobile Content and Service Usage' International Journal of Mobile Communications 5(3) (2007) pp. 281-99

Thomas P., Macredie, R.D. 'Introduction to the New Usability' ACM Transactions on Computer-Human Interaction 9 (2002) pp. 69-73

Turing A. 'On Computable Numbers, With an Application to the Entscheidungsproblem' Proceedings of the London Mathematical Society Series 2(42) (1936) pp. 230-265

Weyer J., Kirchner U., Riedl L., Schmidt J.F.K. Technik, die Gesellschaft schafft: Soziale Netzwerke als Ort der Technikgenese. Berlin: Edition Sigma (1997)

Wright L. 'Functions' Philosophical Review 82 (1973) pp. 139-68

Giuseppina Pellegrino

Mediated Bodies in Saturated Environments: Participation as Co-construction

Introduction

The core thesis of this chapter links the issue of participation with the co-construction of actors and environments through an active shaping of ICT. Users are actors situated at the crossroad of at least two analytical dimensions: the body – more and more intertwined with portable, miniaturized technological artefacts – and multiple technological environments.

On the one hand, the body is the crossroads of several technological embodiments which make it both more artificial and more transparent (cf. Maldonado 2002). On the other hand, this body, hybridised through technological devices, is immersed and surrounded by electronic environments. Such environments are saturated by technologies defined not only as mobile, but ubiquitous. 'Ubiquitous' defines the tension towards a condition of continuous availability, where technologies are at the disposal of actors' interaction anywhere anytime and are able to elicit that interaction in a transparent, unquestioned modality (cf. Greenfield 2006).

Participation is carried through the encounter between actors and environments. Such an encounter makes participation in the broadband society (based on advanced network technologies, e.g. wireless, New Generation Networks, mobile broadband and so on) an issue where materiality and immateriality, opacity and transparency are complexly intertwined.

The aim of this chapter is to identify consequences of current and envisioned technological developments for participation and interaction. In this respect, the concept of co-construction is considered very relevant to investigate the issue of participation. In fact, participation cannot be separated from the tools, the means which make it possible. Participation is an issue linked with repertoires, routines, shared ways of doing things (cf. Lave & Wenger 1991). ICTs and mediated communication, therefore, are constitutively part of it.

The first step towards such an argument is to analyse and circumscribe what participation means. The chapter then tries to depict contexts and characters which are at the centre of new modes of participation. Firstly is environments, that means the stages where participation takes place. Secondly, is bodies as the 'original' portal of communication and interaction. Finally, consequences will be drawn with reference to ubiquity, connection and connectivity as both catalysts and boundaries to effective participation.

Participation: from (inter)action to co-construction

How is participation mediated and realized through technological infrastructures and communication media? What does it mean to participate in technologically dense environments where everyday activities depend on complex socio-technical arrays?

To answer these questions means one must first of all, understand what participation is and how it is accomplished: participation of whom and participation in what?

Participation is commonly associated with concepts of involvement, activity, and interaction; with community, horizontal communication, symmetry, reciprocity, and forms of government like democracy. In this chapter I assert that participation has to do with some sense of 'togetherness', defined as co-construction. This meaning of participation goes beyond the common idea of participation as linked with interactive technologies, and more user-friendly contexts in human-computer interaction. In fact, I argue interactive technologies do not guarantee better involvement and more effective results in the way these technologies are used and appropriated.

Studies of user identity and participation (Symon & Clegg 2005) show the highly constructed and political 'nature' of the active involvement required by users of computer-based systems in organizations. As a consequence, the effectiveness of user participation and the same concept of participation are open to contention in processes of technological change.

Co-construction means concurrency of processes: the convergence of different settings under the sign of a pervasive technologisation of bodies and environments; the constant mixture of face-to-face and mediated communication in everyday life; the increased importance of mobility, convergence and saturation in envisioning current and future environments of interaction. Participation as co-construction means new boundaries and constraints associated with opportunities emerging from new socio-technical assemblies. Some of these opportunities have to do with the assumption (mediated) communication and information retrieval are more and more at the hand of users. This changes the modes and scopes of participation, as suggested in the remainder of the chapter.

Therefore, participation as defined here means:
- to evoke a sense of 'togetherness', shared meanings, routines and tools, as it happens in the Communities of Practice learning process (Lave & Wenger 1991);

- to be able to exploit opportunities coming from a process of functional convergence through which artefacts are multi-functional and multi-task oriented;
- to take into account speed and quality of change processes;
- to distribute resources across contexts;
- to select opportunities according to personalized patterns of appropriation;
- to emphasize the political, contended nature of participation, also shaped through public discourse around new technological settings (cf. Iacono & Kling 2001).

Environments: mobility, convergence, and saturation

Scenarios of participation are based on three key-words which define three trends in contemporary technoscapes (Appadurai 1996). They are mobility, convergence, and saturation, which 'design' the context of participation at multiple levels.

Mobility

The adjective 'mobile' refers to a powerful discourse at the core of contemporary societies where flux, mobility and hybridation configure a new paradigm (Sheller & Urry 2006; Urry 2002). The mobile phone as socio-technical artefact, in this sense, is one of the icons of such a discourse. The shift of the mobile phone from work to everyday life – driving its fast growth throughout the world (cf. Castells et al. 2004; Feijòo et al. 2006; Fortunati 2001) was accompanied and signalled by a correspondent translation in the name of the technology, emphasizing its direct link with mobility. However, mobility is not a singularity, but a multiplicity: "the concept of mobilities encompasses both the large-scale movements of people, objects, capital and information across the world, as well as the more local processes of daily transportation, movement through public space and the travel of material things within everyday life" (Hannam et al. 2006, 1).

What does this mean in terms of participation? First of all, mobility is a relational concept: "while things are always on the move, they can appear in a fixed and stable manner because mobilities are all different, and we relate to them in different ways" (Adey 2006, 90). Participation has to do with the paradoxical nature of mobility: for example, qualifying the phone as 'mobile' is not unproblematic since the distinction between fixed and mobile technologies is more and more blurred (Fortunati 2001). If we look at the concept of 'relational politics of mobility' (Adey 2006), the image of the 'mobile phone' as portable, miniaturized and an anywhere-anytime device can be restructured so that it comprises situations of stability, immobility and fixity. This paradoxical constitution reflects the "Janus face of mobile phones": "(...) the mobile phone number is the affordance that provides the nomad with a fixed address" (Arnold 2003, 243).

If mobility is a resource, its access and the relationship between mobility and immobility constitute determinants of participation. To participate means, among other things, to be able to move around and to access mobile information while being immobile. Those who are not able to access these different mobilities are excluded from the opportunities mobility itself discloses. Mobility and immobility are sources of potential asymmetries in participation: "The power to determine the corporeal mobility of oneself or of others is an important form of power in mobile societies, indeed it may well have become the most significant form of power with the emergence of awesomely mobile elites" (Urry 2002, 4).

These power constraint forms of participation, in terms of access to uncoerced mobility (and immobility), are unequally distributed. Infrastructures and artefacts which enable mobility make it easier to both be on the move and stay immobile. However, access to change and flux, that means being part of a mobile society, constitutes a source of differentiation in the way participation is performed. For example, at a 'micro-level', the sense of 'togetherness' deriving from constant availability in mobile phone communication affects expectations of participants (cf. Arminen 2005).

Convergence

Different types of convergence can be distinguished for analytical purposes. First of all, media history and ICTs evolution can be re-interpreted as the result of processes of convergence which act at an *infrastructural, architectural and market* level. This is particularly evident for mobile technologies, where the trend is marked by "(...) the progressive blurring of the traditional boundaries between previously separated fixed and mobile markets which is led by the continuous technological developments (...)" (Feijòo et al. 2006, 3). In such a process, big emphasis is put on the 'mobile broadband access' as the next frontier in telecommunications, along with "the evolution of mobile Internet as a converging process of access platforms, technologies, contents and services (...)" (Ramos et al. 2004, 76).

This process of convergence is accompanied by a strong institutional discourse where rules for the competition, representations of the users' needs along with policies to reduce the digital divide are pursued (e.g. policies adopted by ITU, EU and so on).

Additionally there is a *material* profile of the convergence, which has to do with miniaturization and portability of multiple, multifunctional mobile technological artefacts (e.g. I-pods, PDAs, and so on). This aspect of the convergence is particularly linked with the body and redefines materiality and visibility of technology. Size and multi–functionality of portable technological devices make them more and more embeddable, wearable and textured within or around the body.

It is not just the mobile phone which becomes more and more 'filled' with functions and services concentrated in smarter and smarter devices, but also the environment, which becomes increasingly textured and embedded with pervasive, unobtrusive, ubiquitous technologies (cf. Lyyttinen & Yoo 2002a, 2002b; Greenfield 2006).

The last point makes convergence in many senses a *functional* process as well. On the one hand, the mobile phone is increasingly a synthesis and a concentration of communicational routines, functions and uses before belonging to different media (e.g. mobile e-mail through blackberry, video download and upload through camera phones, texting through SMS, static and dynamic pictures through MMS and so on). In this sense it can be defined not only as multi-media and multi-function device, but also as "a meta-device" (Aguado & Martinez 2006, 2).

Consequences for participation concern the need to manage concentrated functions and, therefore, more complex artefacts. Miniaturisation does not always go hand in hand with ease of use. Convergence makes selection a crucial skill to get oriented into a convergent and concentrated world; technology in practice (Orlikowski 2000) is the result of selection and patterns of appropriation through which actors often under-utilize a technological system.

Saturation

Saturation draws on Bowker and Star's (2000) analysis of classifying and standardizing. As they put it:

> "Classification and schemes literally saturate our environment. In the built world we inhabit, thousands and thousands of standards are used everywhere (…) This categorical saturation furthermore forms a complex web. Although it is possible to pull out a single classification scheme or standard for reference purposes, in reality none of them stand alone" (Bowker & Star 2000, 37-38).

According to Bowker and Star, the texture of saturation is "a matter of integration, almost like a gigantic web of interoperability" (2000, 38), and therefore so difficult to see and to grasp in its patterns. This phenomenon can be referred to the mobile phone as ubiquitous technology (Ling 2004) accessible everywhere/everytime. More generally, the concept of saturation describes well the way our bodies and environments are intertwined into chains of socio-technical relationships where technology is imagined and represented as a *continuum*: like in the 'everyware' ubiquitous computing, where technology is said 'to colonize everyday life' (Greenfield 2006). The body is one of the 'intelligent terminals' interacting with the environment. The electronic body and its dissemination across different settings is the other side of the corporeal body: both are more and more 'on the move' as this corporeal body carries with it an increasing 'charge' of electronic information stored and distributed in the environment.

Saturation has also to do with the way the mobile phone shifts patterns of communication, integrating co-presence in proximity and at distance (Urry 2002), as well as establishing the oxymoron of "the presence of those who are absent" (Fortunati 2000, 9). All this contributes to form a 'gigantic web of interoperability' not only from the viewpoint of the materiality of technological infrastructures (the 'cellular grid' with its squared lines, connections and material networks surrounding it) but especially from a symbolic viewpoint.

In terms of participation, saturation implies a higher degree of interdependence between actors and environments: as it draws a complex web of interoperability, it means we are immersed into contexts saturated and filled up with all sorts of technological artefacts. The way we interact with each other increasingly depends on access to resources distributed across technological infrastructures. Participation means to face both with a concentration (cf. convergence) and distribution (cf. saturation) of technological artefacts. This is even more evident when looking at the body.

Hybrid actors: mediating the body/mediated bodies

Participation takes place in mobile, convergent environments, saturated with all kind of socio-technical artefacts. Hybridity is the key-word which, more than others, describes the co-constructed dimension of participation. Actors playing on the mobile, convergent and saturated stage are more and more mediated by technologies, even co-extensive to them.

The body itself can be conceived of as a site of convergence and saturation, the *medium par excellence*, the portal where different languages converge (Fortunati 2005). It concurs to perform participation, as technologies converge on it and it is the result of relationships more and more mediated by technical objects. Such a mediation is enacted at multiple levels: through public discourses where the human body and the machine are constantly compared; through the material heterogeneity where technical artefacts accompany, surround and penetrate the body itself (e.g. implanted microchips); at the level of communicational patterns and routines where the model of body-to-body communication no longer describes the current patterns of interaction and does not constitute the classical prototype of mediated interaction (Fortunati 2005).

Mediating the body through these different and concurrent dimensions produces a multiplicity, which means convergence of some processes on the body and, at the same time, its melting down into a chain of actants, associations and substitutions (Latour 1991; 1992). Heterogeneity is here interpreted as fractionality (Law 1997): the body multiple, not anymore a singularity but *multiplicity of mediated bodies*.

Mediated bodies lose their perceived naturality as an attribute: they are increasingly fractured across technological lines of evolution (Longo 2002), prothesised, extended and therefore transparent, less opaque and differently artificialised than in the past (Maldonado 2002).

On the one hand, therefore, the body is shaped by technologies surrounding it (from medical prosthetic devices to personal communication technologies more or less pocketable, within or very close to the body). This is the first aspect of hybridity, which refers to the interweaving of the natural and the artificial, the human and the non-human. The body itself and its transformations take part of such a hybridity. The sense of 'togetherness' associated with participation is translated into a sense of continuity between the body and the environment.

On the other hand, hybridity means the body is transformed because of changes in forms of co-presence. Participation happens through communicational routines and patterns, more and more mediated, to the extent that "we are mediated even in situations in which we are in co-presence with another person – watching TV together, discussing news-paper stories, listening to radio while driving together, and so on" (Fortunati 2005, 55). This means body-to-body communication as prototypical (Fortunati 2005), a kind of original matrix to derive from all the other types of interaction (cf. Thompson 1995) becomes hybrid in turn. Communication (which is a fundamental way of sharing and participating) is experienced through the intermingling of body-to-body and mediated modes, with the emergence of new forms of interaction. Therefore, participation goes beyond physical co-presence and is experienced through multiple forms of proximity, both physical and virtual (Urry 2002). Social actors are expected to manage hybrid interactions and a continuum between mediated bodies and saturated environments can be traced: co-construction is inextricably linked with technological convergence on the body and environments saturated with technological artefacts. Co-construction means, therefore, to cope with interdependence and hybridized forms of interaction, which are enabled by technology but are also sources of new boundaries to effective participation.

Ubiquity, connection and connectivity: catalysts and boundaries to effective participation

Environments and bodies are more and more co-extensive to technologies. Therefore, they transform the nature and scope of participation. Because participation is increasingly dependent from technologically dense environments, new opportunities and boundaries emerge.

First of all, mediated bodies surrounded by technologically saturated environments can interact through different patterns, where the co-presence characteristic of human interaction is variously transformed. There is a *(mediated) body-to-body communication* which extends the concept of co-presence (through portable, mobile technologies); *an intra-environmental interaction*, which is made of communication pervasively embedded into everyday surfaces and artefacts (e.g. ubiquitous computing); a *mediated body to saturated environment interaction*, where mobility, convergence, saturation, and hybridity are enacted, and where ubiquitous interaction takes place.

The point in question here is how to define co-presence going beyond the corporeal co-presence of face-to-face (body-to-body) interaction. If "mediated communication is an emanation of body-to-body communication and swings between innovation and imitation of the latter" (Fortunati 2005, 54), it is also true that the prototype of body-to-body communication is more and more "evanescent" (Fortunati 2005).

As Urry (2002, 1) puts it, "one should investigate not only physical and immediate presence, but also the socialities involved in occasional co-presence, imagined co-presence and virtual co-presence". Mobile devices which travel with us and follow us while being (im)mobile, allow the emergence of what Urry defines 'virtual proximities', "multiple networks, where people can switch from one to the other (...) through the shift to a personalised wireless world (...)" (Urry 2002, 7). These transformations which enlarge the concept of co-presence, call for a closer analysis of what kind of interaction can be definable as 'ubiquitous'.

Convergence and saturation, hybridity and mobility define this interaction: *ubiquitous interaction is a type of communication performed by mobile actors,* that means human and non human assemblies (hybrids) who are mobile across time, space and context, being this mobility physical or virtual; it is extremely pervasive, to the extent of happening everywhere/every time, making time instantaneous and space simultaneous. Furthermore, it fulfils the potential of virtuality, making the relationship between connectivity and interaction more direct. Ubiquitous interaction, eventually, makes mediated communication more invisible, pocketable and easily taken for granted. Convergence and saturation account for the potential fulfilment of a continuous interaction: if bodies and environments are more and more mediated by technological artefacts, mediated interaction becomes more at hand of actors.

This point concerns basic distinctions among *connectivity* (potential to get connected to a specific medium or technological device supporting communication), *connection* and *interaction*. Going beyond a simplistic correspondence between richness of interaction and technical bandwidth of a medium, Bonnie Nardi (2005) reminded us that "to communicate with ease, we must come to feel connected to each other, we must experience mutual commitment to joint undertakings, and we must gain each others' attention" (Nardi 2005, 91).

If connectivity can be defined as potential to access information and distribute it (De Kerckhove & Viseu 2004), connection is both a pre-requisite and a result for continuous interaction over time and space. In fact, "a feeling of connection is a subjective state in which a person experiences an openness to interacting with another person" (Nardi 2005, 92). Such an openness is reminiscent of the sense of togetherness associated with participation.

Does enlarged connectivity typical of broadband society, based on more powerful technical networks, allow better connection and participation?

Connectivity both enables and constrains connection. Analyzing instant messaging in the workplace, Nardi concluded that "rather than undermining the importance of embodied experience for communication, simulated bodily experiences suggest that the impact of embodied experience is so great that people attempt to mimic it in the mediated context. The quality of experience changes as we move from embodied to virtual, yet the results of the transformation often achieve the intended aims" (Nardi 2005, 123).

But this is only one side of the relationship between embodied and virtual experience, bearing in mind that forms of intermittent embodiment make virtual experience (and togetherness associated) neither more nor less 'real' than that carried out in physical co-presence.

In summary, ubiquitous interaction makes it possible to fulfil a potential which is disclosed into 'virtuality' as a dynamic warehouse of chances/opportunities to communicate. Pervasive connectivity, in fact (especially in the case of augmented ubiquitous environments), increases the number and modalities required to establish connection and interact with other mediated bodies and environments. However, it must not be taken for granted that this connectivity will, by definition, enhance fields of connection (in Nardi's terms) or enable communication. Neither does it guarantee a more effective sense of sharing, togetherness, distribution and access to technologies.

To put it another way, transforming the potential of connectivity into actual interaction and establishing a field of connection is not automatic. Connectivity is both a catalyst and a boundary to effective participation, in the way it can encourage and foster interaction, but also erect barriers deriving from compulsion to proximity, constant availability and limited access to infrastructures.

Furthermore, we should bear in mind that some kind of 'work around' (Pollock 2005) as unexpected, creative use of technology can always occur. It can transform the potential of connectivity into innovative or conservative communicative practices. Participation, therefore, manifests itself also through work around, creativity and resistance to prescribed uses of technology.

Conclusion

By exploring the interrelationships between mediated bodies and saturated environments, this contribution has tried to identify critical profiles of participation in technologically dense environments. Assuming participation means co-construction, the changing conditions under which this co-construction is carried out were also analysed.

Convergence and saturation, which characterise the encounter between mediated bodies and environments, configure actors as constantly on the move, at the centre of processes of mediation which converge on the body and saturate multiple environments with complex socio-technical arrays. Bodies and environments are more and more intertwined with each other through dense technological textures. Participation, therefore, is the ability to manage fundamental skills, such as accessing the 'gigantic web of interoperability' (Bowker & Star 2000, 38) through which interaction and communication are differently performed; selecting options and opportunities embedded into multi-tasking and multifunctional technological artefacts; being aware mobile infrastructures are source of power asymmetries; managing a hybrid body which is more and more mediated.

Participation as co-construction manifests itself through mediated forms of communication and hybrid co-presence, which change the way a sense of 'togetherness' is achieved. In this sense ubiquitous interaction, located at the crossroad of the categories analysed, defines the potential to get connected. Its constitution does not automatically afford communication and participation. Therefore, consequences of the increasing mobility, hybridity, convergence and saturation change the way participation is expected and achieved by social actors. In this sense, ubiquitous communication and improved connectivity do not guarantee better participation and connection. Engaging in mediated sociotechnical relationships means one has to cope with contradictory profiles. Such profiles are a prominent dimension in the process through which actors and environments construct each other.

References

Adey P. 'If Mobility is Everything Then it is Nothing: Towards a Relational Politics of (Im)mobilities' Mobilities 1 (2006) pp. 75-94

Aguado J. M., Martinez I. M. 'The World in Your Pocket: Social Consequences of Mobile Phone Mediatisation in the Global Information Society' Paper presented at the XVI World Congress of Sociology. Durban, July 23-29 (2006)

Appadurai A. Modernity at Large, Cultural Dimensions of Globalization. Minneapolis, London: University of Minnesota Press (1996)

Arminen I. 'Social Functions of Location in Mobile Telephony' Personal and Ubiquitous Computing URL: http://www.personal-ubicomp.com (2005) pp. 319-323 (accessed January 2005)

Arnold M. 'On the Phenomenology of Technology: The 'Janus-faces' of Mobile Phones' Information and Organization 13 (2003) pp. 231–256

Bowker G., Star S. L. Sorting Things Out: Classification and Its Consequences. Cambridge MA: The MIT Press (2000)

Castells M., Fernandez-Ardevol M., Linchuan Qui J., Araba S. The Mobile Communication Society. A Cross-Cultural Analysis of Available Evidence on the Social Uses of Wireless Communication Technologies. Los Angeles, CA: Annenberg Research Network (2004)

De Kerckhove D., Viseu A. 'From Memory Societies to Knowledge Societies: The Cognitive Dimensions of Digitization' UNESCO World Report on 'Building Knowledge Societies' UNESCO URL: http://greylodge.org/occultreview/glor_009/digitization.pdf (2004) (accessed May 2007)

Feijòo C., Gomez-Barroso J. L., Ramos S., Rojo-Alonso D. 'Impact of Fixed-mobile Convergence on Users' Choice and Social Benefits. An Analysis of the Paradigm Shift in Communication Markets' Paper presented at the XVI World Congress of Sociology, Durban, July 23-29 (2006)

Fortunati L. 'The Mobile Phone: New Social Categories and Relations' Proceedings of Sosiale Konsekvenser av Mobiltelefoni Seminar (Telenor). Oslo, Norway (2000)

Fortunati L. 'The Mobile Phone: An identity on the Move' Personal and Ubiquitous Computing 5 (2001) pp. 85-98

Fortunati L. 'Is Body-to-body Communication Still the Prototype?' The Information Society 21 (2005) pp. 53-61

Greenfield A. Everywhere: The Dawning Age of Ubiquitous Computing. Berkeley, CA: New Riders (2006)

Hannam K., Sheller M., Urry J. 'Editorial: Mobilities, Immobilities and Moorings' Mobilities 1 (2006) pp. 1–22

Iacono S., Kling R. 'Computerization Movements. The Rise of the Internet and Distant Forms of Work' eds. Yates J., Van Maanen, J. Information Technology and Organizational Transformation: History, Rhetoric and Practice. Thousand Oaks, CA: Sage (2001)

Latour B. 'Technology Is Society Made Durable' ed. Law J. A Sociology of Monsters: Essays on Power, Technology and Domination. London: Routledge (1991)

Latour B. 'Where Are the Missing Masses? Sociology of a Few Mundane Artefacts' eds. Bijker W. E., Law J. Shaping Technology/Building Society: Studies in Sociotechnical Change. Cambridge, MA: The MIT Press (1992)

Lave J., Wenger E. Situated Learning and Legitimate Peripheral Participation. Cambridge, UK: Cambridge University Press (1991)

Law J. 'Heterogeneities' Lancaster, UK: The Centre for Science Studies Lancaster University (1997)

Ling R. The Mobile Connection: The Cell Phone's Impact on Society. San Francisco, CA: Morgan Kaufman Publishers (2004)

Longo G. O. 'Corpo e tecnologia: continuità o frattura?' eds. Fortunati L., Katz J. E., Riccini R. Corpo futuro. Il corpo umano tra tecnologie, comunicazione e moda. Milan: Franco Angeli (2002)

Lyyttinen K., Yoo Y. 'Issues and Challenges in Ubiquitous Computing' Communications of the ACM 45 (2002a) pp. 63-65

Lyyttinen K., Yoo Y. 'Research Commentary: The Next Wave of Nomadic Computing' Information Systems Research 13 (2002b) pp. 377-388

Maldonado T. 'Corpo: artificializzazione e trasparenza' eds. Fortunati L., Katz J. E., Riccini R. Corpo futuro. Il corpo umano tra tecnologie, comunicazione e moda. Milan: Franco Angeli (2002)

Nardi B. A. 'Beyond Bandwidth: Dimensions of Connection in Interpersonal Communication' The Journal of Computer-supported Cooperative Work 14 (2005) pp. 91-130

Orlikowski W. J. 'Using Technology and Constituting Structures: A Practice Lens for Studying Technology in Organizations' Organization Science 11 (2000) pp. 404-428

Pollock N. 'When Is a Work-Around? Conflict and Negotiation in Computer Systems Development' Science, Technology, & Human Values 30 (2005) pp. 496-514

Ramos S., Feijóo C., González A., Rojo-Alonso D., Gómez-Barroso J. L. 'Barriers to Widespread Use of Mobile Internet in Europe. An Overview of the New Regulatory Framework Market Competition Analysis' The Journal of the Communications Network 3: 3 (2004) pp. 76-83

Sheller M., Urry J. 'The New Mobilities Paradigm' Environment and Planning 38 (2006) pp. 207-226

Symon G., Clegg C. 'Constructing Identity and Participation during Technological Change'. Human Relations 58 (2005) pp. 1141-1166

Thompson J. B. The Media and Modernity. A Social Theory of the Media Cambridge: Polity Press (1995)

Urry J. 'Mobility and Proximity' Sociology 36 (2002) pp. 255-274

Theme II:
Emerging Interpersonal Communications among e-actors

Amparo Lasen

Mobile culture and subjectivities: an example of the shared agency between people and technology

Introduction

The term 'Mobile Culture' refers here to the culture of the mobile phone, understood as a shared set of practices, meanings, relationships, norms, exchanges and rituals (e.g. Goggin 2006), and to the growing importance of mobile technologies, mobility and flows, in their different modalities, in contemporary societies (Urry 2000). Besides being portable artefacts carried by their owners on the move, mobiles also contribute to mobilising bodies, affects and sensations and to creating occasions for contacts, exchanges or monitoring. Different types and scales of mobility are related to mobile phones regarding people, devices and services accessible from different places (c.f. micro-, local and remote mobility, Weilenmann 2003; Weilenmann & Larsson 2001; Luff & Heath 1998). Contemporary technological mediations, uses and practices are shaping what can be called a broadband society. This cannot be properly understood without taking into account this mobile culture in its different meanings. One of the consequences of the pervasiveness and ubiquity of mobile phones nowadays, and of their mediation of people's communications and relationships, is that these devices are also taking part in the shaping, transformation and maintaining of subjectivities, in the way we experience, think about and perceive ourselves, others and the world.

The growing convergence between different technologies and media is one of the main features of these uses and practices. Convergence as a social and technological phenomenon is in itself a form of mobility: a flow of content across multiple media platforms; the migratory behaviour of media audiences; and also lives, desires, memories, relationships and fantasies travelling across different media channels (Jenkins 2006). Convergence is part of the contemporary mobile culture and mobile telephony is a key element in the development of both. However, contemporary social, economic, political and technological dynamics that are increasing convergence and mobility do not imply the absence of other logics and resistances such as technological divergence, conflicts between industry and users, and between companies, or legal issues tending to regulate and limit the flow of contents. Further, differences in class and nationality related to the possibilities and meanings of mobility should be taken into account, along with contemporary practices and political decisions to control, regulate and prevent the mobility of people, goods and ideas, creating significant forms of immobility in order to guarantee the securitisation of modern societies (Turner 2007). Bearing that in mind, beyond economic, geographic, gender and other differences related to personal mobility, there is a radical or essential kind of movement and mobility linked to life and being, as well as to the notion of identity, understood as a multifaceted and unachievable process.

The theoretical sensibility of this paper connects to another kind of mobility, a 'mobile epistemology' in the realm of social theory which acknowledges the fluidity and mobility of social realities, asking for a sociology beyond societies (Urry 2000), the recognition that group formations are not 'buildings that need to be restored' but 'movements that need continuation' (Latour 2005), that social ties are fluid, translations, a movement that needs to be followed, traced, accounted for. The possibility of these movements being tracked and of this fluidity being continued and stabilised is largely ensured by the materiality of objects, bodies and artefacts. In Latour's words, 'technology is society made durable'. In our case, mobile phones are not only mediators of verbal, written and visual communications but artefacts that make and keep inscriptions as numbers, sounds, images and texts. Mobile phones and their ability to inscribe communications, messages, social networks and activities are an example of this ability of objects to stabilise and to make durable and traceable practices, activities and relationships (Ferraris 2005). Thus, in our study these inscriptions allow us to trace some of the complex bonds created in couple relationships.

Drawing on qualitative and ethnographic research on mobile phone uses in Spain and in the UK[1], this chapter explores the role of artefacts in the shaping, transformation and maintaining of subjectivities in order to better understand how mobile phones are taking part in these subjectivation processes nowadays. According to Foucault, subjectivation concerns the 'way a human being turns him or herself into a subject' (Foucault 1982, 208). It is a process of self-formation in which people are active and come into being through a variety of 'operations on their own bodies, on their own souls, on their thoughts, on their own conducts' (Foucault 1988, 18). That is the process of relating to oneself and shaping the self through social practices, disciplines, exchanges, communication, interpersonal relationships and power relations, involving individuals, groups, institutions, and the material and the media environment. This process is never either only individual or only collective, although it involves a principle of internal regulation so much so as to be defined by Foucault as a relation to oneself or as a constitutive moment

---

1 Proyecto Complutense 2006 'La mediación de subjetividades e identidades sociales a través de la telefonía móvil', with my colleagues from the University Complutense of Madrid, Angel Gordo and Lucila Finkel; and previous research in the Vodafone Surrey Scholar Project at the DWRC, University of Surrey (Lasen 2005).

of the self. As Foucault reminds us (Foucault 1982), the word 'subject' has taken on a double meaning: subject to another by control and dependency, and subject as a constraint on the own identity, the conscience and own self-knowledge. Both meanings suggest a form of power that subjugates and constitutes the subject. This chapter brings forward an analysis of how mobile phones, take part in both aspects: self-identity, conscience and self-knowledge; along with control and dependency, as well as different strategies for dealing with these. Concerning mobile phones, two aspects of control and dependency emerge: related to the relations between users and the device itself, this is attachment and dependency towards the object, and also regarding power and monitoring in interpersonal relationships mediated by the phone, such as those between employers and employees, working colleagues, members of a couple relationship, friends etc.

A brief description of some aspects of mobile phone uses and practices in young couples' relationships in Madrid related to mobile phone personalisation will provide an example of how the shared agency between individuals and objects takes place, playing a main role in power relationships and control strategies. Subjects and power relations are effects generated by a network of heterogeneous materials in interaction. ICTs form part of this network. Contemporary subjectivities are being shaped by TV and radio reception, mobile use, blogging, chats, and email, among other activities and applications. All these activities involve the creation, diffusion and reception of sounds, images and texts. The process of constitution, transformation and preservation of subjectivities is an ongoing aspect of everyday life, shaped by the interaction of different strategies of identification, modes of socialisation and personalisation of subjects. As personalisation is a reciprocal activity or stylisation, people personalise their devices such as mobile phones and are, in return, personalised by them. The personalisation of the device concerns ringtones, covers, pictures and video clips, and also the communications made and the information stored, all of which contribute to building a unique and personal device. The personalisation of this particular artefact also redefines what a person entails: self + role + place + time + device + network.

This analysis is situated within contemporary theoretical approaches that challenge views on the status of objects and subjects, such as the Actor-Network Theory, the concepts of Cyborg (Haraway 1991), Post-human entities (Hayles 1999) and Post-Humanism. A recent contribution by Giorgio Agamben is also discussed in which the Italian philosopher revisits Foucault's concept of apparatus (*dispositif*) and considers mobile telephony as, in his words, an 'insidious' example of the particularities of present *dispositifs* (Agamben 2009).

Much thinking involved in preparing this text was triggered by the suggestive and enigmatic concept of 'Dyonisian Materialism' coined by the German philosopher Peter Sloterdijk (1989). This notion calls for a recognition of the physicality of thought, for a consideration of the body and drama as the basis of consciousness and subjectivities, highlighting the material and embodied conditions, as well as the theatrical and performative aspects of consciousness and subjectivity. According to the essential mobility of human life and identities, subjectivity is like 'a plot carried out from scene to scene thanks to the improvisational powers of an ensemble of actors' (ibidem, 96), like the spiritual journey of a hero wearing different and successive masks caught in a fluctuation between the processes of masking and unmasking. It can be considered a drama, as an action driven by conflict that entails the unity of lust, pain and knowledge, revealing the illusory aspect of a unified and autonomous subject. This theatrical experience of the self also means 'the impossibility for self-reflection and identity – in the sense of an experience of unity that could lead to contentment – to occur simultaneously', as any self-reflection moment requires to be aware of the mask, to posit oneself as an other, to regard oneself as an other.

The body is the ability to be affected by the external world. It is understood as the learning to be affected and the skills and developments acquired from this learning. Technologies that extend bodies' abilities contribute to modifying our perception and shaping our bodies forms part of this learning. This notion of materialism, as ecstatic and Dionysian learning, can be explored through the study of the associations between people and technology; for instance, through the affects and emotions involved and through the shared agency and mutual configuration between the materialities of bodies and devices. The thread of this notion can also be followed in the study of the role played by information and communication technologies ('ICTs') and their inscriptions in these processes of masking and unmasking, in the different performances of the self, in the contribution of ICTs to the presentation of the self, as well as in the abilities and occasions for self-observation and reflection afforded by such devices. The notion of Dyonisian materialism according to Sloterdijk's reading of Nietzsche (1989) goes far beyond our topic but offers the possibility of new articulations, views, perspectives along with problems and questionings for the study of the personal, social, political and cultural implications of ICT uses and presence in our lives.

A shared agency between people and technologies

Research on mobile phone uses has already suggested that they mediate the constitution of social identities, for instance through consumption tied to selfhood, and based on the diverse and fluid meaning engendered by mobiles in terms of class, generation, political stance and gender (Nafus & Tracey 2002). Mobile phone use has been related to the presentation of the self (Fortunati 2005) and to the construction of the self characterised by fluid and multifaceted identities (Gergen 2003). Meanings attributed to mobile phones linked to identity, sexuality and desire, which receive a specific value and act as symbolic markers, have been studied in relation to the use of mobile phones associated with gay lifestyles (Cooper et al. 2000). Considerations about identity are raised in studies about the personalisation of the device (Oulasvirta & Blom 2008) and about the management of privacy related to the mobile phone (Ling 2004; Licoppe & Heurtin 2002; Palen & Dourish 2003). Personal and social identities are addressed in research about young people's use of the mobile phone and also related to gender and ethnicity (Lobet-Maris & Henin 2002; Skog 2002; Ling 2001, 2004; Green & Singleton 2007).

Social imagination and the experience, display and sharing of affects, emotions and feelings play an important role in the process of identification and the constitution of subjectivity (Bauman 2003; Maffesoli 1993, 1996). The different ways through which the mobile phone mediates people's subjectivity can also be addressed by studying the affective role of mobile phones: from emotional attachment to the device to affective communication through mobile phones, or through the way phone use alters the display and communication of emotions in public, therefore modifying the perception and categorisation of strangers (Lasen 2006; Tomita 2005). Recent research on mobile phones and affective communication deals with how mobile phone uses play a role in the imagination and the expression, display, experience and communication of feelings and emotions (Ellwood-Clayton 2003; Fracchiolla 2001; Lasen 2005; Lobet-Maris & Henin 2002; Vincent 2006, 2007 and her chapter in this volume; Rivière 2002; Ling 2006).

The production of subjectivities, that is to say, the way we perceive, experience and consider ourselves, others – either familiar or strangers – and the world, is affected, transformed and co-created by our environment. Objects that surround us and interact with us form part of this environment. The issue of the constitution and expression of subjectivity is closely linked to the formation of groups and to the feeling of belonging to a group of people with whom we share experiences, images and ideas. ICTs afford the sharing of experiences and also contribute to their creation. The role of mobile phones in the constitution of subjectivities can be grasped through the different ways in which the device mediates people's relationships, that is, the different ways of acting as an intermediary agent, also in the ways its use modifies the understanding and organising of time and space, and in the way mobile phone uses affect the body and its abilities. The embodied practices and the shared agency between bodies and devices refute the idea of an invasion of bodies passively penetrated by technology. Rather, technological devices are seen as objects that are part of our environment, already part of society, existing as social actants which take part in the transformations, subjections, building and rebuilding of this changing mixture of heterogeneous elements, material and immaterial, called subjects. The materiality of the bodies and objects taking part in the subjectivation process also entails immaterial elements with a virtual dimension, the tendencies and potentialities that have not been yet actualised. Thus, corporeal materiality is not understood as a 'substance but as a *transductive* field in which psychical, physical, technical and affective realities precipitate' (MacKenzie 2002, 35; emphasis in the original). Embodiment is also technical. This process involves capture and containment, the organisation of forces with a degree of consistency such that they are apprehensible as bodies, subjects and objects. Yet the outcome of such processes is neither inevitable nor dictated from the beginning by some overarching structural logic (Latham & McCormack 2004, 718-9). Then, mediation in this case is neither a cause nor an effect: it is a pause, a support, before the advent of a new configuration. Bodies and associations, things and dispositifs are all mediators, at the same time affected and effecting in a mutual shaping relationship made up of affordances and constraints (Hennion 2004). Further, mobile phones are both objects to be used and consumed and are also 'media through which social relations are instantiated and performed' (Green 2003, 44).

ICTs' mediations of relationships and identification are linked to the growing individual effort required to maintain and renew social bonds (Bauman 2003). Social networks are unable to make people's interactions last in time and space without the mediation of objects, without the shared agency between people and technologies. The materiality of objects and bodies is the necessary feature of the duration and continuity of relationships, bonds, practices, as well as subjectivities and identities. Therefore, the growing flexibility, fluidity and frailty of these networks and bonds would rend even more necessary and crucial the mediations provided by these devices.

The approach of Action Network Theory to the understanding of agency and human interactions is well suited to investigating the role of technologies, such as mobile phones, in the subjectivation process. According to this approach, subjectivities are not given but arise in specific material and corporeal relations (Law & Moser 1999; Gomart & Hennion 1999). Identities are created and renewed through common actions and networks of practices. Agency and social identification are the result of negotiations and power balances involving individuals and institutions, but also the objects that constitute our material environment. Subjectivities and technologies are mutually shaped (Latour 2005), as post-human forms of entangled agency (Hayles 1999). People and technologies form part of a network of interests. This is not a network connecting entities already there, but a network which configures the entities involved. The agents, their dimensions and what they do all depend on the morphology of the relations in which they are involved (Callon 1999).

The entity 'me and my mobile' (i.e. Vincent's chapter in this volume) constitutes a particular type of human and nonhuman assembly (Latour 2005; Akrich & Latour 1992). This is constituted in situated practices where other actants – groups, individuals and objects – are involved. Shared agency means that mobile phone uses are considered to be a distribution of competencies and performances between people and devices: the result of what we make our mobiles do and what they make us do. That is, what they allow us to do ('affordances') and what they prevent us from doing, including uses foreseen by the industry, the *detournement*[2] of affordances and constraints, the creation and discovery of uses not intended by the designers, and the resistance to certain uses, affordances and practices. This view of a shared agency allows us to avoid a double pitfall when considering the uses and practices involving technologies: technological determinism and the consideration of technologies as mere neutral tools.

Mobile phones as contemporary dispositifs

Giorgio Agamben revisits this Foucauldian concept in a short text whose English title is *'What is apparatus?'* and considers mobile telephony as an example of contemporary dispositifs. This French word can be translated as a socio-technical system, device, mechanism and plan of action. Foucault's notion encompasses all these meanings (Foucault 1977, 1978). Therefore, dispositifs are networks embedding a multiplicity of elements. Agamben defines it as a collection of practices, knowledge, skills, measures and institutions whose aim is to manage, govern, control and orientate in a useful way people's behaviours, gestures and thoughts. He broadens the scope of this notion to anything able to seize, orientate, determine, intercept, shape, control and assure the gestures, behaviours, opinions and discourses of living beings. Accordingly, mobile telephony and computers join schools, factories, prisons, disciplines, but also writing, navigation and literature in the large category of dispositifs.

Agamben divides entities into two classes: living beings and dispositifs and, as a third part, subjects: the effects of the interactions *corps à corps*, body to body, between the other two. In Agamben's view, shared agency is also a clash, an assembly or association also being infighting and subjection. This agonistic materialism can lead to a better understanding of the shared agency between people and artefacts. However, the finalism of his argument and the unidirectional character of the relationship between people and dispositifs, which does not really account

---

2 Deflection, diversion, rerouting, distortion, misuse, misappropriation, hijacking, or otherwise turning something aside from its normal course or purpose.

for resistance or mutual shaping, undermine the value of such battle, as well as ethnographic study and research of the details of the formation, evolution and working of such mechanisms.

Dispositifs have always existed since the birth of *homo sapiens* and played a crucial role in them becoming human, as Agamben states. The particularity of present times is the gigantic proliferation and accumulation of such mechanisms, parallel to the everlasting production of new artefacts required by late capitalism which trigger a continued and infinite development of subjectivation processes, highlighting the theatrical, dramatic aspect of any personal identity. These processes also entail de-subjectivation dynamics regarding modes of subjections (dependencies, forms of control) and the shaping of the self entailing the loss and destruction of older attachments, forms of power, identities, ways of doing and perceiving. Regarding ICTs, these de-subjectivation processes can be tracked in the usual oblivion of how things were done before owning and using these devices. For instance, in our different studies about mobile phone uses quoted above participants were asked about how they communicated and organised their lives before they had a mobile phone, and in all cases they found it very difficult and even impossible to remember how they did. Another example of de-subjectivation regarding mobile phones is the rapidity in which the presence and use of mobile phones have been accepted in spaces, contexts and situations where its use was in conflict with existing norms of etiquette and with the correct socially expected behaviour, also overcoming the initial reluctance and uneasiness of the users studied (Lasen 2005).

The omnipresence of technical dispositifs, at least in developed societies, entails that any moment of individuals' everyday life is mediated by one or more of them. In this sense, the pervasiveness and ubiquity of the mobile phone make its seizure of individuals more intense than that of other artefacts as is revealed in attachment to the device (Lasen 2005). The mobile is 'embodied in us', in the words of one participant in our research, it is always on, always open. The emergent entity 'me and my mobile' augment the subject's opening and accessibility to the world, to their significant others, and therefore increases the need to manage this accessibility. People's presence is also mediated by the device (Lasen 2006): in urban places, in friends' and loved ones' minds and hearts, in places where their contacts are, in all the phone books where their numbers are, and in all the places where those mobiles are. These characteristics of mobiles increase the decentring and heteronomy of individuals.

Deleuze's reading of the concept helps to clarify these issues: dispositifs are machines that make people see and talk (Deleuze 1992). Not as light makes objects already there visible, but as a way of distributing what is visible and what is not. This is an aspect of what we call the inscriptive power of mobile phones, for instance when they afford the inscription and visibility of users' social networks, of their significant ones' presence, or of their affective bonds inscribed in the images and SMS sent and stored, and even of the intensity, reciprocity or lack of it in these relationships, measured through the register of calls and SMS, as some of the participants in our research do. Agamben regards these technological mediations as control, shaping and contamination, entailing increasing separation between individuals and their environment, and also among them, making personal relationships more abstract. According to him, this alienation is one of the effects of the growing presence and use of mobile phones. This separation and abstraction could also be referred to, with different undertones, as the deployment of multiple mediations. It is not clear in his argument if this abstraction is related to the mediation of artefacts and that therefore its opposite, more concrete relationships, would point to a kind of unmediated communication. Agamben claims that mobile phones contribute to growing abstraction in personal relationships and that modern dispositifs only entail de-subjectivation processes without contributing to the generation of new subjectivities. These statements and the use of terms like 'seizure' and 'contamination' led us to think that this fiction of a substantive, pure, un-mediated and un-attached subject involved in forms of relation and communication without the artefact's mediation, still underlies his argument.

Personalisation and trans-personalisation of the mobile phone

The shared agency of people and their mobiles is caught up in the dynamics of difference and identity, isolation and consolidation. Personalisation of the device is one of the aspects performed as a mutual stylisation produced between the object and its owner. This personalisation is an effect of the reciprocal relationships of bodies, data and performances involving people and artefacts. It entails the realisation and storage of diverse inscriptions: SMS, voice messages, pictures, films, numbers, dates, call register, registered sounds, melodies, ringtones, songs, etc. For instance, a register of significant moments of a couple's relationship is kept on the mobile: the wedding picture on the mobile screen, the date of their first date as a PIN, an old SMS with love contents or related to events such as the acquisition of a flat. The lastingness of these, more or less ephemeral, traces depends largely on the memory size of the device and on the periodic decision taken about what texts, numbers and pictures deserve to be kept. Mobile phone personalisation as a way of individuation, self-representation and recognition not only concerns individuals but also other entities such as couples, as was found in our research about mobile uses and the practices of heterosexual couples carried out in Madrid. Mobiles contribute to individuation of the couple entailing a growing des-differentiation of its members, and to the self-representation of the couple and its recognition by other people and partners too. For instance, the evolution of a relationship can be inscribed and read in the modalities of their mobile phone contract: first the inclusion of the other in the favourite numbers list, then portability to share the same operator and, finally, a family contract[3]. In our study it was found that young adults in Madrid allow their spouses, boyfriends or girlfriends total accessibility to their mobiles. They know the other's mobile PIN, answer and make calls with the other's mobile, give out the partner's number to be called, download contents (music, pictures) to the other's device, read and even delete SMS and numbers (cleanup as they say). Such accessibility seems to be becoming one of the expectations and obligations of being part of a couple. Mobiles embody significant others' virtual presence thanks to the possibility of permanent contact. In this case, the presence is reinforced through the inscriptions they have made in their partners' devices. It is not only the usual traces of other people in our mobiles (stored numbers and SMS, call register, pictures and videos we have made) but the personalisation of the other person's device that can be called 'trans-personalisation': making inscriptions in the girlfriend's or husband's mobile (images, pictures, sounds) and taking decisions about what deserves to be kept or deleted (SMS, numbers) in the other's device.

As a result of this trans-personalisation and shared use of the mobile phone that is characteristic of young couples, the mobile is not perceived as a personal object. By making these inscriptions or by erasing other people's ones, they remind their partners that the device and its management also belong to them, that the realm of relationships and exchanges mediated by the mobile is also their business and do not escape their influence. Therefore, this trans-personalisation reveals a de-differentiation process within the couple stressed by the obligation of the double accessibility afforded by mobile phones: to the person through the mobile, and to the device itself and its contents. These obligations reveal a lack of privacy within the couple, which does not seem to be a matter of concern for them. This reduced concern for privacy is also found in other young people's practices related to media and the Internet, such as blogging and photoblogging or the disclosure and sharing of personal information at social networks sites such as Myspace or Facebook.

In spite of being a 'personal technology', mobiles do not increase personal autonomy and individualisation when used according to the norms and expectations shared among the couple whose aim is to consolidate the new entity and ward off

---

3   Mobile Phone operators in Spain offer a cheaper contract called family contract involving at least two numbers. 'Contract couples' are recognised as a family unit by their phone bill before being united by their mortgage or by the register office.

the risks of a double life, betrayal and unfaithfulness. A notion of trust emerges demanding complete transparency. Anything unknown or inaccessible becomes synonym of hidden and threatening, as it is revealed by the young adults interviewed, who do not understand the objection to total accessibility to the device, unless something must be hidden. The potential of the mobile phone to support and reinforce the individual realm of activities, in this case the differences between those making up the couple, and to manage and extend the mobility of affects and affiliations, is fought and downplayed, whilst its capacities as an inscription and monitoring machine are developed. Both aspects entail learning, conflict and collaboration with the affordances of the device and also with the mobile operator's conditions. Trans-personalisation is also the result of negotiations, conflicts and collaborations between those comprising the couple, related to the meaning and expectations about couple relationships. This is only a small example, briefly described, of one of the multiple aspects of how mobiles are influencing what it is to be part of a couple nowadays, making relationships more complex and open to more participants, but not necessarily more abstract, whatever that might mean.

Conclusions

Alienation, masquerade, separation, the multiplication of mediations and assemblies, multiple body-to-body encounters with different artefacts and their constraints, leaving aside the different value judgements about these situations related to the increasing presence and use of ICT all speak of a decentred subject. As has already been made clear by thinkers such as Latour, Sloterdijk, Haraway or Hayles among others, it is not that ICTs are creating a new situation; rather, they are making more evident the existence of these mediations and the work of producing subjects and subjectivities. Therefore, it is becoming more difficult to maintain the modern illusion of the autonomous and consistent subject, in control of being able to enter into unmediated relationships with others and with their environment.

Peter Sloterdijk observes how contemporary Nietzsche questioning about identity involves the drama of individuation; the 'battlefield' or 'hells' of difference and identity; the concurrent trends towards isolation and consolidation or fusion; and the impossible simultaneity of identity and reflexivity. Mobile phones take part in this battle, i.e. in the constitution and transformation of subjects considered as changing and heterogeneous material and informational entities. This assembly 'me and my mobile' is linked to other entities (e.g. couple, family), according to different situations and affiliations. Mobiles are part of embodiment and subjectivation processes, contributing to the extension of bodily abilities and to the modulation of people's presence, rendering virtually present those who are absent but potentially reachable through the mobile as well as playing a role in the way we modulate our presence in public places (Lasen 2006) or share our attention between different settings and situations. They are also playing a role in the configuration of people's subjections and dependencies, not only related to a growing attachment and dependency to the device, but also by the new social obligations, accessibility and ways of monitoring that they are facilitating. They are also contributing to other aspects of the shaping of the self, for instance regarding the management, communication and display of emotions (Lasen 2005). The inscription power of the device is creating new occasions for monitoring and heteronomy as the example showed in this chapter, and is also providing new possibilities for self-knowledge and reflexivity for mobile phone owners.

The development of convergence multiplies the occasions on which different kinds of artefacts and individuals gather together with the entity 'me and my mobile'. The usual definition of convergence regarding mobile phones refers to their different applications such as voice, text, data, images and music and the possibilities to produce, receive and convey content from and to other media (TV, radio, Internet). But mobiles reveal another modality of convergence susceptible of eliciting conflicts and dissonances. A flow of different interactions and social functions is embodied in the device such as connectivity, co-ordination, everyday organisation, control and monitoring, entertaining, affective communication, emotion management, accessibility, heteronomy and autonomy, etc. All of these aspects are made visible and physical through their inscription in the device as sounds, images, numbers and texts. The two interlinked modes of convergence take part in the processes of individuation, self-representation and recognition that are performed by people and their mobile phones.

References

Agamben G. 'What is an Apparatus? and other Essays' Stanford University Press (2009)

Akrich M., Latour B. 'A Summary of a Convenient Vocabulary for the Semiotics of Human and Nonhuman Assemblies' in Bijker W. E. and Law J. eds. Shaping Technology/Building Society: Studies in Sociotechnical Change. MIT (1992)

Bauman Z. Liquid Love Oxford: Blackwell (2003)

Callon M. 'Actor Network Theory: the Market Text' eds. Law J., Hassard J. Actor Network Theory and After London: Blackwell (1999)

Cooper G., Green N., Moore K. 'Mobile culture: the symbolic meanings of a technical artefact' paper for 'Culture, Psychology and New Technologies' Symposium (December 2000)

Deleuze G. 'What is a Dispositif?' Armstrong T.J. ed. Michel Foucault Philosopher New York: Harvester Wheatsheaf. (1992)
Ellwood-Clayton B. 'Virtual Strangers. Young Love and Texting in the Filipino Archipelago of Cyberspace' ed. Nyíri, K. Mobile Democracy. Essays on Society, Self and Politics Vienna: Passagen Verlag (2003)
Ferraris M. Dove sei? Ontologia del telefonino Milano: Bompiani (2005)
Fortunati L. 'Mobile Telephone and the Presentation of Self' eds. Ling, R., Pedersen, P. E. Mobile communications: Re-negotiation of the social sphere Surrey, UK: Springer (2005)
Foucault M. Discipline and Punish: the Birth of the Prison New York: Random House (1977)
Foucault M. The History of Sexuality, Vol. I: An Introduction, translated by Robert Hurley New York: Pantheon (1978)
Foucault M. 'The subject and the power. Afterword' eds. Dreyfus H. L., Rabinow P. Beyond Structuralism and Hermeneutics Chicago: The University of Chicago Press (1982)
Foucault M. 'Technologies of the Self' eds. Martin, L.H. et al. Technologies of the Self: A Seminar with Michel Foucault London: Tavistock pp. 16-49 (1988) URL: http://www.thefoucauldian.co.uk/tself.pdf (accessed January 2009)
Fracchiolla B. 'Le téléphone portable, pour une nouvelle écologie de la vie urbaine?' Esprit critique. Revue électronique de sociologie 3 :6 (2001) URL: www. espritcritique.org/0306/article2.html (accessed January 2009)
Gergen K. J. 'Self and community in the new floating worlds' ed. Nyíri, K. Mobile Democracy. Essays on Society, Self and Politics Vienna: Passagen Verlag (2003)
Goggin G. *Mobile Phone Culture* London: Routledge (2006)
Gomart E., Hennion A. 'A sociology of attachment: music amateurs, drug users' eds. Law J., Hassard J. Actor Network Theory and After London: Blackwell (1999)
Green E., Singleton C. 'Mobile Selves: Gender, ethnicity and mobile phones in the everyday lives of young Pakistani-British women and men' Information, Communication and Society 10: 4 (2007) pp. 506-526
Green N. Community Redefined: Privacy and Accountability ed. Nyíri, K. Mobile Communication: Essays on Cognition and Community Vienna: Passagen Verlag (2003)
Haraway D. Simians, Cyborgs and Women: The Reinvention of Nature New York: Routledge (1991) pp. 149-181 URL: http://www.stanford.edu/dept/HPS/Haraway/ CyborgManifesto.html (accessed January 2009)
Hayles K. How we became posthuman. Virtual bodies in cybernetics, literature, and informatics Chicago: Chicago University Press (1999)

Hennion H. 'Pragmatics of taste' eds. Jacobs M., Hanrahan N. The Blackwell Companion to the Sociology of Culture Oxford UK/Malden MA: Blackwell (2004)

Jenkins H. Convergence Culture: Where Old and New Media Intersect New York: New York University Press (2006)

Lasen A. 'How to be in Two Places at the Same Time. Mobile Phone Uses in Public Places' eds. Höflich J., Hartman M. Mobile Communication in Everyday Life. Ethnographic Views, Observations and Reflections Berlin: Frank & Timme (2006)

Lasen A. Understanding Mobile Phone Users And Usage Newbury: Vodafone Group R&D (2005)

Latham A., McCormack D.P. 'Moving cities: rethinking the materialities of urban geographies' Progress in Human Geography 28: 6 (2004) pp. 701-724

Latour B. Reassembling the Social, An Introduction to Actor-Network-Theory Oxford: Oxford University Press (2005)

Law J., Moser I. 'Managing, Subjectivities, and Desires' Concepts and Transformation 4 (1999) pp. 249-279

Licoppe C., Heurtin J. 'France: preserving the image' eds. Katz J., Aakhus M. Perpetual Contact. Mobile Communication, Private Talk, Public Performance Cambridge: University Press (2002)

Ling R. 'We release them little by little': maturation and gender identity as seen in the use of mobile technology' Personal and Ubiquitous Computing 5: 2 (2001) pp. 123-136

Ling R. The Mobile Connection. The Cell Phone's Impact on society San Francisco: Morgan Kaufmann (2004)

Ling R 'Life in the Nomos: Stress, Emotional Maintenance, and Coordination via the Mobile Telephone in Intact Families' eds. Kavoori A., Arceneaux N. The Cell Phone Reader. Essays in Social Transformation New York: Peter Lang (2006)

Lobet-Maris C., Henin L. 'Hablar sin comunicar o comunicar sin hablar: del GSM al SMS' Revista de estudios de juventud 57 (2002) pp.101-114

Luff P., Heath C. 'Mobility in collaboration' Proceedings CSCW '98 Seattle: ACM Press (1998) pp. 305-314

Maffesoli M. The Shadow of Dionysus: A Contribution to the Sociology of the Orgy New York: State University of New York Press (1993)

Maffesoli M. The Time of the Tribes: The Decline of Individualism in Mass Society London: Sage (1996)

MacKenzie A. Transductions: bodies and machines at speed London: Continuum (2002)

Nafus D., Tracey K. 'Mobile phone consumption and concepts of personhood' eds. Katz J., Aakhus M. Perpetual Contact. Mobile Communication, Private Talk, Public Performance Cambridge: Cambridge University Press (2002)

Oulasvirta A., Blom J. 'Motivations in personalisation behaviour' Interacting with Computers 20: 1 (2008) pp. 1-16

Palen L., Dourish P. 'Unpacking 'Privacy' for a Networked World' Ft. Lauderdale, Florida: CHI 2003 April 5–10 (2003)

Rivière C. 'La práctica del mini-mensaje en las interacciones cotidianas: una doble estrategia de exteriorización y de ocultación de la privacidad para mantener el vínculo social' Revista de estudios de juventud 57 (2002) pp. 125-137

Sloterdijk P. Thinker on stage: Nietzsche's materialism Minneapolis: University of Minnesota Press (1989)

Skog B. 'Mobiles and the Norwegian teen: identity, gender and class' eds. Katz J. E., Aakhus M. Perpetual Contact: Mobile Communication, Private Talk, Public Performance Cambridge: Cambridge University Press (2002)

Tomita H. 'Keitai and the Intimate Stranger' eds. Ito M., Okabe D., Matsuda M. Personal, Portable, Pedestrian Mobile Phones in Japanese Life Cambridge, MA: MIT Press (2005)

Turner B.S. 'The Enclave Society: Towards a Sociology of Immobility' European Journal of Social Theory 10: 2 (2007) pp. 287–303

Urry J. Sociology beyond societies: mobilities for the twenty-first century London: Routledge (2000)

Vincent J. 'Emotional Attachment and Mobile Phones' Knowledge Technology and Policy 19: 1 (2006) pp. 29-44

Vincent J. 'Emotion and my mobile phone' Conference Proceedings Towards a Philosophy of Telecommunications Convergence Conference organised by T-Mobile Budapest: The Hungarian Academy of Sciences (2007)

Weilenmann A. 'Doing Mobility' PhD Thesis Göteborg: University. School of Business, Department of Informatics. (2003) URL: http://guoa.ub.gu.se/dspace/ bitstream/2077/910/1/weilenmann.pdf (accessed January 2009)

Weilenmann A., Larsson C. 'Local use and sharing of mobile phones' eds. Brown B, Green N, Harper R Wireless world. Social and interactional aspects of the mobile age London: Springer Verlag (2001)

Julian Gebhardt

Alfred Schütz and the Media: The Intersubjective Constitution of Mediated Interpersonal Communication in Everyday Life

Introduction

This chapter will investigate the ontological pre-conditions of mediated interpersonal communication from a decidedly actor orientated vantage point. The focus is put here on one of the most fundamental problems of any kind of social (inter-) action and experience, and consequently of any type of mediated communicative activities: the problem of inter-subjectivity, which may be described here as the problem of co-ordinating reciprocal communicative actions, i.e. such activities in which at least two people are orientating themselves upon each other. The theoretical foundation employed here is the socio-phenomenological concept of the "everyday life-world" as it has been elaborated by Alfred Schütz (1967) respectively by Alfred Schütz and Thomas Luckmann (2003). In a first step I will draw on Schütz' notion of communicative actions as "expressive", "meaningful" and "goal-directed" acts of working. Based on Schütz' concept of everyday life tools as meaningfully constituted artefacts, I will then conceptualize communication technologies as communicative working tools, whose interpersonal usage is based on reciprocal orientations, rules and mutually established social practices. It will be shown in which regards Schütz' work can help us to better understand the constitutional processes of using and adopting communication tools not only in their technological but also and especially in their social and inter-subjective dimensions.

The telematization of human communication and social relationships

The media world is undergoing a massive change. Ever more media are penetrating people's everyday life and never before have so many media been used in order to establish new forms of social relationships and to maintain existing social bonds (e.g. Rheingold 2000; Jones 1998). This development of an all-encompassing "mediatization" of everyday life, culture and society (Krotz 2001) is not only marked by the circumstance that interpersonal communication is increasingly mediated through communication technologies. It is also characterized by the fact that people are relying on an ever more broadening spectrum of verbal, written and other audiovisual means of communication (e.g. Fortunati 2005; Pellegrino 2006).

While socio-scientific research projects are increasingly focussing on this all-encompassing "telematization" of communication (Höflich et al. 2004) it has hardly been possible to get an adequate theoretical or empirical grasp on how these new forms of mediated interpersonal communication can be captured and explained. Shortcomings in research include not only the question of which individual and social changes will accompany the ongoing media and communication related developments. They also include the question of how these changes may be interpreted and explained from an actor orientated vantage point – neither with regard to the processes of establishing and maintaining mediated communication nor to the processes of integrating new communication technologies into people's everyday life communicative practices. As a consequence, many researchers still use rather restricted and deterministic concepts of both media and mediated communication, either overestimating the so-called objective technological features of a given communication technology (e.g. Rourke 2004; Short et al. 1976; Daft et al. 1986; Dennis & Valacich 1999; Culnan et al. 1987) or largely overemphasizing the individual characteristics of so-called rational agencies free to choose how, why, where and when they want to realize their communicative goals with a certain medium (e.g. Dimmik et al. 2000; Leung 2000). While the above mentioned research approaches surely provide important hints to understand mediated interpersonal communication, they hardly do justice to the complex and inter-subjective nature of these activities (e.g. Scott & Timmerman 2005; O'Sullivan et al. 2004). Phenomena that need to be clarified – such as the reciprocal co-ordination of mediated communication or the constitution of media-related social practices – are often taken for granted but not promoted to be the actual research subject. In the following paragraphs it will be shown how Alfred Schütz' approach to sociology can help us to better understand such issues.

Human communication in everyday life

The main focus of Alfred Schütz was to theoretically reconstruct the meaningful constitution of social life (e.g. social relationships, societal institutions, sign systems, manufactured artefacts) in such a way as it is experienced in the subjective consciousness of actors living and acting in the everyday life-world. Although Schütz (1967) begins his action-related "hermeneutics of understanding" (Knoblauch 1995, 13) with the subjective consciousness of human actors, he never loses sight of the social and, therefore, intersubjective character of this reality scope, which he conceptualizes as a thoroughly "communicative environment" made up of interrelated and meaningfully constituted communicative actions (Renn 2006). A central concern for Schütz (1967, 139ff) is the question how actors generate and experience the "subjective meaning" (Weber 1947) underlying their social actions and how they can achieve to refer to each other in meaningful and reciprocal ways in spite of the fact that they don't have any direct access to the other's inner states of mind but having to rely on specific "vehicles of thoughts" (e.g. signs and symbols) and other "bodily signs and symptoms" (e.g. smiling, trembling, wincing, etc.), which are referring to (or apprehending) the other's subjective inner life (see also Schütz 1970, 200ff).

The first question to ask here is how communicative actions can be conceptualized both in a subjective and, most and for all, intersubjective respect and how a mutual understanding of each other is possible although the subjectively intended meaning which Ego connects with its actions, does not apply to Alter in the same way in which this meaning is constituted in Ego's consciousness. To address these questions, I will now turn to Schütz' concept of communicative actions as specific types of working and will then sketch his concept of reciprocal understanding. According to Schütz (1970, 125ff) communicative actions can generally be defined as "expressive acts", which – like other social acts as well – are "goal directed", "meaningful" and "intrinsically orientated" towards someone else (here: the interpreters), whereby following a specific form of reciprocal orientation. By this is meant that whenever a communicative action is performed, it is not only targeted at something (here: the desire to be understood) but is also intended to receive some kind of "reply" – whatever this reply may be[1]. The notion of communication as social acts of working is expressed by Schütz (1970, 205) as follows:

> "Social actions involve communication, and any communication is necessarily founded upon acts of working. In order to communicate with others I have to perform overt acts in the outer world, which are supposed to be interpreted by others as signs of what I mean to convey. Gestures, speech, writing, etc., are based upon bodily movements. So far, the behaviouristic interpretation of communication is justified. It goes wrong by identifying the vehicle of communication, namely the working act, with the communicated meaning itself."

---

1 Schütz and Luckmann (2003, 462) differentiate the term "communicative conduct" and "communication action" by pointing out that only the latter one – with regard to the actor's intention – is explicitly aimed at changing the environment: "It must […] be intentionally designed in the action plan – regardless of whether the execution will be successful or not. Hence, leaving footmarks in the snow does not meet these criteria whereas intentionally creating a path in the snow does. This shows that this action mode, too, cannot unequivocally be linked to criteria of conduct but has rather to be considered in terms of the meaning it has for the actor."

[Unless otherwise marked all citations quoted here (originally in German language) have been translated into English by the author.]

With regard to the different spheres and layers of meaning on which an understanding of another's communicative actions may be based, according to Schütz (1970, 162ff), one can differentiate between three levels of understanding – each built on top of the other: For one, any "act of understanding" can be targeted at the meaning of the used signs and symbols itself. On this level, the listener identifies the spoken words as sound patterns of a particular language system, within which they have a specific "objective meaning" regardless of who delivered the words (e.g. a parrot, a tape-recorder or a human being), whether they were spoken or written (e.g. on paper or on a stone board) or in which context this happened (e.g. a funeral or a scientific conference). The meaning the words may have for the speaker, however, is not yet an issue for the listener. Only on a further level of understanding, the listener's perception is no longer targeting the mere "external event" (here: the verbal speech-act), but also considers the person performing this event, which, at the same time is perceived as a "moving body", capable of "reasonable" actions. However, at this stage it is also of no concern to the listener what caused the speaker to speak the words here and now and under these circumstances. A "genuine subjective understanding" is performed only when the listener directs his attention no longer exclusively to the spoken words or the speaker but rather on what may have motivated him or her to speak these words. In this case Ego is dealing with Alter's subjective consciousness (e.g. his plans, goals and intentions) to which he or she will refer via its external, outwardly projected manifestations (e.g. spoken or written words, facial expressions, gestures, etc.).

While a subjective understanding, according to Schütz, always necessitates an understanding of the "subjective motives" underlying a communicative action, it has already been mentioned that the subjective meaning which Alter associates with its (verbal) actions, cannot be perceived by Ego in the same way in which it constitutes itself in Alter's consciousness[2]. That actors may still be able to establish a mutual understanding and to reciprocally adjust their actions is due to the circumstance that, in everyday life, they reduce their expectations with regard to what is considered a "real", genuine subjective understanding (see Schneider 2002, 243). Accordingly, a complete mutual understanding of each other is neither possible nor necessarily intended by the actors. This has been echoed for example in semiotics, especially in the writings of Umberto Eco (1984). Schütz's concept of understanding, in this sense, does neither describe a complete comprehension

---

2   Motives are defined by Schütz and Luckmann (2003, 254f) as „understandable and ascertainable reasons" for an action. However, motives are not to be confused with the causes of an action (see 255): "Causes (...) do not have the comprehensibility of reasons: They are passions, prejudice, habits as well as pressure stemming from social circumstances."

of the unique subjective motives of another, nor the identical comprehension of the performed actions (see Schütz 1974, 160). What understanding means here may rather be characterized as a cognitive activity which Schütz (1970, 184ff), referring to Mead (1934, 129ff), describes as a mental process of "putting oneself in the place of the other". Here Ego reconstructs Alter's activities on the basis of his own experiences, focusing his or her attention on a more or less adequate recognition of "typical motives" of "typical actors" in "typical situations" which, in most cases, may be sufficient for realizing a practical purpose at hand. On this basis, Ego and Alter suspend the differences in experiencing and interpreting the world as they are resulting from their different "biographically determined situations" (e.g. experiences, orientations, plans, relevancies, etc.) by reciprocally claiming that they could perceive things, persons and events of the outer world, respectively their representations in signs (see also Peirce 1958) in an "empirically identical" manner.

The so-called "thesis of the alter ego" is of fundamental importance here (Schütz 1970, 183ff). On this basis Ego does not only take it for granted that he or she could see the world in the same typical way as Alter if he or she would only be in his position ("idealization of the interchangeability of the standpoints"). He or she also takes it for granted that their different perspectives are irrelevant for mastering a given situation ("idealization of the congruency of the system of relevancies"). Of course the accuracy of such interpretations is closely related to the question how familiar or unfamiliar the actors are with each other. The degree of "anonymity" and "intimacy" of reciprocally applicable typifications about each other's communicative habits, plans and interests is therefore of decisive importance[3] – not only with regard to the chances of establishing and maintaining reciprocal understanding in general but also with regard to the peculiar processes of mastering the reciprocal "codes" in human communication (e.g. Eco 1976). That such idealizations are however fragile and cannot indefinitely claim their validity always enters into consciousness whenever an attempt of establishing a reciprocal understanding is prone to fail or has already failed. This is of particular importance especially in those situations, where communication partners do not share a same physical environment and can therefore only rely on the subjective descriptions of their counterparts, like it is the case in court hearings, in journalistic news reports but also in e-mail, chat or telephone conversations. So far, following conclusions may be drawn.

---

3 Typifications are defined by Schütz (1971, 213) as "pre-set contexts of meaning", in which the actor classifies contemporary items of experience (persons, actions, etc.) and interprets them as being typical for a specific circumstance.

In everyday life a perfect and ideal understanding of each other is not possible either in face-to-face or in mediated communication (e.g. Durham 2004). Although actors, based on their experience and routine in interacting with each other, have indeed become accustomed to the circumstance in which they will understand others and in which they could be understood by them, intersubjectivity is not something to be taken for granted. It must be established constantly through processes of co-operation and idealisation (see Schneider 2002, 250). This has been demonstrated for example in conversational analysis, especially by the work of Paul Grice (1975) on the "cooperative principles" of reciprocal conversations. These findings are of a particular importance in view of those research approaches (e.g. "Cues filtered out", "Channel-Reduction-Models", "Social Presence") which implicitly assume that the problem of inter-subjectivity represents a media-specific communication problem, while losing sight of the fact that it is a communication-immanent phenomenon which does not principally dissolve by itself in face-to-face encounters either. An adequate analysis of the specific scopes and limits of reciprocal communication, therefore, has not only to differentiate carefully between different levels and stages of understanding but has also to investigate the specific type of social relationship in which the communication partners are actually interacting with each other in sometimes more and sometimes less anonymous or intimate ways. Such levels of understanding do not only imply different expectations regarding the role behaviour of the participating communication partners but do also necessitate a whole spectrum of different conversational competencies. This applies to those communicative actions which are motivated by the wish to express oneself in a clear and unequivocal manner. It also applies to those encounters where communication partners – for whatever reasons – refer to rather "vague" (e.g. Keefe et al. 1999) and "ambiguous" (e.g. Gaines 2003) communication styles.

Spatial, temporal and social structures of human communication

The reality scopes in which Schütz (1970, 72f) was interested in with his analyses of human communication and social interaction represents the "world of daily life" which he named following Husserl's (1954) concept of the "life-world". Its "ontological" (temporal, spatial and social) structures (see Schütz & Luckmann 2003, 53ff) take a special ranking here because they do not only represent the basic parameters of human experience in general but also of the problems discussed here of using and adopting communication technologies in particular.

A unique property of everyday life can be seen here in the circumstance that it represents a reality which, from its beginning, is experienced as a "pre-organized" and "pre-defined" reality in which one has to act mutually with (or against) others. According to Schütz and Luckmann (2003, 70) the actors` actions and experiences in this reality scope are steered by the so-called "pragmatic motive" which does not only encompass a "pragmatic" form of orientation (the "natural attitude") but also a specific form of attention to life (being "wide-awake"). These modes do not only comprise a specific form of orientation in time and in space but also a specific perception of the social world. From a temporal point of view, daily life is structured in the dimensions of past, present and future and its subjective correlations to remembrance, accomplishment and expectation (see Schützeichel 2004, 141). Its spatial structures may be differentiated into different zones of human acting, namely the world of "actual", "re-attainable" and "potential" reach. Regarding this Schütz and Luckmann (2003, 77) particularly emphasize the "manipulatory zone" of action which comprises those spheres of life which can be affected either directly (the "primary manipulatory zone") or indirectly (the "secondary manipulatory zone"), whereby the borderlines for the latter can "only be determined by the status quo of the technological development in a given society" (Schütz and Luckmann 2003, 80). Here they are referring to such technological achievements as the bow and arrow, gunpowder, smoke signals and the telephone.

The spatial and temporal structures of everyday life are significant because they are directly related to the question how communication partners will experience each other physically in space and in time. Broadly speaking one can distinguish here between so-called "immediate" (face-to-face) and mediated (e.g. telephone, e-mail, letters) "communicative environments" (Schütz 1970, 192). These environments are not only marked by different levels and degrees of "immediacy", "interactivity" and "intensity" but also confront communication partners with each environment-specific opportunities and limitations of human understanding (see Schütz & Luckmann 2003, 541ff). The "communicative immediacy" (Schützeichel 2004, 142) of these environments, however, is not only marked by different levels of their "spatio-temporal" mediation but also by different degrees of their "social" mediation. The term social mediation refers to the level of intersubjectivity, anonymity, and familiarity by which the actors will and can experience each other, e.g. as close friends or as perfect strangers.

Whereas the problems of mediating communication in space and in time will be discussed in the next section, I will now turn to the question how different levels of "social immediacy" will affect communication within a given communicative environment. Basically, two modes, reciprocally experiencing one another may be distinguished here (see Schütz 1970, 184ff): On one hand, one may perceive others as so-called "fellowmen" in a typical "thou-orientation" (here: within a "we-relationship"). On the other hand, it is possible to experience them as "contemporaries" in a typical "they-orientation" (here: within a "they-relationship").

In principal, these modes of mutually addressing each other do not only refer to specific types and degrees of "knowledge-proven" and "content-filled" typifications about the other's communicative purposes, habits, preferences, etc. They do also point to relationship specific types and degrees of cognitive "engagement" and "concern," with which the actors (e.g. as close friends, intimate lovers, well known colleagues, etc.) are usually addressing each other. Whereas communication partners in typical "we-relationships" are usually applying a broad and differentiated "stock of knowledge" about the other's subjective consciousness, the counterparts in "they-relationships" will typically rely on rather restricted and narrow concepts of each other. The decisive characteristic of the "thou-orientation" as opposed to the "they-orientation" is the circumstance that actors, in the latter mode, will typically not refer to the subjective "being there and being as such" of a specific, unique individual (e.g. my friend X, who has a penchant for irony, a certain communicative style, a predilection for certain communication devices, etc.) but only to the behaviour of typical and anonymous others (e.g. a typical butcher, policeman, waitress, etc.).

According to Schütz and Luckmann (2003, 118ff) these modes, at the same time, are closely related to typical forms and expectations regarding the processes of establishing and maintaining reciprocal understanding – both in an objective ("they-relationship") and subjective ("we-relationship") respect. While a profound exploration of the other's subjective intentions is typically not expected in the context of a "they-relationship" Schütz and Luckmann (2003, 120), the mere attempt of penetrating the other's inner consciousness – within this type of reciprocal orientation – may be perceived as disturbing or even violating a given encounter. The opposite may be true for typical "we-relationships", where the counterparts are typically expected to show some interest in the other's subjective inner life (see Schneider 2002, 265). Of course this can happen in a sometimes more and sometimes less attentive and intensive way – depending on the situational requirements and specific interests within a given context.

These findings, at the same time, indicate that the type of social relationship, the communication partners are actually engaged in, is relatively independent of their physical presence in space and time. A friend typically remains a friend regardless of whether he actually encounters Ego face-to-face, speaks to him by telephone or sends him an e-mail. On the other side, an unknown person will intermediately remain strange whether Ego meets him or her on the street, in an online-chat or another communicative environment. Thus, also the way in which a face-to-face encounter, an exchange of letters, a telephone call or an e-mail exchange is experienced (e.g. as personal, factual or anonymous) does not exclusively depend on the technological features of the employed communication devices but, in the first instance, on reciprocally valid orientations and contextual necessities of a given encounter, even if such mutually established types of orientation may differ from time to time and in relation to certain "diachronic" developments and accompanying "uncertainties" regarding the actual status of a given relationship (e.g. Knapp & Vangelisti 2004).

The spatio-temporal mediation of communicative actions

Although the type of social relationship and corresponding forms of addressing and experiencing oneself and others are of decisive importance with regard to the "outcomes" of human communication its chances and limitations are also deeply marked by its spatio-temporal structuring. Of most importance here is the question of how communication is affected when it is not established in "direct" (face-to-face) encounters but in a technologically "mediated" ones (Schütz 1970, 219), e.g. in e-mail conversations or telephone calls. Regarding this, Schütz and Luckmann (2003, 106ff) provide two basic features for differentiation: On the one hand, the level and degree of "bodily symptoms" with which the communication partners are able to perceive each other (acoustically, visually, tactile, and olfactory) and, on the other hand, the degree of "synchronisation" with which they can participate in the other's streams of consciousness (see Schütz 1970, 216f).

Concerning the degree of perceivable "bodily symptoms" the following may be noted: Bodily symptoms represent an important function with regard to the processes of identifying oneself and others because communication partners in the "vivid presence" of a face-to-face encounter, and opposed to technologically mediated communicative environments, may still have doubts about all kinds of things but not about the actual presence of the other (see Schütz & Luckmann 2003, 572). This can be seen as a reason why the matter of trust in computer mediated communication has always been such a relevant research topic (e.g. Walther & Bunz 2005). Moreover, Ego – while having full access to the range of bodily symptoms of another person – is not only able to perceive Alter's engagement and concern but is also able to determine whether this happens with little or more attention (see Schütz 1974, 234). The degree of perceivable bodily symptoms is also important with regard to the question how a given communicative encounter is experienced and interpreted (see Schütz & Luckmann 2003, 106). Since Ego, in a face-to-face environment, can not only capture the objective meaning of Alter's purposely delivered expressions (e.g. voice, facial expressions and gestures), he or she is also capable to assess those things the other is conveying via non-motivated bodily movements (e.g. blushing, crying, trembling, etc.). Additionally, in a shared spatio-temporal environment, Alter and Ego can ascertain their reciprocal perceptions by just referring to present objects in the same environment, meaning that they are able to continuously check if their interpretations and corresponding actions are thereof adequate. This is of particular significance in those situations where language "'fails' for one or the other reason" (Schütz & Luckmann 2003, 346).

With regard to the possibilities for "synchronizing" the inner streams of consciousness and concomitant outwardly projected actions, the following may be remarked. The more direct and closely related in space and in time each action steps can be interlinked with, the better chances there are, for mutually and attentively "tuning in" (Schütz 1970, 216) on the other's inner life and corresponding actions. This means that actors are able to initiate potential corrections of their actions not only after a certain action has been performed and after the other has answered in one way or another, but rather in the simultaneity of their mutual experience. Accordingly, the question whether one understood the other correctly or not, in case of synchronised communications (e.g. face-to-face, chat, telephone) may be solved directly and simultaneously, whereas in asynchronous forms of communication (e.g. letter, e-mail, SMS) this is only possible on the basis of the "frozen results" (Schütz & Luckmann 2003, 577) of a certain action, whereby it can be hardly denied that they are receiving "another weight, another meaning" then.

Concerning the degrees of "bodily symptoms" and "synchronization" within the context of a given communicative environment it may be concluded, that face-to-face encounters of this kind are, in principle, "superior" to technologically mediated ones. However, it would be misleading to consider latter forms of communication as principally "deficient" or "problem-ridden", like it has been argued for example by the adherents of "media richness" and other related research concept. On the one hand, a number of empirical research studies clearly indicated that people are definitely capable of adapting to a whole variety of media-specific "coordination devices" (Knoblauch 1995, 54), e.g. linguistic, para-linguistic and other prosodic communication techniques, in order to adequately co-ordinate their actions in mediated communicative environments (e.g. O'Sullivan et al. 2004; Auer 1990). On the other hand, it is evident that deficits in the degree of bodily symptoms and synchronisation may be pragmatically compensated via the above mentioned typifications and idealizations regarding the communication partner's intentions, plans and habits (e.g. Dickey et al. 2006). What is even more crucial here is the circumstance that, from an actor-orientated vantage point, the so-called "weaknesses" of a given communication technology may just be regarded as their actual "strength". This is because, by using different communication media, actors are able to objectify their communicative intentions beyond the borders of time and space without having to display their subjective constitution. This means that they can use communication technologies as "strategic" interaction tools with the aid of which they may either offer or refuse certain levels of accessibility to the range of their bodily symptoms and inner streams of consciousness (e.g. Dobos 1997; Scott et al. 2005; Ling 2006). Especially if one considers Erving Goffman's (e.g. 1959; 1967; 1969) detailed and enlightening analyses of what it takes to act within the "interaction order" of co-present face-to-face encounters, one becomes aware of the burden relieving effects certain communication technologies may provide – beginning from "face-work" up to different techniques of producing and sustaining the "territories of the self".

Does this mean that the ever broadening spectrum of different communication technologies can be regarded as a large and well-equipped tool-box, from which actors can arbitrarily choose which communication tools they want to use in order to get into touch with each other? Each time depending on their will to either present or refuse certain levels of accessing the spectrum of their bodily symptoms and inner streams of consciousness? This will be explored in the next section.

Communication technologies as societal tools of working

Based on Schütz's (1970, 205f) notion of communicative actions as specific "acts of working", I will now outline a concept of communication technologies which helps us to capture them as time and space transcending working tools, which are used in order to solve typically recurring everyday life problems. Such problems can be seen in the wish to contact others with whom we do not share the same physical and spatial environment, Schütz and Luckmann (2003, 49ff) illustrated this by the example of the letter and Schütz (1974, 117f) by the example of the telephone. From an actor-orientated vantage point one can say then that communication technologies, like other tools as well, are not only perceived as mere technological objects of the outer world but as meaningfully constituted artefacts, which inherit a certain "typical" function (Schütz & Luckmann 2003, 46) and which are experienced as "typical" means to achieve "typical" ends within the context of establishing and maintaining reciprocal communication. This idea is elaborated by Flanagin and Metzger (2001, 24) who are referring to such media-specific "images" in the sense of "collectively held notions of how a medium is used" in the context of specific communicative practices. Such norms and social expectations, in a certain sense, are not only binding and restricting mediated communication. In the first place, they do enable actors to anticipate the possible (re-)actions of their counterparts and on this foundation to plan the goals, means and consequences of their own communicative actions (see Höflich 1996, 93f).

Schütz and Luckmann (2003, 399) clearly indicate how such tool-related orientations regarding how, where, when and why a certain tool can be used in order to solve whichever type of problem becomes institutionalized to a point where they tend to prevent "independent" and "subjective" modifications. However, it has also to be pointed out here, that the societal adoption of tools in general and of communication tools in particular does not represent a stable and temporarily fixed issue. It has rather to be seen as a socially constructed process (see Berger and Luckmann 1966) during the course of which the "practical function" (Schütz 1970, 74f) of a certain tool is negotiated, fixed and altered according to the lifeworld specific problems. Furthermore it challenges the various communications members of a given society are usually confronted with at a certain point in time. This may be illustrated for example by the historical adoption processes of a whole variety of everyday life communication technologies – starting with the telephone which in the early stages of its societal diffusion was used as a mass medium (to transmit opera concerts), but which successively established itself as a medium of interpersonal communication (see e.g. Aaronson 1977) via the internet which was originally developed as a military communication facility up to the "classic" handwritten letter which is no longer perceived as a mere space and time transcending communication tool but as a meaningfully constituted artefact, with the help of which one may express a specific relationship between oneself and others (see Taylor & Harper 2002).

Particularly true in phases of accelerated media developments, at the same time this means that people have to adapt not only continuously to new problem solving expertise and concomitant communicative competences, but also that they continually have to check and modify their hitherto proven problem solving strategies. This can be explained on the example of adapting "new" written forms of communication (e.g. e-mail and SMS) and the conceptual modifications in experiencing "older" ones, e.g. letter, fax, and postcard (see Höflich & Gebhardt 2004). The "interpretative flexibility" (Pinch & Bijker 1987) of technological artefacts can be stressed by the findings of research projects which were conducted in the context of the "Cultural Studies" and other ethnographically oriented ICTs adoption studies (e.g. within the so-called "domestication" paradigm). They all are clearly indicating that the societal adoption and diffusion of technology has to be regarded as a dynamic and thoroughly socially defined process of co-constructing and re-shaping its societal meaning (e.g. Berker et al. 2005; Haddon 2004; Morley & Silverstone 1990; Silverstone et al. 2001; Hennen 1992).

That it seems however impossible to define "the" communicative function and meaning of a certain technology becomes obvious if one recognizes that tools, following Schütz and Luckmann (2003, 45ff), do inherit at least three different contexts of meaning, which are attached to them by different actors, groups and other societal parties: Firstly, tools are afflicted with an "originally intended meaning", which their producers (e.g. developers, designers, service companies) had in mind, when they constructed a certain communication technology. Those meaning endowing acts can be described as a result of anticipating "typical" relevancies (e.g. problems, needs, goals, orientations) of "typical" users and potential customers (e.g. managers, students, seniors, etc.) in order to offer relevant technological solutions and in doing so to allow for their rapid societal integration (e.g. Agar 2003; Fortunati 2006). Secondly, technological artefacts are assigned with those "subjective" meaning contexts, which are developing in the practical context of their social usage (e.g. at home, at work, in public, etc.) and which do often manifest themselves in specific technological (life-) styles with which a single actor can express certain subjective values and orientations as well as certain affiliations to particular groups and social collectives (e.g. Ellrich 2003; Lobet-Maris 2003). Thirdly, tools adhere certain "objectified" meaning contexts, which are associated with culturally shared interpretations of their "practical relevance" – either for everyone (e.g. the telephone) or only for specific members of a given society (e.g. IM, Skype, etc.). While it might sound trivial, it still cannot be stated enough that those different meaning contexts can vary considerably, especially with regard to the "meaning supplies" as they are offered by professional ICT developers and those applied in people's everyday life (e.g. Tomlinson 2006; Jenson 2005; Haddon 2006; Green et al. 2001).

Concerning the meaningful constitution of communication technologies as societal tools for establishing and maintaining reciprocal communication, the following conclusions may be drawn. It was illustrated that the processes of using and adopting a certain communication tool are closely related to the subjective problems, needs and competences of an individual actor who will impart a certain subjective meaning to them in the context of his or her everyday life coping with reality and the communicative problems he or she is confronted with. It also became apparent, however, and this is particularly important with regard to those research approaches which are dealing with the relationship between subjective communicative needs and related forms of media usage (e.g. the "Uses-and-Gratifications-Approach"), that such meaning-endowing acts will never develop in a social vacuum but do always refer to collectively established notions of how, when, where and why and also with regard to whom a certain technology can be used as a reasonable problem-solving everyday life tool (see Westerik et al. 2006). This, at the same time, means that all theoretical approaches, which are trying to explain the constitutional processes of using and adopting communication technologies as a means of establishing and maintaining reciprocal communication must inevitably go wrong, by solely referring to the communicative needs and problems of a single user without looking at their social and therefore intersubjective foundations.

Conclusions

As could be illustrated on the basis of the life world-concept of Alfred Schütz (and Thomas Luckmann) mediated communication can generally be described as a specific type of reciprocal action (see Knoblauch 2001), to be more precise: specific social acts of working. They are meaningfully planned and their in-order-to motive is to bring about changes in the external world (here: to outwardly project the contents of one's own consciousness for the use of others). Their intersubjective constitution does not only refer to their expressive intention but also to the technological means to mediate these intentions in time and space. The concept proposed here does not only allow one to investigate the inter-subjective constitution of mediated communication in everyday life from an actor orientated vantage point. It also allows us to bind the limitations and possibilities of such actions not exclusively to the individual characteristics of a single user or to the specific features of a given communication technology but also to the specific type of social relationship, within the communication partners interaction with each other in differing degrees of anonymity and intimacy – both in a meaningful and culturally pre-defined way. Accordingly, the reflections presented here may be considered as an attempt to conceptually integrate both the technological, actor-oriented and social pre-conditions of mediated communication and in so doing to offer a research agenda within which the processes of using and adopting communication technologies in people's everyday life can be investigated in a way which acknowledges the complexity of the research phenomenon in question.

References

Agar J. Constant touch. A global history of the mobile phone. Cambridge: Icon Books (2003)

Aaronson S. H. 'Bell's Electronic Toy. What's the Use? The Sociology of Early Telephone Usage' ed. Pool I. de Sola The Social Impact of the Telephone. Cambridge et al.: MIT Press (1977)

Auer P. 'Rhythm in telephone closings' Human Studies 13 (1990), pp. 361-392

Berger P. L., Luckmann T. The Social Construction of Reality: A Treatise in the Sociology of Knowledge. New York/Frankfurt: Fischer (1966)

Berker T., Hartmann M., Punie Y., Ward, K. eds. Domestication of media and technologies. Maidenhead: Open University Press (2005)

Culnan M. J., Markus M. L. 'Information Technologies' eds. Jablin, F. M., Putnam L. L., Roberts K. H., Porter L. W.: Handbook of organisational communication: An interdisciplinary perspective. Newbury Park: Sage Publications (1987)

Daft R. L., Lengel R. H. 'Organizational Information Requirements, Media Richness and Structural Design'. Management Science 32 (1986), pp. 554-571

Dennis Allan R., Valacich J. S. 'Rethinking Media Richness' ed. Sprague R. H. Proceedings of the 32nd Hawaii International Conference for System Sciences (HICSS 32). Los Alamitos et al.: IEEE Computer Society (1999)

Dickey M. H., Wasko M. M., Chudoba, K. M. 'Do you know what I know?: A shared understandings perspective on text-based communication' Journal of Computer-Mediated Communication, 12: 1 (2006) article no. 4 URL: http://jcmc.indiana.edu/vol12/issue1/dickey.html (accessed December 2008)

Dimmick J. W., Kline S., Stafford L. 'The Gratification Niches of the Personal E-Mail and the Telephone. Competition, Displacement, and Complementarity' Communication Research 27 (2000), pp. 227-248

Dobos J. 'Gratification Models of Satisfaction and Choice of Communication Channels in Organizations' Communication Research 19 (1992), pp. 29-51

Durham P. Speaking into the Air: A History of the Idea of Communication. Chicago: University of Chicago Press (2004).

Eco U. A theory of Semiotics. Bloomington: Indiana University Press (1976)

Eco U. Semiotics and the Philosophy of Language. Bloomington: Indiana University Press (1984)

Ellrich L. 'Identitätskonzepte der neuen ‚digitalen Elite'' eds. Winter C, Thomas T., Hepp A. Medienidentitäten. Kiel: Von Halem Verlag (2003)

Flanagin A. J., Metzger M. 'Internet Use in the Contemporary Media Environment' Human Communication Research 27 (2001), pp. 153-181

Fortunati L. 'Is Body-to-Body Communication still the Prototype?' The Information Society 21 (2005), pp. 53-61

Fortunati L. 'Understanding Mobile Phone Design' ed. Pertierra R. The Social Construction and Usage of Communication Technologies: European and Asian Experiences. Singapore: Singapore University Press (2006)

Gaines E. 'The Necessary Ambiguity of Communication' eds. Prewitt T., Deely J.: Semiotics 2002. New York: Legas Publishing (2003)

Goffman E. The presentation of Self in Everday Life. Garden City: Doubleday, Anchor Books (1959)

Goffman E. Interaction Rituals: Essays on Face-to-Face Behavior. Garden City: Doubleday, Anchor Books (1967)

Goffman E. Strategic Interaction. Philadelphia: University of Pennsylvania Press (1969)

Green N., Harper R, Murtagh G., Cooper G. 'Configuring the Mobile User: Sociological and Industry Models of the Consumer' Personal and Ubiquitous Computing 5 (2001), pp. 146-156

Grice P. H. 'Logic and Conversation' eds. Cole P., Morgan J. Syntax and Semantics vol. 3. New York: Academic (1975), pp. 41-58

Haddon L. ed. Information and communication technologies in everyday life: a concise introduction and research guide. Oxford et al.: Berg (2004)

Haddon L. 'The Innovatory Use of ICTs' eds. Haddon L., Mante E., Sapio B., Kommonen K.H., Fortunati L., Kant A.: Everyday Innovators. Researching the Role of Users in Shaping ICT's. Dordrecht: Springer (2006)

Höflich J. R. Technisch vermittelte interpersonale Kommunikation. Grundlagen – organisatorische Medienverwendung – Konstitution "elektronischer Gemeinschaften". Opladen: Westdeutscher Verlag (1996)

Höflich J. R., Gebhardt J. 'Changing Cultures of Written Communication' eds. Harper R., Palen L., Taylor A. The Inside Text: Social, Cultural and Design Perspectives on SMS. Dordrecht: Springer (2004)

Hennen L. Technisierung des Alltags. Ein handlungstheoretischer Beitrag zur Theorie technischer Vergesellschaftung. Opladen: Westdeutscher Verlag (1992)

Husserl E. Die Krisis der europäischen Wissenschaften und die transzendentale Phänomenologie (Husserliania VI, ed. Walter Biemel). Den Haag: Nijhoff (1954)

Jenson S. 'Default Thinking: Why consumer products fail' eds. Harper R., Palen L., Taylor A. The Inside Text: Social, Cultural and Design Perspectives on SMS. Dordrecht: Springer (2005)

Jones S. G. ed. CyberSociety 2.0. Revisiting Computer-Mediated Communication and Community. London et al.: Sage (1998)

Keefe R., Smith P. Vagueness. A Reader. Cambridge: MIT Press (1999)

Knapp M. L., Vangelisti A.L. Interpersonal Communication and Social Relationships. Allyn & Bacon (2004)

Knoblauch H. Kommunikationskultur. Die kommunikative Konstruktion kultureller Kontexte. Berlin et al.: Walter de Gruyter (1995)

Knoblauch H. 'Communication, Contexts and Culture. A Communicative Constructivist Approach to Intercultural Communication' eds. Di Luzio A. et al. Culture in Communication. Analysis of intercultural situations. Amsterdam et al. John Benjamins Publishing Company (2001)

Krotz F. Die Mediatisierung kommunikativen Handelns: der Wandel von Alltag und sozialen Beziehungen, Kultur und Gesellschaft durch die Medien. Wiesbaden: Westdeutscher Verlag (2001)

Leung L., Wei R. 'More than just talk on the move: uses and gratifications of the cellular phone' Journalism & Mass Communication Quarterly 77 (2000), pp. 308-320

Ling R. '"I have a free phone so I don't bother to send SMS, I call" – The Gendered Use of SMS Among Adults in Intact and Divorced Families' eds. Höflich, J.R., Hartmann M. Mobile Communication in Everyday Life: Ethnographic Views, Observations and Reflection. Berlin: Frank & Timme (2006)

Lobet-Maris C. 'Mobile Phone Tribes: Youth and Social Identity' eds. Fortunati L., Katz J.E., Riccini R. Mediating the Human Body: Technology, Communication and Fashion. Mahwah: Erlbaum (2003)

Mead G. H. Mind, Self, and Society, edited by C.W. Morris. Chicago: University of Chicago Press (1934)

Morley D., Silverstone R. 'Domestic communication – technologies and meanings.' Media, Culture & Society 12 (1990), pp. 31-55

O'Sullivan P., Hunt S. K., Lippert L. R. 'Mediated Immediacy. A Language of Affiliation in a Technological Age' Journal of Language and Social Psychology 23 (2004), pp. 464-490

Pellegrino G. 'Ubiquity and Pervasivity: On the Technological Mediation of (Mobile) Everyday Life' eds. Berleur J, Nurminen M., Impagliazzo J. Human Choice and Computers Boston: Springer (2006)

Peirce C. S. Selected writings, edited by P.O. Wiener. New York: Dover (1958)

Pinch T. J., Bijker W.E. 'The Social Construction of Facts and Artefacts: or How the Sociology of Science and the Sociology of Technology might Benefit Each Other' eds. Pinch T.J., Bijker W. E. The Social Construction of Technological Systems. Cambridge et al.: Cambridge University Press (1987)

Renn J. 'Appresentation and Simultaneity. Alfred Schütz on Communication between Phenomenology and Pragmatics' Human Studies 29 (2006), pp. 1-19

Rheingold H. The Virtual Community. Homesteading on the Electronic Frontier. Cambridge: MIT Press (2000)

Rourke L., Anderson T., Garrison R., Archer W. Assessing Social Presence in Asynchronous Text-based Computer Conferencing. PhD presented at the University of Alberta (2004) URL: http://communitiesofinquiry.com/documents/SocialPresenceFinal.pdf (accessed January 2009)

Schneider W. L. Grundlagen der soziologischen Theorie Bd. 1. Wiesbaden et al.: Westdeutscher Verlag (2002)

Scott C. R., Timmerman E.C. Relating Computer, Communication, and Computer-Mediated Communication Apprehensions to New Communication Technology Use in the Workplace. Communication Research 32 (2005), pp. 683-725

Schütz A. The Phenomenology of the Social World. Evanston, IL: Northwestern University Press (1967)

Schütz A. On Phenomenology and Social Relations, edited by H.R. Wagner. Chicago et al.: University of Chicago Press (1970)

Schütz A. Gesammelte Aufsätze. Das Problem der sozialen Wirklichkeit Bd.1. Den Haag: Nijhoff (1971)

Schütz A. Der sinnhafte Aufbau der sozialen Welt. Eine Einleitung in die verstehende Soziologie. Franfurt: Suhrkamp (1974)

Schütz A., Luckmann T. Strukturen der Lebenswelt. Frankfurt: Suhrkamp (2003)

Schützeichel R. Soziologische Kommunikationstheorien. Konstanz: UVK (2004)

Short J., Williams E., Christie B. The Social Psychology of Telecommunications. London: George Allen & Unwin (1976)

Silverstone R., Hirsch E., Morely D. 'Listening To A Long Conversation: An Ethnographic Approach To The Study Of Information And Communication Technologies In The Home' Cultural Studies: Theorizing politics, politicising theory 5 (2001), pp. 204-227

Taylor A., Harper R. 'Age-old Practices in the "New World": A Study of Gift-Giving Between Teenage Mobile Phone Users' Proceedings of ACM SIGCHI Conference New York: ACM Press (2002), pp. 439-446

Tomlinson J. '"Your Life – To Go": Der kulturelle Einfluss der neuen Medientechnologien' eds. Hepp A. et al. Konnektivität, Netzwerk und Fluss. Wiesbaden: VS Verlag (2006), pp. 69-79

Walther J.B., Bunz U. 'The rules of virtual groups: Trust, liking, and performance in computer-mediated communication' Journal of Communication 55 (2005), pp. 828-846

Weber M.: Wirtschaft und Gesellschaft. Tübingen: J.C.B. Mohr (1947)

Westerik H., Renckstorf K., Lammers J., Wester F. 'Transcending Uses and Gratifications: Media use as social action and the use of event history analysis' Communications 31 (2006), pp. 139-153

Jane Vincent
'Me and My Mobile'

Introduction

The demand for mobile phones has consistently exceeded all business forecasts for growth since the launch of a public mobile phone service that began in Scandinavia in the 1970s. By the end of 2008 it is anticipated there would be over 4 billion mobile phone users around the world – around half of the world's population (Mobile Data Association 2007; GSMA 2009). There are more Internet-enabled mobile phones than desktop computers and mobile phones now offer an array of media contents and multimedia capability in addition to basic talk and text. In the UK, there are now more actively used mobile phones than there are people indicating that many people have more than one (Short 2007). There is also little doubt that mobile phones have become extremely private and personal communications devices much used throughout the world and it is this personal relationship between 'me and my mobile phone' that is the subject of this chapter. In it I draw on my own research and research by others into the social practices of mobile phone users that explore the growing attachment people appear to have to these highly sophisticated electronic computational devices. Increasingly diverse in their capabilities mobile phones now enable services convergent with a plethora of digital media and have a growing role in the social presence of the e-actor in broadband society.

The chapter will explore how the relationship between the e-actor[1] and their mobile phone is becoming more and more vital in managing their lives. This chapter will examine in particular the transition from the almost exclusive use of the mobile phone for individual-to-individual communications to its additional use as a me-to-machine interface. It will conclude with a consideration of the fit of these sophisticated mobile phone e-actors in broadband society.

Research Methodologies

The exemplars in this paper are taken from four studies led by the author (Vincent & Harper 2003; Vincent & Haddon 2003; Vincent 2004; Haddon & Vincent

---

1 The term 'e-actor' refers to the human user of electronically-mediated communications and is explained further in research by the COST261 and 298 Work Group 2 (see: www.cost298.org) (accessed May 2008).

2007) that explored the use of mobile phones, primarily in the UK. These form part of a series of research studies conducted by DWRC[2] since 1997 for a variety of organisations within the mobile communications industry, all of which explored certain aspects of the social practices of mobile phone users, particularly in the UK. The first two of the studies discussed in this chapter examined how people's use of mobile phones might shape the ways they would use the new 3G mobile communications technologies. The data for these studies were collected from questionnaires, focus groups, 24-hour diaries and interviews (the first included respondents from Germany as well as the UK) and workshops with industry and academic experts. Most respondents were between 18 and 50 years old. During 2004 and 2007 the use of mobile phones by children aged 11-16 was examined using focus groups, 24-hour diaries and interviews (Vincent 2004; Vincent 2005a; Haddon & Vincent 2007). In excess of 400 respondents contributed to these qualitative examinations of mobile phone use by people of all ages in the UK and the findings contributed to the development of the research questions for each subsequent study. The overarching research focus for all the studies was to learn more about how the mobile phone, and to some extent information communications technologies, fit into the communications repertoire of the day-to-day lives of the respondents.

Theoretical Perspectives

The theoretical perspectives for this analysis of these various studies build on the work of the interactionist theorists and, in particular, Goffman (1959) and Hochschild (1983). Particularly relevant to my research is Goffman's (1959) dramaturgical explanation of our actions and way that he separates the 'frontstage' behaviours shown in public from those that are 'backstage' that are not made explicit or shared without consideration. However, unlike some others researching mobile phones, for example Ling (2001) and Höflich (2005), I do not use observation as a source of data in my research. Watching and recording what others do is of interest particularly when exploring public 'front stage' behaviours; however, I assert that because the observer does not know why people are doing these things an incomplete picture will most likely be obtained. In the interviews and data collection the DWRC research explored the respondents' reported actions more deeply than might be possible from an observational study thereby finding out the reasons for some of the social practices involving their mobile phones. This exploration

---

2 The DWRC Digital World Research Centre Faculty of the Arts and Human Sciences University of Surrey www.dwrc.surrey.ac.uk

into the more private reasons behind mobile phone use has also been discussed by Fortunati (2005) who, in her examination of the mobile phone and the self, has exposed the backstage, private, activities of mobile phone users, suggesting that Goffman's categorisation may need updating with so much of this backstage activity being now performed frontstage in the public sphere. Examples of this have certainly emerged from my research and are discussed below. Indeed, they could be demonstrative of a new set of behaviours that relate to the mobile phone's omnipresence in society and in the lives of individual and groups of mobile phone users. These new social practices are comparable with the concept of the mediated space or 'middle stage' developed by Meyrowitz (1985) in his examination (before mobile phones) of the impact of electronic media. This mediated space has been recognised in previous research on mobile phones being called a 'buddy space' (Rheingold 2003), 'third space' (Kruse & Ström-Carlsson 2003) or 'ghost place' (Katz & Aakhus 2002). What these authors have identified, irrespective of the name, is that the stage on which mobile phone activity is performed is not necessarily physically located and is, to a large extent, electronically mediated. Fortunati's aforementioned examination of the emotions associated with mobile phone use and public space alerts us to the loss of the intimacy of the backstage and also that 'we have lost awareness of social space as a place of control' (Fortunati 2005, 217). This refers to the amount of previously private and intimate conversations that are no longer carried out in privacy. Whilst acknowledging the existence of the electronically mediated space that exists for other communications there does appear to be a new mobile phone 'stage', a place where special moments may occur between people via their mobile phones, moments that are both private and intimate but that may be acted out in a public place but only because they are done so on a mobile phone. Examining electronic mediation in this way is one approach, but another is to look in more detail at how the intrusion of the intimacy of the privacy of the backstage is being managed by the mobile phone users and for this I turn to Hochschild's (2003) theory of emotional labour. Hochschild's studies of emotional labour and emotion work built on her initial analysis of airline cabin crew and their obligation as employees to be always courteous to passengers; this resulted in the outward expression of what might be, on occasions, a false emotion in contradiction to the true feelings of the flight attendant. As Hochschild (2003) says, this has even been described by some as 'going robot', something they do automatically rather than in a planned way. I assert in this chapter that there are similarities between this managed emotion, the emotion work as described by Hochschild, and the ways that people have learned to use their mobile phones, the key to this being that the mobile phone is mediating a multitude of relationships and communications that range from the highly desirable to the most disliked. In so doing the mobile phone enables multiple moments involving others when there is a discrepancy between what one wants to feel and what one actually does feel – a situation described by Hochschild (1983) as 'a moment of "pinch"'. The act of managing this discrepancy, such as in the managing of a relationship with someone, could last a short while, minutes, or even years. Thus the interactive theoretical basis of both Goffman, with regard to some people's willingness to conduct private (backstage) matters on a public stage via the mobile phone, and Hochschild, with regard to the corresponding need to manage one's emotions in response to these communications, provide the key theoretical perspectives in my discourse.

Examining the Research Findings

Although the range of findings in the numerous DWRC studies were quite varied three themes emerged in the first study (Vincent & Harper 2003) that have recurred in the subsequent studies. These themes were, first, the emotional attachment that many respondents appeared to have with their mobile phone that was different from that with any other computational device, second, that although the mobile phone was used for social relationships it was used to intensify existing relationships rather than create new and, third, that the traditional barriers between private and public behaviours were being continually challenged by the social practices of mobile phone users.

In this section I use these themes to explore the topic of this chapter, 'me and my mobile' by offering exemplars from the aforementioned research projects. In particular, highlighting how the emotional discord caused to some extent by the conflation of the social and emotional needs of the respondents has, to a degree, been played out in the respondents' lives via their use of mobile phones.

Emotional Attachment

When asked if they have an emotional attachment to their mobile phone many people deny it but nevertheless they use emotion words to describe the ways they use their mobile phone. To some extent it was because they had not ever thought about their mobile phone in this way, preferring to consider it in terms of how much it has helped them to enjoy their life more, *'But it's not changed who I am'* (Vincent & Harper 2003, 18). Indeed, many of the respondents said that whilst mobile phones are important to them they do worry about getting too dependent on them. Exploring when and where they might be when they did not have their mobile phone it transpired that it had become so valuable to some they could not afford to lose it. One respondent explained *'I don't take it to the club 'cause it would be terrible if I lost it'* (Vincent & Harper 2003, 18). This apparent value paradox was similarly recounted by children, some of whom would leave it at home if they went to an amusement park *'They fly out of your pocket on the roller coasters and then you've lost it forever'* (Vincent 2004). Others would not take it to school on gym day if it meant they would have to leave it in their bag in the changing room. There was little sympathy for someone who had their mobile phone stolen in this way as they all knew that changing rooms are an easy place for thieves. In these instances, they were most often with a group of friends or a responsible adult who would look out for them or they were in a place where family or friends who were not with them would know where they were or, indeed, someone would have their phone with them. In her research on those going to nightclubs, Moore described situations where students would text a parent when they got back after a night out although they lived nowhere near them. In this way they knew that someone they could rely on would alert their university that they might be missing or in trouble if they did not make contact. However, not all nightclubbers leave their mobiles at home, especially if they are used to decide on the venue for the evening and Moore also describes how some use their mobile phones for safety, *'just having it with me makes me feel better' (Male clubber MASH 12 July 2003)* (Moore 2005, 231).

This attachment to and dependence on the mobile phone is particularly related to its individual-to-individual use and this was of great significance in the earlier studies. To some extent this dependence has been both assuaged and augmented by the convergence of ICTs in more recent years. The use of social networking sites for maintaining social contact has reduced the amount of talking in favour of instant messaging but this has in turn reinforced the value of the mobile phone when access to the Internet via a personal computer is not available. In particular, children were very dependent on their mobile phones for lifts from parents and would phone and speak to their parent, rather than text, to make sure they had received the message about when to collect them. Although they clearly depended on the mobile phone some were also irked by their parents using the mobile phone to check up on them. *'My mum rings me every five minutes when I get on the train – it's really annoying' (girl 14)* (Vincent 2004, 7). Today, arrangements between parents and children, and between friends and family for meeting up socially, for lifts or for what to do in an emergency all revolve around having a mobile phone and back-up plans are more about what to do when your mobile phone battery goes flat or you lose your mobile phone than what to do if your car breaks down. Respondents would say that they panic when the battery runs out, and having a mobile phone for when their car breaks down was a common example of its use for safety and security.

Borrowing and sharing mobile phones has become more prevalent during the course of the studies and whilst the content of messages and phone directories on a device may be jealously guarded they are often the first thing friends will look at if they pick up a mobile phone and it is switched on. The intimacy of this sharing, perhaps reflecting the nature of the relationships within the group of users, is an example of how previously private 'backstage' behaviours are now more in the public sphere.

This enriching of individual-to-individual contact via the mobile phone would appear to be the main reason why the mobile phone is owned and for most it would appear that they are much less price-sensitive about this type of usage than they would be for using the mobile phone for games or to send and receive information via data calls (Vincent & Harper 2003; Haddon & Vincent 2007).

The cost of maintaining the mobile phone is key to how much it is used and in the UK the monthly charge, be it contract or pay as you go, is the deciding factor for many users with regard to what they use their mobile phone for. For example, for children, who may only have less than £5 per month to spend, the mobile phone represents a status symbol, a rite of passage to teens as well as being an essential link to parents and some friends for safety and emotional support. Most people will at least maintain their mobile phone to ensure they do not miss an incoming call, especially now that it is possible to make an emergency transfer charge call if you have no credit and, at worst, the fact that a mobile can make an emergency call even without a functioning SIM provided that the battery is charged, is now more widely known and reduces the need to ensure the phone is cash charged.

However, the need to stay in contact highlights the attachment to the mobile phone and, regardless of the cost, many people say they could not live without it.

"It's just so easy to keep in contact, so convenient…you get to a stage when you couldn't do without it…I'd feel really, really lost without my phone now' Sharon" (Vincent & Haddon 2003, 46).

Intensifying Social Relationships

UK mobile phone numbers are rarely published in telephone directories and are mostly only given out by people to someone they know or have met, or perhaps for a specific purpose to avoid missing an appointment or an important delivery. The list of numbers in the mobile phone directory were, and still are, frequently not reproduced elsewhere causing tremendous upset if the phone is lost or the memory wiped in some way. This directory represents the friends, family, acquaintances and for some the business contacts that are current at that moment in the mobile phone owner's life. Accordingly, their mobile phone is rarely used to communicate with people they do not already know, or have some form of relationship with, and for many the mobile phone is the main focus for maintaining their social relations. Indeed, as the mobile phone increases the frequency with which people can be in contact it has the effect of increasing the connectivity between these people more than providing opportunities for creating new contacts. As the findings from the first study stated, "Mobile devices do not enable more social relations but more intensive relations with already existing contacts" (Vincent & Harper 2003, 8).

Interestingly, although many of the respondents did use their phone for business use and, indeed, it was often paid for by their employer, they chose to share examples of social uses of the mobile phone much more than business uses in the focus groups and one-to-one interviews. Some respondents considered that the mobile phone was not yet a device on which they felt comfortable talking to important clients.

> *"I've got a mobile here and yet I just got up and went to another room to make a call to a prospective client on a fixed phone – I called him on his mobile!"* (Vincent & Harper 2003, 9).

The findings with regard to the ways that the social uses of mobile phones might impact on business uses was borne out in the follow-up study in the next year (Vincent & Haddon 2003). Asking people to talk about how they used their mobile phones for business use frequently resulted not in a discussion of client relationships nor in the type and content of the calls but, again, was quickly diverted to talk about social relationships carried out via the mobile phone that occurred during work time. It appears that even when the mobile phone is intended primarily as a business tool it becomes a means of balancing work and home life and of keeping in touch with family and friends at any time of the working day.

> *"I'll go to lunch and leave my mobile behind, switched on, on my desk. Colleagues know I'm coming back and I can see what calls I've had while away' John"* (Vincent & Haddon 2003, 27).

Similar findings are reported in a recent report from Australia which states that 'more than half of the respondents believe that the mobile helps them to balance their family and working lives' (Wajcman et al. 2007, 23). For some mobile phone users their social life is also their work life and the two are inextricably linked and for others the role of the mobile phone is highly questionable for important business calls.

> *"I was trying to get hold of someone quite prestigious in a national organisation and when I rang his office I was given his mobile phone number to call. I checked if it would be OK to call on his mobile and was assured that it was. Imagine my surprise when I rang him to find he was on the beach on holiday in Cornwall! I felt really bad and apologised expecting to get short shrift and no chance of a business meeting if I called him again. But no, he was happy to talk to me and chatted about the proposition and we agreed a meeting time. There's no way I'm getting a mobile phone if people like him think they can call me when I'm on holiday! Nigel"* (Vincent & Haddon 2003, 68).

It is the potential for an always-on, always-connectable device that makes it so compelling for friendship but, at the same time, these are the very reasons that make it less convincing as a business device, and for some they simply prefer to have conversations using a landline phone.

> *"It's just on my desk to be charged up. 90% of the time I use a landline. My friends sometimes leave messages but I usually phone on a direct line and get through or talk to friends and people in the office face to face. Stuart"* (Vincent & Haddon 2003, 62).

Always being in touch with those who are closest to you personally was worth the occasional interruption from work but this intensification of social relationships appears to have been reinforced by the increasingly widespread use of image and music downloads between mobile phones and other digital devices using Bluetooth and infrared. A few respondents in the first study had found ways to download and transfer data between mobile phones such as this example from a man in one of the focus groups:

> *"It was her idea, I'd only just got the phone at the time and her eyes lit up! – She suddenly realised that she had the means of doing this and we gave it a go and it worked... I don't know how it happened" (transferring images between cameras)* (Vincent & Haddon 2003, 38).

In the later studies this experience extended to between mobile phones and computers as well thereby expanding participation in the broadband society. The fact that there are more Internet enabled mobile phones than there are Internet enabled personal computers bodes well for this continued exploration and play that the respondents discussed in this paper have demonstrated.

Improvements to mobile phone capabilities for still and moving images as well as the intensification of the use of social networking sites has significantly changed the social practices of mobile phones since they were first used in the 1970s and only offered voice capability. Even as recently as the DWRC study in 2003 camera phones were still in their infancy, whereas now it is almost impossible to buy a mobile phone that does not have a camera capability. Improvements in the mobile communications networking provision and the use of Bluetooth and infrared technologies mean that people have less need to send images over the network but can instead download them direct between phones and other ICTs. Social networking sites like bebo.com; myspace.com; flkcr.com; facebook.com and youtube.com abound with images recorded on the mobile phone. Images are used that were intended for personal intimate use to those with malicious intent such as happy slapping or to bully through to those that are use to promote career opportunities in music and film businesses. One teenager gave an example of how the images are used on social network sites:

"Nina: This girl fell asleep and she had paint all over her face...and we all took photos... and shared them around and put them on Bebo...and she got very upset...
Ruth: And so we took them off.
Nina: When they get upset...then you delete them...but ...(...) You keep going until they're upset" (Focus Group 2: 13-14yrs) (Vincent & Haddon 2003).

This integration of ICTs into so many day-to-day activities has led to the mobile phone being part of a much larger digital portfolio enabling it to be used as much now as a 'me to machine' interface as it has been for an 'individual-to-individual' device.

"If you're on the computer downloading on Microsoft Word, you can put it onto your phone. And then if you want to take it to another computer it's like a memory stick" Sandra (14) (Vincent & Haddon 2003, 20).

A major factor in this adaptation of use has no doubt been the free-of-charge data transfer of images, music and to some extent messaging. Whilst mobile phones are not yet on a par with PC Internet access and games consoles people do use them in this way to while away the time much as they also use them as MP3 players and radios. As one of the findings of the most recent study of children showed, they used the mobile phone to play games to escape from unwelcome situations that they described as 'boring'.

"But it was striking how many times young people of various ages specifically said that they played when they were 'bored'. It is worthwhile looking at what this means in more detail since children seemed to use the word far more often than many adults. Apart from car journeys, young people could be bored when doing homework and bored when visiting parents' friends – or as Nina put it 'if you're somewhere where you don't want to be'. Using the mobile game was an escape to something more interesting" (Haddon & Vincent 2007, 15).

The additional functionality enabled by the convergence of electronic mediated communications devices focuses attention on the mobile phone, suggesting that it may have a unique place in the communications repertoire. The ability to keep in contact with close friends and family at all times not only intensifies the social contact between individuals but within and between their social groups in the worldwide network of the broadband society.

Private and Public Behaviours

The examples highlighted above of changes in social practices enabled by the free transfer of images and music has also enabled the foregrounding of previously backstage behaviours, moving them into the public space. The sharing of intimate communications amongst friendship groups is one example of the boundaries changing between the previously private domains and the public sphere. Whilst the mobile phone continues to be 'my mobile', the data on it such as images, music, video or messages are freely shared but usually only at the behest of or with the permission of the owner. In the first of my DWRC studies on mobile phones we reported that:

"Mobile phones result in more private behaviours in public spaces than ever before, with gradually fewer boundaries to acceptance of where and when people can use their mobile phones. This is a world wide phenomenon, though the extent to which it occurs varies between different countries" (Vincent & Harper 2003, 7).

The use of mobile phones in public spaces is so commonplace now that mobile-free zones are being created in social venues, on some public transport, in offices and so on. Although mobile phone use is perhaps controllable in these more (self-)regulated environments the etiquette for mobile phone use still varies. Whilst it would appear that almost anything goes there are individual interventions from time to time in the form of phone rage such as when an actor evicted an audience member whose ringing mobile phone interrupted his performance three times (Shenton 2005). It is reported that the unfortunate recipient of a call in such circumstances in New York would also be fined £50.

Another new use of mobiles in the public sphere is that of citizen journalism – the taking and sending of images and video to the national media during or immediately after major events such as the 7 July bombing in London in 2005 (BBC News 2008), or the reporting of vandalism in your local community (Vincent & Harris 2008). These developing uses of mobiles can push images of backstage personal moments into a global public sphere. In the teens studies this change from camera phone as a multimedia message device to a camera phone as an image recorder and sharer was most notable between the two studies in 2004 and 2007 and, by the latter study, music transfers were even more common than image transfers introducing further convergent uses of ICTs within the broadband society.

The separation of the public from the private in children's use of mobile phones is perhaps more defined by when and where they are permitted to use their mobile phones than whether it is an appropriate use. For example, most children are not permitted to have or use mobile phones at school, rules that they flout from time to time. In all the studies we found that people of all ages take pictures on their mobile phones that they store and share with others, but rarely send in messages. Whilst cost and complexity are factors contributing to this lack of use of multimedia messaging it would appear that the mobile phone is now being used like a digital camera and images are downloaded via memory cards or Bluetooth (or occasionally infrared) onto other mobiles or personal computers. The images are then often shared via social networking sites as discussed above. During the fieldwork for the fourth study a letter was read out to children at a school assembly after a mobile phone video of a fight at their school was placed online, naming the school and resulting in bad media for the school.

Although the predominance of the private vs. public debate emerges when private backstage activities are invading the public sphere, there are also examples of the opposite, namely the public sphere invading the private. Numerous respondents gave examples of being interrupted by friends and family who would contact them when they wanted to be left alone, or if they did not answer the fixed line phone quickly enough they would assume them to be out and on their mobile leaving them to be dashing between fixed and mobile phones in their home, interrupted at least twice for a call that was about nothing in particular. Although as this example given by Janet shows the benefits of keeping your mobile phone with you can outweigh the disadvantages.

> "*Sometimes it infringes on your privacy...I mean you want to be left alone and unless you switch the thing off... I mean, my husband "Where are you, what are you doing"... "Oh, leave me alone, don't drive me mad"...I hate that feeling of someone...you know "What are you doing, who can I hear in the background"...that kind of thing...but then there are certain times when it can be invaluable...like I broke down in the car a couple months ago and I had to ring the AA ... where are there any phone boxes? ... you've got to walk miles sometimes...so... Janet*" (Vincent & Haddon 2003, 55).

I briefly discussed above the issue of the work life balance and as we know from other studies business use at home is less tolerated. Here it is not the public vs. private but two opposing private domains each in conflict with the other; the intimacy of home life and of the social relationships that pertain to it being impinged upon by the external monolithic work domain or simply the intrusion of a caller who assumes their calls will be answered.

Emotional Discord

Managing emotions runs as an undercurrent throughout the various research studies as situations are recounted in which the respondents felt compelled to answer calls in inappropriate locations or at times when they were not emotionally equipped to handle the content of a call.

"People do have a distinct and essentially emotional relationship with their mobile phone. This reflects what the phone enables them to do in terms of being in touch with those they are close to, in the way that the mobile enables emotional and spontaneous behaviours, and in the ways in which people account for and think about their phones" (Vincent & Harper 2003, 17).

It would appear from the existing literature on the use of mobile phones that, even from childhood, the mobile phone has a very personal effect on some people's everyday lives (Goggin 2006; Kavoor & Arceneaux 2006; Levinson 2004; Vincent 2005b). Further, people report that they cannot live without it, that they panic when they do not have it (Vincent & Harper 2003), and many people certainly find it hard to imagine life without a mobile phone as we learned from Sharon above.

Emotional discord occurs when there is an inconsistency between the expectations of the user of the mobile phone and those whom they are communicating with via the device. The loss of the mobile phone would likely cause distress to those who could no longer make contact with their loved ones as well as to the person who lost it. Situations like this are the 'moments of pinch' described by Hochschild and are the point at which emotional discord becomes most apparent, such as when Janet had to take an unwanted call from her husband. It appears that many people accept that these situations occur and they have each developed strategies for dealing with them. In most instances they have developed a 'personal front' (Goffman 1959) for dealing with calls and on occasions when the call intrudes, they convey a false emotional response, disguising their true inner self which may be upset or dealing with other issues at the time. Following Goffman's work on the Presentation of Self (1959), this always-connected state which mobile phones enable, and that some respondents use to manage their lives to a greater or lesser extent, is a form of dramatisation of their social network. Presence in the context of a mobile phone could mean that individuals do not need to be physically co-present in order to feel and behave as if they are actually at the same location. Thus, although Goffman refers to a 'front' as occurring in the observed presence of others (Goffman 1959, 32) I suggest that the mobile phone has become the 'setting' for conveying the 'personal front' of the absent present observers. Goffman describes the 'setting' as the scenic parts of expressive equipment and 'personal front' to refer to the other items of expressive equipment, the items that we most intimately identify with the performer himself and that we naturally expect will follow the performer wherever he goes (Goffman 1959, 34).

As Goffman might say, the mobile phone user has the personal assurance of the constancy of their personal front but their 'setting' varies to accord with the relationship and its location. Thus, they have a front for each relationship described above although they may actually never be co-present with any of the people with whom they are communicating.

Hochschild's explanation of emotion work is also applicable to this behaviour which I suggest is both a display of what she refers to as bodily emotion work and of cognitive emotion. The bodily display is when someone uses hand-held touch to ensure they do not miss a call instead of having the mobile in their handbag or jacket pocket; the cognitive emotion is as they prepare to manage the expectations of callers such as to mitigate a situation whereby they might have an argument about why an earlier call was not taken. As discussed above, it would appear that for some their mobile phone has become an almost indispensable tool when dealing with close relationships. The feeling of security and comfort that they can always contact their close friends and family using the mobile phone cannot be easily substituted.

In summary, the mobile phone lies very much at the heart of the day-to-day activities of many people, not only for maintaining relationships through individual-to-individual voice and text communications but also through the ways the mobile phone links and converges with other ICTs using Bluetooth and infrared capabilities. The mobile phone has become a symbol for its owner whose personal life both backstage and frontstage is played out through the various roles that it performs for them. The mobile phone has become an aide memoire, a memento, a keepsake or repository of memories and at the same time an enabler of social relations and a technological playground as well as a plain old communicator for calls and text.

Conclusions

In this chapter I have examined the ways that various respondents have made use of their mobile phones in their day-to-day lives. The mobile phone is such a vital tool for maintaining connectivity with family and friends that there is a constant connectivity and attachment with the device. This me-to-machine link is reinforced by its use when bored to fill awkward moments, or even to act as a comforter. It is further enhanced by searching for and looking at images, text messages, music and other personal data stored on the device. It would appear from this that the relationship the user has with their device is one of an e-actor who uses it to enable electronically mediated connectivity, rather than merely an actor who is using it to communicate. In other words, the electronic functionality of the mobile phone has become integral to the role that the device plays in their relationships not only with family friends and work colleagues but with the multitude of other ICTs that have now converged with it.

Exploring this through the three themes that recurred in the four DWRC research studies, individual-to-individual communications highlights the vital role that the mobile phone continues to play in maintaining and intensifying social contact, especially within families and close relationships.

However, when talking about their mobile phones people expressed, in emotional terms, how they used their mobile phones, highlighting a situation of emotional discord. What was for some an indispensable tool for maintaining close contact with loved ones and the safety and security of being able to make contact had, for others, created 'moments of pinch'. These were situations in which one was forced to play out a role that demanded a particular emotional response that was different from how one actually felt at the time. In some instances, this discord could be attributed to the shift of private and intimate behaviours previously only carried out 'backstage' now being played out on the more public 'frontstage', such as laughing off the unintended sharing of an intimate text or image or dealing with the downloading of inappropriate photos onto social networking sites.

Compared to the earlier study of 2003 reported in this chapter there is a now a greater sense of ease with the technology, and indeed the excitement that extended to exploring the various functions of the device was typical of the mobile phone users in each of the studies referred to in this paper. It is not just mobile phone technology that can be baffling but all types of ICT; however, finding solutions is rewarding and pleasurable – this me-to-machine activity, the e-actor role for me and my mobile is now manifest.

References

BBC News. URL: http://news.bbc.co.uk/1/hi/in_depth/uk/2005/london_explosions/default.stm (accessed May 2008)

Fortunati L. 'Mobile Telephone and the Presentation of Self' eds. R. Ling, Pedersen, P. E. Mobile communications: Re-negotiation of the Social Sphere London: Springer (2005) pp. 203- 218.

Goffman E. The Presentation of Self in Everyday Life Middlesex: Penguin Books Edition (1959)

Goggin G. Cell Phone Culture Mobile Technology in Everyday Life London: Routledge (2006)
GSMA: GSM Association Web Site (2008) URL: http://www.gsmworld.com/ news/press_2008/press08_31.shtml (accessed May 2008)
Haddon L., Vincent J. Growing Up With a Mobile Phone – Learning from the Experiences of Some Children in the UK, DWRC Report for Vodafone UK, June (2007)
Hochschild A. R. The Managed Heart Commercialization of the Human Feeling. Berkley, CA: University of California Berkley (1983), (20th edition with afterword 2003)
Hochschild A. R. The Commercialization of Feelings: Notes From Home and Work Berkley, CA: University of California Berkley (2003)
Höflich J. R. 'A Certain Sense of Place Mobile Communication and Local Orientation' eds. Nyiri K. A Sense of Place The Global and The Local in Mobile Communication Vienna: Passagen Verlag (2005) pp. 159-168
Katz J. E., Aakhus M. Perpetual Contact: Mobile Communications, Private Talk, Public Performance Cambridge: Cambridge University Press (2002)
Kavoor A., Arceneaux N. eds. The Cell Phone Reader Essays in Social Transformation New York: Peter Lang (2006)
Kruse E., Ström-Carlsson A. A Journey to the Third Place: Market Reality among Early Adopters Stockholm: Ericsson Consumer and Enterprise Lab (2003)
Lasen A. 'The Social Shaping of Fixed and Mobile Networks: A Historical Comparison' ed. Gossett, P. Understanding Mobile Phone Users and Usage Newbury: Vodafone Group (2005)
Levinson P. Cellphone. The Story of the World's Most Mobile Medium and How It Has Transformed Everything! New York: Palgrave (2004)
Ling R. "We Release Them Little by Little": Maturation and Gender Identity as Seen in the Use of Mobile Telephony' Personal and Ubiquitous Computing, Vol. 5 London: Springer-Verlag (2001) pp. 123-136
Mobile Data Association (2007) URL: http://www.themda.org/documents/ PressReleases/ General/MDA_ future_of_mobile_press_release_Nov07.pdf (accessed May 2008)
Meyrowitz J. No Sense of Place: the Impact of Electronic Media in Social Behaviour New York: Oxford University Press (1985)
Moore K. "Sort Drugs, Make Mates": The Use and Meanings of Mobiles in Club Culture' eds. Brown, B., O'Hara, K. Consuming Music Together: Social and Collaborative Aspects of Music Consumption Technologies Amsterdam: Springer (2005)
Rheingold H. Smart Mobs the Next Social Revolution Cambridge: Perseus (2003)

Shenton M. Mobile Phone Rage (2005) URL: http://blogs.thestage.co.uk/shenton/2005/11/ mobile-phone-rage/ (accessed May 2008)

Short M. Communications and Mobility Appleby Lecture Institute of Engineering. Technology September 2007 London (2007) URL: www.iet.tv (accessed January 2008)

Vincent J., Harper R. 'Social Shaping of UMTS – Preparing the 3G Customer'. Report 26, UMTS Forum (2003) URL: http://www.umts-forum.org (accessed April 2008)

Vincent J., Haddon L. Informing Suppliers about User Behaviours to Better Prepare them for their 3G/UMTS Customers UMTS Forum Report No. 34. (2003) URL: www.dwrc.surrey.ac.uk (accessed May 2008)

Vincent J.'11-16 Mobile': Examining Mobile Phone and ICT Use Amongst Children aged 11-16 (2004) URL: www.dwrc.surrey.ac.uk (accessed January 2008)

Vincent J. Growing up with a Mobile paper at Communications in the 21st Century, The Mobile Information Society, Seeing, Understanding, Learning in the Mobile Age 28-30. (2005a) URL: www.fil.hu/mobil/2005 (accessed April 2005)

Vincent J. 'Are some people affected their attachment to their mobile phone?' ed. Nyiri K. A Sense of Place the Global and the Local in Mobile Communication Vienna: Passagen Verlag (2005) pp. 221-229

Vincent J., Harris L. 'Effective Use of Mobile Communications in E-Government: How do we reach the tipping point?' Information, Communication & Society 11 (2008) pp. 395-413.

Wajcman J., Bittman M., Jones P., Johnstone L. and Brown J. The Impact of the Mobile Phone on Work Life Balance. Preliminary Report June 2007 Australian Research Council Linkage Project (2007)

Theme III:
Exploring the notion of e-actors within the information society

Vsevolod M. Zherebin

Information Society as the Law-Governed Result of the Evolution of Information

Introduction

This chapter attempts to consider and interpret the phenomenon of information in the process of its evolution. The discourse considers the topic from its beginning, until the emergence of the modern social forms and formation of the information society. The thesis substantiated herein is that information, in spite of the accepted conception, is not an attribute of the matter in general but it appears only together with the animate life which forms an inherent part. The process of the evolution of information and modern concepts of it from the point of view of the general information theory are considered. Furthermore, the evolution of information, the development of its concepts and the growth of the information possibilities of society are developed in the text and examined in parallel.

Nowadays the most advanced countries of the world are entering a phase of development which has acquired the general name of the information society. The information society is the post industrial society that has essentially new and increased information resources and possibilities. The information society may be considered to be a result of the combination of two lines of development, namely, the line of development of a human society as such – the social, cultural, economic, scientific and technical and, on the other hand (and this follows from the name) the line of development of the information possibilities of society. Whilst the evolution of human society has been studied comparatively well, it is impossible to assert the same about the history of development and changes in the forms and character of the information and the role it plays in the whole process. This chapter examines these topics from the point of view that it is the evolutionary approach to the phenomenon of information that makes it possible to see more clearly the process of the growth of the information possibilities of mankind.

The general idea of information

Today we freely operate within the circle of concepts connected to information as well as in the ways of its storage and processing. Without special effort, for example, we may differentiate and give definitions to various kinds of the economic and social information. However, the interpretation of the category of information as a whole, in a generalised sense of this concept, is a much more difficult business. The origin of the concept of information remains uncertain, and the term itself is understood ambiguously by different researchers. Even from prominent scientists one has on occasions heard statements such as: 'Actually, nobody can tell, what this information is'. At the same time the authority of information in today's society achieves a grandiose scale, becoming more and more imperative in character. All this forces one to perceive information as a phenomenon that is extremely capacious, many-sided and having an almost mystical complexion.

Thus before building the system of conceptions related to the formation of information society, it is reasonable to try, first of all, to give a more complete and understandable interpretation of the term 'information' itself. As a first approximation information may be defined as some data about things, properties, relations, phenomena, actions, and laws etc., which are required and perceived by some object or objects and used for realization of their purposes or requirements. Such a strict definition, (which is representative of many other definitions of similar kinds) is useful but it is also insufficient. It is more of a consumer definition that says very little about the nature of information as a phenomenon. In the next section of the chapter some different notions of information are explored.

Phases of study and different notions of information

The term 'information' became commonplace in the sciences and public life in the middle of the twentieth century and quickly found the widest application that confirmed the necessity and also the timeliness of its appearance. However, some vagueness in the outline of this polysemous concept, and the huge richness of its contents have created significant difficulties achieving an uniform interpretation and selection of one common measure and universal unit of information.

Strong and weak points of the approach of Shannon (1948) and his followers, who connected information, first of all, with the probability method of estimation of the reduction of the level of uncertainty during a choice, have already been repeatedly discussed in scientific literature and do not demand the further explanation. Also the attempts to construct a formal semantic theory of information based on Shannon's ideas begun by Carnap and Bar-Hillel (1953) and continued by a line of other researchers have not resulted in a final desirable outcome.

Undoubtedly an invaluable role in the development of information theory was played by various research and conceptions obtained on the basis of cybernetic ideas, the general theory of systems and consideration of information in the aspect of control (e.g., Wiener 1967; Ross Ashby 1956; von Bertalanffy 1968). After that the concept of information was interpreted as a tool of management and control or as data necessary to perform functions of systems, to make decisions and to solve problems.

However, even those approaches, (that in part built on Shannon's principles), despite their great theoretical and applied value, could not give answers to several important questions concerning, in particular, the correlation between the form and semantic contents of messages. They have not made it possible to develop a uniform measure and a richer universal definition of information, which could satisfy the demands of the majority of researchers and users.

One more step was made in the study and comprehension of information after the appearance of informatics as the science of computers and other information technologies applications. Shortly after that science was divided into two branches: informatics of control and scientific informatics.

Nevertheless, one can now conclude that theoretical concepts and the aforementioned interpretation of the meanings of information that existed earlier do not allow one to describe it completely; further it has enabled one to only estimate separate sides and qualities of the overall category. Attempts to overcome these boundaries are still pursued today within the framework of scientific direction under the auspices of 'the general theory of information' – studies that are now developed mainly by biologists and philosophers.

Concepts of the general theory of information

One of the well-known experts in the field of the general theory of information, Yankovsky, writes that during the last decades the necessity to realise the organisation of processes of movement has become obvious and that analysis of this has obtained the general name 'information'. Meanwhile, the concept of information in many respects remains intuitive and receives different semantic contents in various branches of human activity (Yankovsky 2000).

Thus we find that this category may receive different definitions depending variously on solving problems, scientific directions, spheres of human activity and depth of philosophical comprehension. In the Internet, for example, today one can find as many as 34 formulations of such definitions and it undoubtedly may be extended.

The beginning of the development of the general theory of information in Russia in many respects may be connected to the name of Ursul (1975). In the West the biological views on information were presented first of all by Machlup and Mansfield (1983), however the papers of these scientists mainly examined the opinions of western representatives of the biological science.

Although the scientist himself did not assert as such Vernadsky (1989) can be attributed as one of the exponents of the general theory of information. The scientific predictions of Vernadsky were contained in his ideas of the noosphere; that is the state of biosphere which occurs as a result of the interaction of its laws with the activity of human mind and concerns global consequences of the informatisation process. This idea of noosphere is completely in harmony with the modern notion of information society – a society characterised not only by a high level of informatisation and value of knowledge in the economy and in social life, but also as the post–industrial society, taking place in the qualitatively new and contrasting points of social and economic development.

In his developed and complete doctrine of the biosphere as a living substance organising the terrestrial capsule and of the evolution of biosphere into noosphere, Vernadsky unites in a uniform process, analyzing the biological life and the life of human society in a common way. In his theory, examining the interrelation between the informatisation and the biosphere, he attaches determining importance to the informatisation and knowledge. The great interest by today's representatives of the general theory of information and, in particular, of its teleological direction is served by these definitions. Yankovsky associates the category of information with the concept of information interaction and explains that any interaction between objects during which one object gets some substance, and the other does not loose it, may be named an information interaction. In this case the transmitted substance is to be called information (Yankovsky 2000).

The concept of the operator of information is another parallel development within this examination of information. Creating his teleological theory of information, Korogodin (1991) proceeds from the situation of achievement of some event as the purpose, from the concept of purposeful action and its complex characteristics, and also from the operator of information formed for the achievement of this purpose on the basis of concentration of the necessary information. The information is defined as the set of rules, methods and data necessary for constructing the operator of information, formed for achievement of the purpose under consideration. The concept of the operator of information is also used by other experts working in the field of information theory. Sosnin (1999), for example, puts forward that information is a set of receptions, rules or the data necessary for construction of an operator. In other words information is the guide for action.

The evolutionary approach and the rise of information in the nature

The essence of information may be better understood and interpreted by observing it in the process of evolution. Indeed, 'information' is inherently connected to the existence and ability to live of living organisms, including human beings as well as societies. It is important not to forget that when its evolution is considered historically information is not only social, but also biological; perhaps even, primarily, a biological phenomenon.

In an integrated view this evolutionary chain would appear to be as follows: the biological information, leading to the transition to the social information, its gradual transformation into the major resource of society (informatisation), formation of the information society and, hence finally, the creation of the noosphere as a new stage of development of the biosphere.

This suggested approach can be considered as the evolutionary concept of research and the interpretation of information within the framework of the general theory of information.

Contrary to the opinion of many scientists who postulate that in the nature there are three super-categories: matter, energy and information, it is suggested here that information does not belong to the super-categories of this level. Rather, it should be regarded as an attribute only of the living matter, not of the matter in general.

The present forms and kinds of information that might be of common interest were generated together with the origin of life. By this is meant presumably social information, which after its development turned from the biological into the social. Life arose at a period of a very complex combination of conditions, (temperature, pressure, chemical compounds of environment, gravitation, presence of energy sources etc.), that was close to unique. Directly opposite to the lifeless matter which is indifferent to the states it passes through, (firm, liquid or gaseous) living organisms may exist only in rather narrow limits of values of these conditions and their combinations. They must adapt in order to maintain homeostasis. Accordingly, living creatures were initially supplied by the nature with the aspiration to self-preservation and survival. It is suggested here, that apparently, this aspiration marked the beginning to the phenomenon of purposefulness in the nature. It was in this context that living creatures were provided with sense organs, the memory as an ability to fix the important events and situations and a nervous system for the reaction to external disturbances. As a result living organisms got an opportunity to perceive, register changes in external conditions and react to them. It is further expounded here that it was those data about conditions and changes in the environment, which formed the basis of the initial information and served as the starting point for creation of the information of the next subsequent types.

According to Grobstein's theory (1964) 'the strategy of life' consists in the constant development of living matter representing a steady, creative evolutionary process of its antagonism to the 'monstrous power of the lifeless nature'. From here we may judge, that life should always adapt to big and small changes of the environment and continue thus until the values of these changes obtain a catastrophic character and became unacceptable from the point of view of the limits of short term possible alterations in the structures and properties of alive organisms. The continuous reception of data about the environment serves the base condition for their survival and development. Thus, originally information was the need and consequence of the adaptation of living organisms to changes in conditions of their environment. Further, together with their development in the courses of ontogenesis and phylogenesis, in their struggle for existence and energy sources, during training and mutual informing, the growth of abilities in processing and accumulation of information took place. With development of the nervous system and acquisition by animals of that which Lorenz (1973) named the 'parliament of instincts', living creatures obtained new possibilities for the effective use of information.

Almost in the same way the biologist Korogodin (1991) considers this problem, when he suggests that our conviction in that information is the basis of life, represents, in its essence, only the ascertaining of this fact. He further outlines that in the nature there is not any information system which, if not being alive, was not made by hands of the human being (Korogodin 1991).

Academician Moiseev (1990), considers, even more definitely, information to be an attribute of the living matter. Arguing about the information, he writes that the concept of information could be imaged as somewhat 'historical'. Necessity of its introduction arises only at the description of rather late stages of development of the material world, only when life arises in it. Moiseev (1990) concludes that the information appears only when we begin to study purposeful objects (i.e., objects capable to act purposely).

Thus, the point of view expressed herein is that information is simultaneously an attribute, a need and a product of ability to live off the living matter. Information has arisen and was originally used in connection with the need of living organisms to adapt for changes in the environment – this conclusion may be drawn from aforementioned 'general strategy of life' of Grobstein (1964).

Information in the processes of ontogenesis and phylogenesis

For the realisation of their general strategy and performance of vital functions, living organisms must have data about the condition and changes in the environment. These changes result in development of devices for perception, processing and storage of these data (i.e., sense organs, nervous system and finally brains). Living organisms were also provided with complex emotional capabilities for the initial estimation of the importance of received signals and production impulses in order to determine the necessary reactions to them. The fixation of reactions to incoming signals was necessary, firstly, from the point of view of survival and adaptation of separate organisms during their life (ontogenesis), and secondly, for actualization of the long-term mechanisms of heredity and adaptation in populations, genus, species, orders and other biological groups (phylogenesis).

Development of the living matter is, certainly, not only the result of its opposition to the lifeless nature as well as it is the consequence of its interaction with the biosphere. For instance, Grobstein (1964) suggests that heterogeneity of the biomass is the result of its prolonged interaction with biosphere – the interaction which in essence is the self-doubling of making the biomass units based directly or indirectly on replication enclosed in molecules of information. For the successful struggle for survival between separate specimens and different kinds of living creatures they should be supplied with both the current situational information and the long-term stored information. The latter is also promoting a choice of rational variants of reaction to incoming signals and disturbances. The long-term information here is that which is accumulated during the life of organisms (life experience), and also transmitted from generation to generation at the level of genetic hereditary attributes and acquired instincts. It must be noted that there is some kind of competition between long living and short-living kinds of living beings. Here again the nature provides the reliability of development of biosphere with the help of the application of various ways of adaptation. Long living organisms for the period of their life are capable of saving up more experience, than short living, but organisms with short period of life have an opportunity to provide faster transfer of the information saved to the subsequent generations on the genetic line.

In order for incoming information to be recognised and for proper reactions to them to occur, the memory of living beings must have registered various kinds of relationships and a record of events that have already happened. On the basis of these registrations, and in particular on condition of their repeatability and high intensity of emotional colouring during their perception, reflexes in living beings began to be formed. It was during this development of the nervous system and intelligence of living creatures that they became more and more complicated and obtained new possibilities.

At the same time their life experience together with that partly transmitted from the previous generations was summarized and found expression in the complication and increase of the number of their instincts. Created by that experience, (conditioned and unconditioned reflexes) and as discussed earlier, Lorenz's elegant phrase 'the parliament of instincts' (1973) together with the improved nervous system and the saved genetic information they became, apparently, the main constituents of the basis on which, in particular after the occurrence of natural language, the process of formation of logic and human abstract thinking began.

Transition from the biological to the social information

It is possible to distinguish several stages in the development of forms of existence, perception and use of information. Firstly, was the initial natural image information directly perceived with the help of sense organs. Then it was followed by the indicative (attribute) information, i.e. information connecting some phenomena together, for example, a flash of lightning is an attribute of a peal of thunder following behind it. Then the signal-communication information arose in biological groups: broods, flocks, packs, herds. Initially it may be warning shouts of alarm, exclamations of pain or, on the contrary, satisfaction. The modelling of the meaning of such signals (necessary reactions to them) was registered in the memory of animals together with those that occurred at the beginning in the operational stage, and thence into the long-term memory.

The ability to transform received signals into signs already meant transition to a higher level of communication and, in many respects was the consequence of growth of the number, and simultaneously the intelligence, of members of the community. Signs may be considered as signals which were fixed with accepted meanings by the community.

The growing number of living organisms and formation of different kinds of communities, realization of their mutual actions, increase of frequency of contacts between them, and the perfection of their abilities to be perceptive, recognize, store and process data, intensified the information interaction activities. The gradual transition was carried out from mainly signal, primitively sign forms of communication to the formation for this purpose and use of more and more advanced signs and whole sign systems. This notion is clearly articulated by Ursul, when he argues that the evolution of sociums (communities) is connected just to the development of means of information interaction of its participants, and in particular of construction and use of their combined memory. The speed of this evolution is much higher than the speed of evolution of individual organisms. It is connected with that the means of information interactions used by a community may include not only means integrally inherent in its members, but also introduced in it from the outside. Advanced communities may purposefully develop external means of information interaction used by them (Ursul 1990).

The basic type of information used in the human society is the information expressed in natural languages. One of the characteristic features of the language of information is that it may be analyzed on three semiotic levels: syntactical, semantic and pragmatic (Morris 1938; Cherry 1978). The development of languages passed several important stages each of which increased to an important extent possibilities of communication between people in space and in time. The main stages were as follows: spoken language, writing and book-printing. Nowadays, however, the natural language and language information have entered a new stage of existence – an electronic and digital one.

On the final account, it was the formation and use of language which made the information: perceived by all members of communities, freely enough transmitted in time and in space, suitable for use in different sorts of communities and society in general, i.e. allowed transform it into the social information.

Informatisation and the formation of information society

During the past several decades there has been a period when the information engineering and technologies were developing impetuously. The accumulation of knowledge was intensified, the possibilities and the significance of their use in the life of humans and society increased. One would expect this process to result in the informatisation of society, and indeed is has already done so, and further in same cases in the formation of information society. In fact, Ursul (1990) notes how the informatisation of society is understood now as the process of more and more full mastering by the society information as a resource of development by means of informatics with the purpose of cardinal increase of the intellectual potential of civilization and on this basis – humanistic reorganization of the whole life and activities of the human being.

Human's vital activity, to a very great extent, consists of reception, storage, transformation and transfer of information. In any event, very many of our physical actions are also connected to the processing of information. Constantly progressing processes of informatisation gradually relieves people of the increasing number of physical operations connected to the processing and use of information. The impact of informatisation is so radical, that it may even bring some people to the hypodynamia. However, certainly, the main impact of informatisation consists in the release of the intellectual apparatus of men from routine operations and in increase opportunities for creative work. Now informatisation is understood as the development and application of the most advanced means and technologies of information processing, first of all, electronic and digital, including computers, Internet, mobile telephones, united by the general name of 'information and communication technologies' (devices and services).

Notwithstanding this the notion of informatisation may be understood more widely as a general historical process of the perfection of human abilities to process information. In this case one may also attribute to the informatisation the invention and application of writing, book-printing, telegraph, telephone, arithmometer etc. As it can be seen, the paradigm sequence: 'information – informatisation – information society' has its historical principle of construction. In detail, the initial part of this sequence would appear to suggest that it is the originating of information – development of the biological information – transition to the social information – past stages of informatisation – modern electronic and digital informatisation.

The next step of informatisation is the information society. One speaks about the information society when one means first of all social and economic aspects of development of mankind, this stage of development is named as knowledge society if the information-intellectual saturation of society is emphasized. Under economy of knowledge as a constituent of the information society it is reasonable to mean, first of all, such an economy in which the share of knowledge in the structure of total cost of the national product considerably surpasses the ratio which generally takes place now.

Major kinds and the general definition of information

As research shows, it is expedient to attribute to the major categories of the information first of all the following: current information, knowledge and genetic information.

A Russian philosopher Zhdanov (2001), who distinguishes three kinds of information in the context of his reasoning: genetic, logic and figurative, defines the first point by saying that the genetic information enables an organism to carry out the special characteristic only for the ways of its self-organizing that are alive, in particular, providing preservation and transfer in time of the data and programs of adaptation, adequate reaction and development of living organisms (Zhdanov 2001).

In the initial biological sense the reception of information is, first of all, the process of scanning and perception by an object, the conditions of environment and their changes, with allocation of elements, significant from the point of view of realisation of strategies incorporated in it by the nature. The data received as a result of this process is the current information. These data may influence on the perceiving object in various ways: to cause only an emotional reaction, to require in the answer some physical actions, to promote structural – functional restructuring of the object, and also may be accumulated, collected and inherited. Almost the same properties and functions (excluding the last) also form the basis of the current social information.

As to knowledge, today both everyday life and scientific knowledge are received and stored data about objects, processes, phenomena, laws of the nature, and also about their presence, properties and relations, allowing receive or improve our comprehension of them. Usually knowledge is considered as the long-term potential information, however in some cases (for example, some discoveries) it may be used at once after its reception. Scientific knowledge is the result of process of recognition of environmental reality. This process is very well determined by Klaus (1967) who writes about knowledge as of: '… perfection of the structural model of the world.' Scientific knowledge is that kind of information which, as it is known, makes a basis of scientific, technical and social progress of mankind. An interesting approach to knowledge as a resource was shown by Machlup (1980) as well as by Porat and Rubin (1977). They offered the methodology and a mathematical procedure for estimation of the contribution of knowledge in the total cost of national product. In that project Leontiev "input-output" tables and technological factors were used.

During evolution, beginning from the time of appearance of primitive alive creatures and up to now, kinds, forms, the role and significance of information, and also the range of spheres and directions of its use were changing and extending so much, that now it is practically impossible to give this concept a uniform, universal and strict definition. Such definition should unite its biological, social and even technological sense. Attempts to develop such definition (cf. Shannon 1948; Yankovsky 2000) lead to quite an abstract and senseless interpretation of information, or demand a lengthy additional explanation and decoding.

Therefore, taking into account what was told above about the basic kinds of information used in the human society, it is suggested that one may in the following way formulate its combined definition to include several constituents: *information is, first, data about the current situation, and this includes data about conditions and changes of the environment, its separate objects and phenomena; secondly, the data formed and used for the organization and control of our actions; in the third, the data received and accumulated as knowledge; and, at last, the data and programmes incorporated in human beings by the nature and ensuring their biological development and in a large extent, determining their behaviour (the genetic information).*

Thus, having arisen in the biosphere information, following the progress of mankind, becomes the determining factor of its development. Intensive processes of informatisation proceeding concurrently result finally in the formation of the information society, as a new form of existence of mankind. As this society knowledge and intellect begin to render it becomes the deciding influence not only on its own development, but also on the character of the continuing biosphere and geological processes, reaching further towards the stage of development named noosphere. Up to the present time there is already a whole philosophical trend of noospherism led by the followers of Vernadsky and Ursul. Indeed, this is an optimistic philosophical theory because in it an accent is made on the developmental tendency of mankind. More recently noospherism is being more and more opposed by the proponents of finalism, who emphasize that during mankind's development its accumulation of the capital of knowledge will lead to the exhaustion of resources of the planet and pollution of the environment, and that finally it will lead it to degradation and destruction (Nazarov 1984).

References

Carnap R., Bar-Hillel Y. An outline of theory of semantic information Boston, MA: The MIT Press (1953)
Cherry C. On Human Communication 3rd ed. Cambridge, MA: The MIT Press (1978)
Grobstein C. The strategy of life San Francisco, CA: Freeman (1964)
Korogodin V. I. Informazia i fenomen zhizny [Information and the phenomenon of life] Puschino: Puschinsky Nauchny Zentr (1991)
Klaus G. Sila slova [The power of the word] Moscow: Progress (1967)
Lorenz K. Behind the mirror: A search for a natural history of human knowledge Fort Washington, PA: Harvest Books (1973)
Machlup F. Knowledge and knowledge production Princeton, NJ: Princeton University Press, Princeton (1980)
Machlup F., Mansfield U. eds. The studies of information: Interdisciplinary messages New York: J. Wiley & Sons (1983)
Moiseev N. N. Chelovek i noosfera [The individual and the noosphere] Moscow: Molodaya Gvardia (1990)
Morris C. W. Foundations of the theory of signs (1938)
Nazarov V. I. Finalism in modern evolution theory Moscow: Nauka (1984) (in Russian)
Porat M., Rubin M. The information economy, in nine volumes Washington, DC: Government Printing Office (1977)
Ross Ashby W. An introduction to cybernetics London: Chapman & Hall (1956)
Shannon C. E. 'A mathematical theory of communication' Bell System Theoretical Journal 27 (1948) pp. 379-423, pp. 623-656
Ursul A. D. Problema informazii v sovremennoy nauke [The problem of information in modern science] Moscow: Nauka (1975)
Ursul A. D. Informatizatia: Vvedenie v sozialnuyu informatiku [Informatization of the society: Introduction to social informatics] Moscow: Akademia Obschestvennih Nauk (1990)
Vernadsky V. I. Biosfera i noosfera [The biosphere and noosphere] Moscow: Nauka (1989)

Sosnin E. A. 'Informazionny operator i reclamnaya deyatelnost [Information operator and advertise activities]' published in Ekonomika reclami Tomsk: Tomsky Universitet (1999)

von Bertalanffy K. L. General system theory: Foundations, development, applications New York: George Braziller (1968)

Wiener N. Cybernetics or control and communication in the animal and in the machine Cambridge, MA: The MIT Press (1967)

Yankovsky S. Konzepzii obschey teorii informazii [Concepts of the general theory of information] Moscow: Publ. House Beta-Izdat (2000) URL: http://n-t.ru/tpe/ng/oti.htm (accessed September 2008)

Zhdanov G. B. 'Vibor estestvoznania: 8 prinzipov ili 8 illuziy razionalizma [The choice of natural sciences: 8 principles or 8 illusions of rationalism]' Filosovskie nauki. Problemi razionalnosti (2001)

Olga Vershinskaya

Theoretical Approach to the Concept of Humans as E-actors

Introduction

Dealing with digital information has become a part of our lives as we come to the end of this first decade of the twenty-first century. For many years now we have discussed the social consequences of the dissemination of ICTs and the appearance of e-actors, discussion of whom is the topic of this chapter, and who have come about as a direct consequence of ICTs. Talking of social consequences, the most generic definition concerns the social transformations that are related to the possibilities, rights and interests of a person. The main subjects of the social consequences of ICT research at the beginning of this century are numerous, for example, information inequality; usage of ICT by children and youth; emergence of electronic networks and more (Haddon 2004). Studying e-activity, in other words the human interaction with broadband technologies, is a rather new direction of research. Although looking at ICT from the point of view of its user already has a history of research there was still no need for holistic theory to support it. There is already a large number of studies, in the field of Socio-Technical Studies (STS), as well as different theoretical approaches to technology uses in sociology and anthropology (Actor-Network Theory for instance).

This chapter is an attempt to offer a general approach to e-activity research by the development of the concept of the human as an e-actor. This topic of e-activity is one possible perspective to study changes in the relationships between society and ICTs. The appearance of e-actors is a direct consequence of ICT dissemination, and although it can be studied within this framework of analysis, an action-oriented multidisciplinary approach to research is suggested in this chapter. It is based most particularly on noosphere theory, semiotics, the theory of socio-cultural reproduction and the social portrait genre. Different approaches "to draw" or explicate e-portraits will also be explored. For example the e-portrait as a part of the social portrait, as a list of e-activities performed or as a type of user are discussed. The pragmatic value of e- portraits is considered. Finally e-activity as a part of the twenty first century computer culture is analyzed, with the importance of the cultural and psychological aspects of social dynamics being particularly highlighted.

Concept of the e-actor

Today the concept of an actor is one of the basic sociological concepts, and indeed, it is used as often as the concepts of subject and object. But an e-actor as opposed to the well understood term actor is a new a concept that applies specifically to the electronic sphere. The e-actor is an actor who is acting in an electronic space. The very concept 'actor' comes from the verb to act and thus implies studying activity and thus e-actor implies studying this activity in a digitally mediated space. There are individual actors who are representing nobody but oneself, and there are collective actors representing institutions and organisations.

A social subject as an active participant, not society as a whole, became the subject of sociology in the second half of the 20th century and we look to Bourdieu and Giddens as the founders of this approach (Bourdieu & Passeron 1979; Giddens 1990). These concepts of social actor and social subject are often used as synonyms too, but they are in fact not similar at all in their relation to social acts and their meaning is not transferable in this way. The concept actor has a meaning only together with a certain social act or acts, while the concept of subject stresses the rationality of the mind and the ability to make a choice. A subject can become an actor concerning some act and an actor can be considered as a subject if certain characteristics of mind are present. In one case, for example, only some actors could have properties of subjectivity and in another case only some subjects could be actors of certain acts. This leads to an infinite number of possible situations and these are further extended by the concept of the e-actor as an actor acting in virtual space. Thus we can study e-actors in many ways, using different formats of behavioural research, consumption and media studies to name but three.

Levels of analysis

It would appear that there are many action-oriented theories that could be applicable for e-actors research. However, the aim of the paper is not to discuss them all but to suggest a multidisciplinary approach based on the three semiotic levels of analysis. Semiotics, the well known general theory of signs, introduced by Charles Pierce and Charles Morris in the second half of the nineteenth century (Morris 1938), analyses signs firstly at the syntactic level – which studies relationships between signs, structures of their combinations and rules of signs transformation regardless of their meanings. Secondly, the semantic level, which analyses meanings of signs, their interpretations and combinations. Thirdly the pragmatic level studies relationships between signs and their users and interprets the messages signs carry. These three levels: syntactic, semantics and pragmatics are three interrelated parts of this science of semiotics that treats each sign system as a model of a certain fragment of the world.

E-activity too can be studied at the three levels. The first level, similar to syntactic, is purely functional, monitoring possible e-actions and new possibilities. At the second semantic level, factors which determine use or commitment of an e-action are studied. And at the third, pragmatic level relationships between users and e-actions they perform are analysed. Thus we are able to study users as consumers and producers, the growing feature of the broadband world.

An informational explosion is the essence of postmodernism. The postmodern tradition in art and literature is similar to post-industrial tradition in economics and sociology. The basic features of the information environment in both cases are the same: a fragmentary and eclectic character with no well-defined borders and a narrowing of the realms of stable traditions. For postmodernists there is no reality, there are only descriptions of reality; there is no truth, there are only versions of truth. The truth is defined with the help of utility. There is nothing real as everything has been fabricated.

E-activity is activity in a fabricated world but consequences of this activity are quite practical, they happen in the real world.

There are two basic functions of knowledge: 'to know for the sake of knowledge' and 'to know to be able to do' (Teilhard de Chardin 1999). ICTs enhance the second, pragmatic function of knowledge. An action-oriented approach to research is the pragmatism as articulated by Mead (1938). The word "pragmatism" comes from the Greek word "action", pragmatic means practical. At this pragmatic level of research we relate each concept, each action with its consequences, all kinds of consequences such as applied, moral, imaginary and so on (Dewey 1916). E-activity is terra incognita from this point of view. For instance, from a moral point of view "correct" behaviour is the one which leads to the benefit of others and oneself. Non-ethical behaviour in the electronic world includes such types of e-activity as dissemination of viruses with the help of e-mails, dissemination of the wrong information through Internet or plagiarism – declaring oneself the author of another's information.

There are many other problems connected with e-activity not widely discussed. For instance the little studied problems of those who are over-informed or involvement into the world of illusionary communication. Progress of ICT makes illusionary reality become more and more trustworthy and that makes it easy to cheat the human psychology causing the number of psychological and ethical problems to grow.

Transition of the old pre-digital e-activity days to these new e-actor times represents a significant social transformation. Drawing now on the noosphere theory that was posed by the Russian academician Vladimir Vernadsky in the beginning of the twentieth century, we learn that the biosphere is gradually transforming into a noosphere – a manmade sphere, an artificial non-natural world. Noos is 'mind' in Greek, and the concept "noosphere" was actually suggested by a French researcher Le Royin in 1926. Using this concept Vernadsky developed a theory of the noosphere (Vernadsky 1988). The existence of this manmade world implies the necessity to direct, to regulate the evolution of the society using intellect and knowledge. A man of the noosphere with his abilities to deliver perturbations in the form of technical intrusions can easily break the natural equilibrium in many ways.

Vernadsky's theory is not well known globally among academics, today his concept of "watched over development" is mostly connected with ecological problems. However in essence, "watched over development" is an alternative to a market non-regulated development in all spheres of academic endeavour. The basic idea of "watched over development" is the same for all subjects and for all countries. The basic principle of the noosphere theory is the necessity to define the limitations, the highest permissible values in the sphere you are dealing with in order to know what it is not possible to do. Global cooperation and global discussions should be at the very core of making decisions, Vernadsky claimed. Eighty years ago he explained that the formation of collective intellect is vital for the humankind and today electronic networks, commonly accessible data banks and global possibilities of data exchange are all indicators of collective social intellect formation. Cooperation between and within societies becomes as important a market force for change as competition when global common interests appear.

The speed of technology change is constantly growing which makes it necessary to learn all the time, to constantly and perpetually update one's e-skills. Acceleration of change such as we have witnessed with the introduction of digital technologies, transforms society into an ever learning society. The life-long learning paradigm becomes important not only in educational discourse. The ability to learn quickly becomes very important in all echelons of society and all walks of life. There appears a new social differentiation between computerised and not computerised people, many of whom have much less ability to learn quickly.

It is important to analyse e-activity along all these lines in order to define limitations and to define what is not possible to do. In many ways the use of ICTs helps to implement and maintain "watched over development". The artificial digital world is a part of modern society, part of our postmodern environment. There are new social trends, new standards of behaviour, new notions of comfort, new types of activity, new types of poverty, not only in purely economic and income terms but also in the perspective of e-deprivation.

This idea of e-deprivation is a relative concept. To have no computer is considered by many to be a deprivation in modern society. However, this deprivation, one's e-poverty, is subjective – you may feel deprived because you are bothered by the fact that your personal computer is much less advanced than your neighbour's for instance. The time you actually spend using ICTs can also be an indicator of e-deprivation. There are many questions: why are people hindered in their ability to go online, have they got appropriate social networks in their lives etc. We can also expect indicators of e-deprivation to be different in different countries as they depend on what is considered deprivation in the national broadband society. Levels of e-deprivation can also vary.

The very concepts of equality and justice are changing in broadband world as the social development changes. The aspect of usage becomes more important in information society than the aspect of ownership.

It is for all these different perspectives of human e-activity that we have to study a human being "as a whole" towards achieving an understanding of the digital world.

As discussed above the noosphere is the sphere of human activity and accordingly it also includes e-activity. Indeed it is most apposite that the basic principles of noosphere theory are so suitable for studying social development and e- activity. There are two key factors to explore at this point. First is the contention that awareness of consequences is awareness of the future. Each human action has consequences, so, it is postulated, a person should be always aware of the results of his/her activity, aware of different possibilities of his/her behaviour and consciously choose the most suitable alternative from the point of view of the future. Social consequences of ICT dissemination are widely studied. Secondly, in order to survive in an artificial man-made world, a system of regulations and limitations of human behaviour should be developed. Limitations of behaviour concerning ICTs are poorly developed today.

There are other problems too. For instance, change and stability. There is no doubt that change is here, but there are stable things too. Each culture has its own models of production and consumption of knowledge and information. Quality of informational flows depends much on the national socio-cultural features. Stable paradigms of informational behaviour exist, which are transmitted from generation to generation (Bourdieu & Passeron 1979). Types of informational interactions are stable: people are either informationally active or passive, interested or disinterested regardless of the informational channel. ICTs enhance human possibilities but above all they enhance them for informationally active people. But can we assert that e-active people were always informationally active?

Still another problem – the ability to make a choice and to project one's lifestyle. It does not fully depend on ICTs, rather it is a characteristic of a person. To take an holistic view we have to take into account that there are several basic lifestyles that can be characterised by different attitudes (Meyer & Schulze 1997). Following this approach there are certain characteristics of lifestyle that are particularly relevant to the development of humans as e-actors. These manifest in certain attitudes to everyday life described here as follows:

- traditional attitude to family and gender roles, established lifestyle with financial independence, conservative pattern of values for all areas of life;
- emancipated attitude to family and gender roles, successful and consumption-oriented lifestyle with financial independence. Search for meaning and personal freedom within social network, openness to new experiences;
- achievement- and status-oriented attitude when profession and career take priority over one's personal needs and family, pronounced status thinking, pleasure in what is achieved through one's own efforts;
- post-modern attitude when the guiding principle is the development of individual personality in the context of diverse experiences, rejection of traditional norms and values, heightened sense of communication.

Becoming a lifestyle in itself, e-activity combines different attitudes. It does not necessarily reject traditional norms and values, but usage of ICT implies openness to new experiences and a heightened sense of communication.

If we go beyond behaviour looking for the motivations, trying to understand why this action was performed, e-activity can be well charted using domestication methodology. Roger Silverstone and Leslie Haddon's domestication methodology is one of the most well known social theories in this sphere. It emerged at the start of the 1990s (Silverstone & Haddon 1996). Domestication as a concept originated from anthropology, consumption studies and modern media studies (Haddon 2006). All kinds of social processes around ICTs are studied with the help of qualitative methodology, in-depth interviews and participant observation. Different questions can be explored: how patterns of use develop, how a person finds time for ICT usage; does ICT resolve conflicts in the family; is it used as a means of control; what are ownership relations; is ICT treated as a threat or as a new opportunity by different family members; is it used only for entertainment or/and for work; what do people do with technologies and services etc. With the help of this methodology we are able to study the meaning of ICT to a person, to understand usage patterns and to study different social relations. This approach fits well in the exploration of the e-activity of family members, because it allows one to study different generations of e-actors and it corresponds well with other approaches. Case studies of households give rich evidence of ICT usage.

We have explored how to approach an understanding of the close relationship between human activity and the electronic activities of broadband society by combining different traditions of research. In order to conceptualize e-actors research further I propose that we describe each e-actor with the help of his/her e-portrait.

The concept of the "e-portrait"

A concept through which we are able to understand more about a person as an e-actor is his/her electronic portrait. A person's e-portrait is a part of their social portrait. Social portrait is a genre of sociological research in which characteristics of a certain social group are described in maximal detail (for instance the 'social portrait of a young mother' or the 'social portrait of a believer'). At first such research implied questioning a large number of representatives of the chosen social group using a wide range of indicators. The idea was to get a full and comprehensive description of the social characteristics of this group. One of the first sociological study of this kind was carried out at the end of the nineteenth century in the USA (Du Bois 1995). It was called 'The Philadelphia Negro: A social study' and analysed the living conditions, work, income, education. More than 9000 African-Americans were studied for fifteen months and the results published in 1899. Another widely known study of this kind is the social research conducted in Pittsburgh, 1909-1914, into the workers of the steel industry who comprised 80% of the city workers. Later in the beginning of the 20th century the Chicago school introduced another sociological genre – case study. This genre is not based on big quantitative samples though the objects are more or less the same. Characteristics of the social group are extracted out of a single description of one particular case. Today the social portrait genre implies both methodologies of statistical/quantitative and qualitative research.

Building on this diversity of methodological approaches to examine social portraits we can use different approaches for constructing an e-portrait. The simplest approach is to present a person as a number of figures, such as their identification number, individual tax number, a set of pin codes etc. which represent the person in an electronic world. Those figures help digital identification of each person and this quickly leads one to consider the growing danger of the possibility of global digital control that is widely discussed elsewhere such as in literature on surveillance society (Lyon 2001). However, such a portrait is not likely to be very informative for studying e-activity as a sociological phenomenon.

Another approach is to draw an e-portrait based on types of e-activities and their intensity. There are several main groups of e-activities: retrieval of information, communication, organisation of services (travel arrangements, booking tickets and hotels, buying goods etc.), entertainment and working. Each e-actor performs a number of activities, which can be listed and classified. One actor is all in e-business, another in entertainment, still another uses a balanced list of different activities. Such characteristics like paintings give us a picture of a person showing what part of his/her life has become digital.

It is clear that talking about users as e-actors will differ completely along the lines of user type. The intensity of e-activity can be also defined by the type of user. There are many classifications of users, each one of which says something of the users' actions in their particular network. Making use of different typologies we shall have different e-portraits. Each class of users is a characteristic of e-activity.

E-portraits can be used in many different ways. For example by studying consumption of e-services we can monitor transformation of the traditional service sector. We can use e-portraits as a measure of social differentiation. We can study e-activity as a lifestyle; we can consider e-actors at home or at the working place, we can study issues involved in measuring and characterizing users. Humans as e-actors research is important both to understand what is happening to social and economic life, and to what effective practical interventions can be made into the worlds of production and consumption of ICT.

Conclusion

In this new century we have new literacy, new ethics, new identities, new elites and new culture. Besides two traditional types of culture: culture of face to face, direct communication and book culture, culture of written language, a new type of culture appeared – screen or computer culture based on the convergence of computer, video and telecommunication technologies. Dynamic dialogical type of interaction between computer text and the user is the main indicator of this computer culture. Interactivity, feedback with the screen is the basic change. This new type of culture is actively interacting with the two traditional types. This interaction leads to fundamental changes in culture but it does not deform it – computer culture is complimentary to traditional culture (Razlogov 2006) as it brings entirely new possibilities. A new type of communication appears, international by nature and thus a new type of thinking appears, oriented on self development and combining the logical and the emotional. Computer skills are not enough, to conduct e-activity – one has to have advanced information skills such as awareness of an information need, definition of the sources of information, comparison of information from different sources and choosing the best, using the information when making a decision and disseminating it to the interested people. There are many new qualities of e-information consumers, not least the ability to act in a transnational environment, the ability to collect information for the task and the ability to find colleagues in an electronic world. Computer culture is not only screen culture, such new concepts as "digital me", "e-self", "e-lert" or "e-fit" imply new social phenomena which can be described with the help of e-activity research.

A range of activities previously considered predominantly technical or economic or cultural are now converging. The importance of creativity and knowledge to contemporary economic success gives a turn to the analysis of psychological and cultural forms to be found everywhere. The importance of informational, psychological and cultural aspects of social dynamics is growing and it is now recognised that there are more and more social and humanitarian problems being caused, or at least influenced, by the dissemination of ICTs. The importance of e-activity grows apace in a broadband society, and in studying virtual reality as a part of the manmade sphere we have to study things which change and remain stable and concentrate on new limitations.

Fundamental questions about how to understand transformation of traditional life caused by e-activity are raised by scholars from the humanities, social sciences, communications, media and management studies and from this the action-oriented multidisciplinary theory is being born. It will be some time before such a theory is fully developed. Suggested levels of analysis outlined in this paper combined with the concepts of e-activity, e-actor and e-portrait should in some way bring this theoretical debate a step nearer to this aim.

References

Bourdieu P., Passeron J. C. The Inheritors: French students and their relation to culture Chicago: The University of Chicago Press (1979)
Dewey J. Essays in Environmental Logic Chicago: University of Chicago Press (1916)
Du Bois W. E. B. The Philadelphia Negro: A Social Study Pennsylvania: University of Pennsylvania Press URL: http://www.webdubois.org/wdb-phila.html (1995) (accessed January 2009)
Giddens A. The Consequences of Modernity Cambridge: Polity Press (1990)
Haddon L. 'The Contribution of Domestication Research to In-Home Computing and Media Consumption' The Information Society 22 (2006) pp. 1-9
Haddon L. Information and Communication Technology in Everyday Life Oxford: Berg (2004)
Lyon D. Surveillance Society: Monitoring Everyday Life Maidenhead: Open University Press (2001)
Mead G. The Philosophy of the Act Chicago: Chicago University Press (1938)
Meyer S., Schulze E. 'Dialectical coherence of technology and the private household: concept and adjustment' EMTEL Meeting Barcelona (7th November 1997)

Morris C. 'Foundations of the theory of signs' ed. Neurath O. International Encyclopedia of Unified Science vol. 1 no. 2. Chicago: University of Chicago Press (1938)

Razlogov K. New audio visual technologies Moscow (in Russian) (2006)

Silverstone R., Haddon L. 'Design and the domestication of information and communication technologies: Technical change and everyday life' eds. Silverstone R., Mansell R.. Communication by Design Oxford: Oxford University Press (1996)

Teilhard de Chardin P. The human phenomenon Eastbourne: Sussex Academic Press (1999)

Vernadsky V. Philosophic thoughts of a natural scientist (in Russian). Moscow: Nauka (1988)

Theme IV:
E-actors in the institutional context: Policies and regulations from e-actors' point of view

Lilia Raycheva

Television: The Good, the Bad and the Unexpected Challenges of ICT to Contemporary Television

Introduction

In March 2000, the European Council in Lisbon set up an agenda for economic and social renewal of Europe. Realizing that the continent is facing a paradigm shift driven by globalization, the EU Heads of States and Governments agreed to make the EU "the most competitive, dynamic and inclusive knowledge-driven economy by 2010". It was also noted that "the knowledge economy is profoundly changing the types of skills required for work and that information technologies can help reduce long-term structural unemployment" (EuC 2000). In 2005, following the Commission's mid-term review of the Lisbon agenda, a comprehensive strategy for the Information Society 2005-2010 was launched.

Later, the *"i2010 – an European Information Society for growth and employment"* initiative was adopted by the European Commission on 1st June 2005 as a framework for addressing the main challenges and developments in the sector of information, communication and media industries up to 2010. The initiative contains a range of EU policy instruments envisaged to encourage the development of a competitive digital economy, such as regulatory instruments, research and partnerships with stakeholders. It also promotes ICT as a key driver of social inclusion and of better quality of life.

i2010 has three main policy objectives:

- to create a single European information space, which will secure an open and competitive internal market for the digital economy (electronic communication and media services) both for industry and consumers.
- to strengthen investment in innovation and research in ICT and to encourage the industrial application of ICTs.
- to foster inclusion, better public services and quality of life through the use of ICT (EC, 2005a).

The creation of single information space has started with upgrading of EU rules on audiovisual content services. Practices have demonstrated considerable progress: telecommunication providers already offer broadcasting services and content providers supply communications services. The goal is for the consumers to be able to watch audiovisual content anytime, anywhere, and on all technical platforms (TV set, computer, mobile phone, personal digital assistant, etc.). Broadband, triple play and quadruple play, fixed-mobile convergence, fiber rollouts, mobile TV are the new challenges to media markets. Next-generation networks, capable of offering speeds that can support Internet and high-definition TV (IPTV, VOIP, mobile TV, and Web 2.0) are on the way. All these exciting varieties of technological options and services need regulatory certainty in the developing common internal market for electronic communications (Reding 2007).

Modern technologies have considerably facilitated collecting, storage, processing, and distribution of data volumes, reducing tangibly their entropy. However, under the conditions of this new communication environment orientation in the vast quantities of information is particularly important, as well as its rationalization and conversion into knowledge, or as John Naisbitt puts it: "We swim in information, but starve for knowledge" (Naisbitt 1984, 17). Which brings us to the "informational paradox of more information = less information" in the uncontrollable commercialization of the media (Cuilenburg 1998, 81).

This gives rise to the question: How well does the traditional media system, with its main social pillars such as plurality and diversity, fit into the newly developed situation, in which geopolitical boundaries become ever more conditional?

Relevant information about research and activities in this area can be found in:

- Media and Information Society (Council of Eutrope):
  http://www.coe.int/t/dghl/standardsetting/media/
- Information Society and Media Directorate-General (European Commission):
  http://ec.europa.eu/dgs/information_society/index_en.htm
- Europe's Information Society Thematic Portal:
  http://ec.europa.eu/information_society/activities/ict_psp/index_en.htm
- MEDIA Programme:
  http://ec.europa.eu/information_society/media/index_en.htmInternational
- Information and Communication Technologies: Pervasive and Trusted Network and Service Infrastructures:
  http://cordis.europa.eu/fp7/ict/programme/challenge1_en.html
- Information and Communication Technologies: Networked Media Systems:
  http://cordis.europa.eu/fp7/ict/netmedia/home_en.html
- Telecommunication Union:
  http://www.itu.int/net/home/index.aspx

The perspective of mediamatics

Theoretical verification and legal regulation of the traditional mass media developments have difficulty keeping up with the headlong progress of new technologies. And if half a century ago Arthur Clarke's fantasies about a satellite communication ring had a strongly futuristic twang, in less than a decade digital technology brought revolutionary changes in the radio and TV production and dissemination processes all over the world. In a matter of several years analogue communications will be a history. The type and pace of these changes will present mankind with challenges of many an aspect.

Of all factors affecting the building rate of the new type of society, the technological one is undoubtedly the most active. Arrangement and processing of information have been optimized and the speed of communication has increased. Mass-scale advent of digital electronics and computer software in the everyday life presumes introduction of new schemes and mechanisms for the creation, distribution and consumption of information. The range of traditional communication products and services is steadily expanding. Moreover, the satellite links, digitalization and new information technologies have brought to the fore the question of convergence in communications development on various levels.

In its 1997 *Green Paper* the European Commission defined convergence as follows:

- ability to transfer kindred services on different platforms;
- bringing together of such large-scale public works as the telephone, television or personal computers.

The *Green Paper* also identified the basic characteristics of the Internet and the digital technologies that challenged the applied grounds for the existing media regulation in a converged marketplace: the overcoming of scarcity, the interactive merge between publisher and consumer, the user-driven status, and the decentralized (horizontal) communication. Thus, it prompted the media industries to acknowledge that in the vast growing technological era they would be predominantly governed by market mechanisms and economic objectives for achieving wider social, economic and general policy aims (EC 1997a, 18).

The *Green Paper* has set clear goals to the convergence policy in audiovision. The information and communication technologies have outpaced regulation and have set up an economic basis for the convergence of entire industries: the electronic, entertainment, media. In this sense, Santiago Lorente sees two stages in technological development: convergence between telecommunications and informatics (telematics) and between telematics and audio-vision (mediamatics) (Lorente 1997, 119).

Being the backbone of the knowledge based society broadband is providing access to advanced public services and diverse multimedia content for information, entertainment, training and work. Broadband access has become a prerequisite for a wide range of issues: from economic growth to social inclusion. The move to broadband will fundamentally add to Internet experience new phenomena, such as "user-generated" content sites and advanced "digital ecosystem" technologies. (EC 2006a).

The Single European Information Space is the pillar of i2010 that combines regulatory and other instruments for creation of a modern, market-oriented regulatory framework for the electronic communications, including the audiovisual policies, the radio spectrum management, and the process of switchover to digital TV. The switchover from analogue to digital broadcasting is expected to create new distribution networks and expand the potential for wireless innovation and services. Just prior to the reform of the EU telecom rules, on 29 March 2007, the European Commission published its 12th report on the EU telecom market. It pointed out that although the consumers have more choice in a sector worth almost €290 billion in revenues, which accounts for about 2.2% of the annual European GDP, the full potential of the EU internal market still remains untapped (EC 2007a).

Despite the general progress of broadband developments, access to the new services in remote and rural regions appears to be limited because of high costs due to low density of population and remoteness. With this in mind, the European Commission published in March 2006 the communication *"Bridging the Broadband Gap"*, which refers to the territorial differences in broadband access, speeds, quality of service, prices and use between urban and rural/remote areas, as well as between more/less developed areas in Europe (EC 2006b). This is a direct move for the protection of fundamental democratic achievements, such as freedom of expression and access to information.

The European contemporary audio-visual policies

Protection of the freedom of expression and promotion of media pluralism are two of the most important democratic pillars in contemporary society. The necessity of sustaining these social achievements was underlined already in the first pan-European documents. In 1950, these intentions were outlined in the *Convention for the Protection of Human Rights and Fundamental Freedoms.* Article 10 of the *ECHR* provides the right of everyone to freedom of expression, which includes "to hold opinion and to receive and impart information and ideas without interference by public authority and regardless of frontiers". This freedom is subject to certain restrictions that are "in accordance with law" and "necessary in a democratic society" (CoE 1950).

About half a century later, Article 11 (Freedom of expression and information) of the *Charter of Fundamental Rights of the European Union* reaffirmed that:

1. Everyone has the right to freedom of expression. The right shall include freedom to hold opinions and to receive and impart information and ideas without interference by public authority and regardless of frontiers.
2. The freedom and pluralism of the media shall be respected (EU P 2000).

Within the meaning of the *Treaty of Rome* – the EU founding document – broadcasting is considered a service. The requirement for freedom of movement of goods and services across the frontiers of the Member States is a basic requirement for achieving the pan-European objectives (EU 1957). Some thirty years later, revising the *Treaty of Rome*, the *Single European Act (SEA)* added new momentum to European integration by completing the internal market (EU 1986). According to the *General Agreement on Trade in Services (GATS)*, since January 2000 the audiovisual services sector has become the subject of multilateral trade negotiations. The sector includes motion picture and video tape production and distribution services, motion picture projection services, radio and television services, radio and television transmission services, and sound recording (WTO 2000).

As the main intergovernmental organization at pan-European level dealing with the democratic dimensions of communication, which serves 800 million Europeans from 47 member states, The Council of Europe has been consistently active in setting common standards for media developments. The attention to these developments has become particularly strong since the 1990s, with the rapid progress of information and communication technologies, which stimulated the media concentration process (CoE 2007).

The acts of the Council of Europe important for the audio-visual developments are the legally binding European treaties or conventions, many of which are open to non-member states, as well as the acts of the:

– Parliamentary Assembly;
– Committee of Ministers;
– Steering Committee on the Media and New Communication Services (CDMC);
– Standing Committee of Transfrontier Television;
– European Court of Human Rights.

Mostly significant for the audiovisual sector are the *European Convention for the Protection of Human Rights and Fundamental Freedoms* and *The European Convention on Transfrontier Television.*

The *European Convention on Transfrontier Television* opened on May 1989 for signature by Member States and by the other States Parties to the *European Cultural Convention* and by the European Community. May 1, 1993 marked its entry into force. Currently, the number of parties, brought to this instrument, is 32. The *Protocol* amending the *ECTT* was opened for signing by the Parties to the *Convention,* in Strasbourg, on 1 October 1998. Since its entry into force on 1 March 2002, this *Protocol* has become an integral part of *ECTT.*

The aim of the *ECTT* is to facilitate, among the Parties, the transfrontier transmission and the retransmission of television program services. It lays down a set of minimum rules in areas such as the responsibility of broadcasters in regard to programming matters, including the European content of programming; advertising, teleshopping and sponsorship as well as the protection of certain individual rights. Application of the *ECTT* mostly relies on mutual co-operation between the Parties (CoE 1989).

A *Convention* body, the Standing Committee on Transfrontier Television composed of representatives of the Parties, is responsible for following the instrument's application and may intervene with advisory opinion for friendly conciliation of any difficulties. In cases where disputes cannot be resolved through friendly settlement, arbitration is contemplated, resulting in legally binding decisions.

The European Union (EU) as one of the largest economic and political entities in the world is a supranational and intergovernmental alliance of 27 states with 495 million people (Eurostat 2007) and a combined nominal GDP of 11 294.6609 € ($15,183.404) billions in 2007 (EU GDP 2007).

Alongside the European Parliament and the Council of the European Union, the European Commission is one of the three main institutions governing the EU. The primary role of the European Commission is to propose and implement the legal basis for the EU. It monitors the Member States' compliance with the Union's agreed Treaties and Directives, taking action against those in default. The Commission is intended to be a body independent of the Member States. It consists of 27 Commissioners, one from each Member State of the EU, supported by an administrative body of the Directorates-General (EC 2007b).

The EU Directorate General for the Information Society and Media was expanded as from January 2005 to include the media (which were formerly under DG for Education and Culture). DG InfSo deals with the research, policy and regulation of the areas of information, and with communication technology and media. It defines and implements the regulatory framework for services based on information, communication and audio-visual technologies. Its regulation has cultural, societal and economic objectives, and covers some of the largest economic sectors in Europe. Furthermore, it fosters the growth of the content industries drawing on Europe's cultural diversity. *i2010 – European Information Society for Growth and Employment* is currently the main ruling policy document of DG InfSo (DG InfSo 2005).

Following the rigorously developing TV and radio market, a need of setting some minimum regulatory standards applicable to all Member States was felt. Thus on 3 October 1989 the European Union came up with the *Television without Frontiers Directive 89/552/EEC*. This *Directive* constitutes a legal *EU* framework aimed at coordination of certain provisions laid down by law, regulation or administrative actions in the Member States concerning the pursuit of television broadcasting activities. It aims to ensure free movement of broadcasting services within the internal market and at the same time to preserve certain objectives of public interest. It is also intended to promote the distribution and production of European audiovisual programs and to ensure, whenever possible, that they are given a majority position in program schedules of the television channels (EC 1989).

Only half a decade after the entry into force of the *TVWF Directive,* intensive developments in the audiovisual sector determined the necessity in further extension of the rules regarding some of its general provisions. These included: advertising, teleshopping and sponsorship; promotion and distribution of the European cultural productions; access of the public to major (sports) events, protection of minors, and right to reply.

Parallel to these developments, a report *Europe and the Global Information* (largely known as the *Bangemann Report*) proved to be extremely influential in starting out the discussion on the future European communications policy, by pointing out that the building of European information society would be market-driven (EC 1994).

Thus, on 30 June 1997 the *Directive 97/36/EC* of the European Parliament and of the Council amended the *Council Directive 89/552/EEC*. Among the above mentioned provisions, it introduced a special article concerning the setting up of a Contact Committee under the aegis of the Commission (EC 1997b).

In the process of implementation of the *TVWF Directive* it was impossible to adopt decisions, contradictory to the norms of the *ECTT*. As an illustration of the coordinated actions of the European Union and the Council of Europe in the audiovisual area can serve the fact that the *Amending Protocol of the ECTT* was adopted after the revision of the *Directive* in 1997. This *Protocol* practically reflected the amendments to the *Directive*. The current discussions of the review of the *ECTT* are in tune with the latest revision of the *TVWF Directive*, already adopted in 2007. As a matter of fact, this process has started quite long ago: since

2001 the effectiveness of the articles of the *Convention* and the *Directive* has been thoroughly analyzed.

In another five years after the *TVWF Directive* was amended, the European audiovisual sector has dramatically changed. The convergence of technologies has provided interweaving of linear and non-linear services. The expansion of fixed broadband, digital TV and 3G networks was rapidly changing the viewers' habits. The vertical structure of audio-visual programming was being steadily displaced by horizontal fragmentation of the audiences, who wished to follow their own viewing time schedule. Technological progress has made a strong impact on the business models of the media industry. A need for modernization and adjustment of the regulatory framework was felt in this new situation of rigorous market and technological developments.

After a large and intensive discussion more coherent measures for reinforcing the pan-European audiovisual policy were proposed to the Community legislator, taking into account the objective of creating a pro-competitive, technologically driven and growth-oriented environment for the development of the audiovisual sector. A broad consensus on the scope, European works, co- and self-regulation, independence of the national media regulators has been achieved. Thus, the amending *Directive* was adopted on 11 December and entered into force on 19 December 2007. Member States have two years to transpose the new provisions into national law, so that the modernized legal framework for audiovisual media services will be fully applicable throughout the European Union by the end of 2009.

The *ECTT* and the amending *Protocol,* on the one hand, and the newly adopted *Audiovisual Media Service Directive* (which has replaced the *Television without Frontiers Directive)*, on another, have similar objectives, although the intention of the *AVMS Directive* as an instrument of the European Commission is to create a common market in broadcasting.

The *AVMS Directive* offers an updated and comprehensive legal framework that covers all linear (broadcasting) and non-linear (on-demand) audiovisual media services, as well as provides less detailed and more flexible regulation and modernizes rules on TV advertising to better finance audiovisual content. The *AVMS Directive* also upholds the basic pillars of Europe's audiovisual model, such as cultural diversity, media pluralism, protection of minors, consumer protection, and intolerance of incitement to racial and religious hatred. It acknowledges that "Audiovisual media services are as much cultural services as they are economic services. Their growing importance for society, democracy – in particular by ensuring freedom of information, diversity of opinion and media pluralism – education and culture justifies the application of specific rules to these services." In particular, the new *Directive* underlines the importance of promoting media literacy, development of which can help people "exercise informed choices, understand the nature of content and services and take advantage of the full range of opportunities offered by new communication technologies" (EC 2007c). Thus, they will be better able to protect themselves and their families from harmful or offensive material.

The field both of the *ECTT* and the *AVMS Directive* is very flexible and dynamic. That is why the work on their improvement is an ongoing process. In particular, the harmonization of both instruments by the participating Parties concern:

– the scope of the *Convention* and *Directive* (the broadening of traditional television broadcasting towards the ICT audio-visual services);
– the duties of the Parties to the *Convention* and the *Directive*;
– the broadening of the jurisdiction and scope of the regulatory practices, involving co-regulation and self-regulation;
– the freedom of reception and retransmission, including intended and unintended transfrontier distribution;
– the developments of advertising techniques (advertising, sponsorship, tele-shopping, product placement, etc.);
– the protection of rights granted by the *Convention* and the *Directive* (such as the right to information and cultural objectives, media pluralism, right to reply, protection of minors and respect for human dignity), etc.

The rapid change of the audiovisual market requires a thorough refining of the existing norms in the *Convention* and the *Directive* under a broad consensus. The problem is whether the regulatory changes should anticipate or follow the practices.

European DVB-T policies

The recent years have witnessed some stepped–up efforts on the part of the Council of Europe and the European Commission directed at speeding up the process of transition from analogue to digital television by publication of various acts. In 2002 the Commission issued a *Decision* aimed at establishing a policy and legal framework in the Community for ensuring coordination of policy approaches and, when appropriate, harmonised conditions with regard to availability and efficient use of the radio spectrum. This was considered necessary for the establishment and functioning of the internal market in Community policy areas, such as electronic communications, transport, and research and development (R&D) (EC 2002a).

On the same day – March 7th, 2002 – the European Commission published three interrelated EC Directives, known as the *Access Directive* (2002/19/EC), the *Authorisation Directive* (2002/20/EC) and the *Framework Directive* (2002/21/EC).

The *Access Directive* (which does not refer to access by end-users) focuses on the harmonization of the way in which Member States regulate access to and interconnection of electronic communications networks and associated facilities. Its aim refers to establishing a regulatory framework, in accordance with the internal market principles, for relationships between the suppliers of networks and services that would result in sustainable competition, interoperability of electronic communications services and consumer benefits (EC 2002b, 19).

The aim of the *Authorisation Directive* is to implement an internal market in electronic communications networks and services through harmonisation and simplification of the authorisation rules and conditions. This is necessary in order to facilitate their provision throughout the Community. The *Directive* applies to authorisations for the provision of electronic communications networks and services (EC 2002c, 20).

And *the Framework Directive* is aiming at establishing a harmonised framework for the regulation of electronic communications services, electronic communications networks, associated facilities and associated services. It also lays down the tasks of the national regulatory authorities and establishes a set of procedures to ensure the harmonised application of the regulatory framework throughout the Community (EC 2002d, 21).

Following these Acts, the European Commission published *Guidelines on Market Analysis and the Assessment of Significant Market Power under the Community Regulatory Framework for Electronic Communications Networks and Services* (EC 2002e).

In 2003 the Committee of Ministers of the Council of Europe adopted a *Recommendation Rec(2003)9 to Member States on Measures to Promote the Democratic and Social Contribution of Digital Broadcasting.* The Governments of the Member States were reminded in it to "create adequate legal and economic conditions for the development of digital broadcasting that guarantee the pluralism of broadcasting services and public access to an enlarged choice and variety of quality programmes, including the maintenance and, where possible, extension of the availability of transfrontier services". The Governments should guarantee the protection of the interests of the public, as well as to set out clear and fair principles of operation to the broadcasters and especially to the public service media (CoE 2003).

During the same year the European Commission adopted an important document: *Communication on the Transition from Analogue to Digital Broadcasting (from 'Digital Switch-over' to 'Analogue Switch-off').* According to it, "digital TV needs new drivers beyond traditional pay-TV and improved differentiation from analogue television, achieved through some combination of more free-to-air, including terrestrial digital TV programming; better picture quality; data and interactive services; mobile and portable services" (EC 2003).

Two years later, (in 2005), the rapid development of ICT was a precondition for the Commission to adopt a *Communication on Accelerating the Transition from Analogue to Digital Broadcasting*. This Communication sets out the Community policy objectives for the transition. It identifies the spectrum gains as one of the major advantages of the switchover, especially the "additional spectrum capacity released by the switch-off of analogue terrestrial television" and the fact that "it will be important not to constrain unduly the reuse of these bands for new and innovative services". The Communication on digital switchover set out 2012 as deadline for analogue switch-off (EC 2005b).

In the process of preparation for the regional Radiocommunication Conference, which revised the regional Agreement on the European Radio Broadcasting Zone of Stockholm, 1961 amended by the Regional Administrative Conference of the Council Members of the European Radio Broadcasting Zone of Geneva, 1985, the European Commission adopted another *Communication on the EU Spectrum Policy Priorities for the Digital Switchover in the Context of the Upcoming ITU Regional Radiocommunication Conference 2006 (RRC-06)*.

According to this Communication, the Member States should be obligated to ensure that the RRC-06 will not create undue obstacles to the strict application of the EU *Framework and Authorisation Directives on Electronic Communications Services* and other applicable EU legislation regarding future allocation and assignment of the spectrum dividend. The Communication also addresses the relationship between the RRC planning approach and the market and policy developments. In particular, it points out that access to the spectrum dividend has to comply with Article 9 of the EC *Framework Directive* (2002) whereby *"Member States shall ensure that the allocation and assignment of such radio frequencies by national regulatory authorities are based on objective, transparent, non-discriminatory and proportionate criteria"*. In addition, Article 7 of the *Authorisation Directive* (2002) imposes further requirements on the procedure for limiting the number of rights of use to be granted for radio frequencies, when appropriate (EC 2005c).

Digital dividend

One of the key questions in the context of the switchover refers to the task of the best use of the spectrum dividend. Prior to the ITU Regional Radiocommunication Conference 2006 (RRC-06), the Radio Spectrum Policy Group (RSPG), established to assist the Commission on radio spectrum policy issues, advised to distinguish three categories of spectrum demands:

- Spectrum needed for the improvement of terrestrial broadcasting services;
- Radio resources needed for "converged" broadcasting services which are expected to be primarily "hybrids" of traditional broadcast and mobile communication services;
- Frequencies to be allocated to new "uses" which do not belong to the broadcasting family of applications (EC 2005c).

The digital dividend resulting from efficiencies in spectrum usage is supposed to allow the creation of new distribution networks and expansion of the potential for wireless innovation and services. The aim is to support the mobile reception of video, Internet and multimedia data, as well as the development of handheld TV broadcast (DVB-H), along with high-definition Television (HDTV).

The ITU's Regional Radiocommunication Conference (RRC-06) in Geneva outlined the 'all-digital' terrestrial broadcasting in the frequency bands 174-230 MHz and 470-862 MHz in Europe, Africa, Middle East and the Islamic Republic of Iran by 2015. The new Digital Plan based on broadcasting standards known as T-DAB (for sound) and DVB-T (for TV) provides also for sufficient flexibility for adaptation to the changing telecommunication environment (ITU 2006).

In 2007, the ITU held its World Radiocommunication Conference 2007 (WRC-07) under the motto: *Bringing all radio services together.* The Conference adopted an international treaty, known as *Radio Regulations Governing the Use of the Radio-Frequency Spectrum and Satellite Orbits.* These regulations were revised and updated to meet the global demand for radio-frequency spectrum efficiency. Digital broadcasting was among the 30 agenda items addressed at WRC-07 (ITU 2007).

In the final documents of RRC-06 and WRC-07, as well as in other documents, special attention was attached to various aspects of the digital dividend. Priority has been assigned to the public orientation of the digital dividend usage. According to the EC *Communication on Reaping the Full Benefits of the Digital Dividend in Europe: a Common Approach to the Use of the Spectrum Released by the Digital Switchover,* the transition from analogue to digital broadcasting and HD services has been regarded as a possibility to increase the media pluralism, growth in media content production, and the higher-quality and more interactive services for viewers. Thus, digital dividend is related, above all, to the support of existing broadcasting services in a fully digital environment, with special attention to public service obligations (EC 2007d).

At the beginning of 2008, the Committee of Ministers of the Council of Europe adopted a *Declaration on the Allocation and Management of the Digital Dividend and the Public Interest*. According to it, the Member States must declare that they "should acknowledge the public nature of the digital dividend resulting from the switchover and the need to manage such a public resource efficiently in the public interest, taking account of present and foreseeable future needs for a radio spectrum CoE 2008).

In March 2008, the DVB World Conference 2008 in Budapest was held under the motto *Convergence or Divergence?* In her speech at the Conference headlined "Digital TV, Mobile TV: Let's push for open technologies in Europe and worldwide", the EU Commissioner for Information Society and Media, Viviane Reding, confirmed that the process of transition to digital television in the European Union should stand for a short-time simulcast.

"The digital dividend resulting from the switch-off is expected to give a major boost to wireless communications, including to broadcasting applications. Thus, even before 2012, the high-quality radio spectrum that will become progressively available on the Continent can be used in the interest of the European citizens and consumers. On this issue, we should avoid useless disputes between broadcasters and telecom/wireless companies and look at how to create a win–win situation," underlined commissioner Reding (Reding 2008).

Conclusion

The significance and role of television in the contemporary world has been growing tremendously with the development of new platforms for distribution of audiovisual content. The television not only continues to inform the audiences, but to shape their views too. Moreover, it catalyzes rather than reflects the public processes, thus creating preconditions for reformatting society to the extent that it begins to reflect the developments on the TV screen. This mutual interpenetration is aided by diffusion of some other kindred activities with the media world. The political elites are quick to use the media for their PR purposes. For the economic elites, the media are the main distributors of their advertisements. The needs of the public are increasingly forced out of the media. Paradoxically enough, the governments engage in regulatory protection of the public service television which is supposed to be its most vehement critic. Self-regulation has failed to become the public ombudsman and corrective of the commercial influence yet. Even enhanced interactivity could hardly pull the recipients out of their assigned role of users and consumers. The Internet environment is aiding the fragmentation of audiences, but still fails to change the prevailing vertical communication model. The moment it succeeds, this would probably bring in large functional restructuring of the traditional mass-media system.

Analogue switch-off is not a simple matter. A poorly managed process can have unpredictable consequences and turn into a liability to both Government and broadcasters, should some households be left without television services. It is for this reason that careful planning (technological, financial, regulatory, and social) is necessary to ensure that possible negative consequences are avoided. In an open market, viewers ultimately determine the speed of DTT penetration. Pan-European moves for further promotion of the efficient usage of the radio frequency spectrum in the audiovisual sector is of major economic, social and cultural importance.

The rapid technological developments of the information and communication industries outline some major aspects of concern. Politically, the development of free and unhindered transmission of audiovisual services on pan-European level governed by a common legal framework is important for pursuing EU objectives. In view of the democratic, social and cultural significance of the media, policymakers and public authorities should enforce adequate measures to ensure transparency in the media sector and prevent the conflicts of interest which pose a threat to the independence and plurality of the media.

Technologically, digital technologies, broadband and web casting increase the number of channels, providing the viewers with multiple choices of programs and audio-visual services. The contemporary audiovisual reality becomes more and more complex with the interweaving between linear and non-linear programming as well as between broadcasting and audiovisual service. A key question in the context of the digital switchover refers to the task of the best use of the spectrum dividend.

Economically, the expanding tendency towards deregulation and privatization in broadcasting leads to predominance of the commercial structures and dependence on market mechanisms. Thus, the merger control at the European, as well as at national level, should be complemented, where appropriate, with specific measures to protect and promote media pluralism.

In regulatory terms, the tendencies to merging media, telecommunications and entertainment industries lead to changes in the legal basis of the regulatory approaches (in structure and duties of the regulatory authorities, in methods of regulating (regulation, co-regulation and self-regulation) and in audiovisual content, subjected to regulation). In this sense it is of great importance to outline the parameters of the "regulatable" content".

Socially, the quantity of programs on offer leads to fragmentation, demassification of the audiences of the traditional broadcasting (one-to-many), thus opening ground for non-broadcasting and interactive audiovisual services. Further on, the Information Society services offer their products in a "one-to-one" mode. Through citizen journalism citizen media individuals can produce and disseminate information and opinions that are marginalized by the mainstream media. The broad impact of media on the general publics in real time is reduced due to asymmetric communication offered by diverse electronic sources. This new communication environment needs an energetic developing of media literacy programs.

Professionally, the rapid introduction of the technological innovations is challenging the traditional formats, styles, and modes of programming. The process of media convergence as well as the interactivity tendencies raises serious questions in the managing of editorial content. The significance of self-regulation and application of ethical codes of conduct become ever more important for the journalist practices. Public service broadcasters should contribute to media pluralism by providing a diverse range of quality programs. Media organizations should develop media accountability systems in order to strengthen professional values, editorial and journalistic independence and quality journalism.

Television is still the most significant source of information and entertainment for 98% of the European households that watch television on the average for more than 3 hours per day. However, having in mind the rapid technological developments in a highly competitive market, a major concern about the vitality of the new regulatory rules may be for how long the pillars of Europe's audiovisual model (cultural diversity, protection of minors, consumer protection, media pluralism, and intolerance against racial and religious hatred) will be protected. And all this makes ever more obvious how compression of historical time dictates the new pace of the communication process with the good, the bad and the unexpected challenges of ICT.

References

Council of Europe. Convention for the Protection of Human Rights and Fundamental Freedoms as amended by Protocol No 11 (1950) URL: http://conventions.coe.int/Treaty/en/Treaties/Html/005.htm (accessed April 2007)

Council of Europe. European Convention on Transfrontier Television (1989) URL: http://conventions.coe.int/Treaty/EN/Treaties/Html/132.htm (accessed April 2007)

Council of Europe. Recommendation of the Committee of Ministers to member states on measures to promote the democratic and social contribution of digital broadcasting (2003) URL: https://wcd.coe.int/rsi/common/renderers/rend_standard.jsp?DocId=38043&SecMode=1&SiteName=cm&Lang=en (accessed April 2008)

Council of Europe. An Overview (2007) URL: http://www.cid.bg/en/right/genoverview.htm (accessed April 2007)

Council of Europe. Declaration of the Committee of Ministers on the allocation and management of the digital dividend and the public interest. (2008) URL: https://wcd.coe.int/ViewDoc.jsp?id=1252459&Site=CM&BackColorInternet=9999CC&BackColorIntranet=FFBB55&BackColorLogged=FFAC75 (accessed November 2006)

Cuilenburg J. V. 'New Perspectives on Media Diversity. Toward a Critical-Rational Approach to Media Performance' eds. Zassoursky Y., E. Vartanova E. Changing Media and Communications. Moscow: Publisher ICAR (1998)

DG Infso (2005) URL: http://en.wikipedia.org/wiki/Directorate-General_for_Information_Society_and_Media (accessed April 2007)

EU GDP, International World Monetary Fund (2007) URL: http://www.imf.org/external/_pubs/ft/weo/2008/01/weodata/index.aspx (accessed April 2007)

European Commission. Council Directive 89/552/EEC of 3 October 1989 on the coordination of certain provisions laid down by law, regulation or administrative action in member states concerning the pursuit of television broadcasting activities. (1989) URL: http://ec. europa.eu/comm/avpolicy/reg/tvwf/index_en.htm (accessed April 2007)

European Commission. Europe and the Global Information Society, the Bangemann Report. (1994) URL: http://europa.eu.int/ISPO/infosoc/backg/bangeman.html (accessed April 2007)

European Commission. Green Paper on Convergence of the Telecommunications, Media and Information Technology Sector, and the Implication for Regulation towards an Information Society Approach. Com(97) p. 623 (1997a) URL: http://europa.eu.int/ISPO/_convergencegp/greenp.html (accessed April 2007)

European Commission. Directive 97/36/EC of the European Parliament and of the Council of 30 June 1997 amending Council Directive 89/552/EEC on the coordination of certain provisions laid down by law, regulation or administrative action in Member States concerning the pursuit of television broadcasting activities (1997b) URL: http://ec. europa.eu/comm/avpolicy/reg/tvwf/index_en.htm (accessed April 2007)

European Commission. Decision No 676/2002/EC of the European Parliament and of the Council on a regulatory framework for radio spectrum policy in the European Community (2002a) URL: http://www.anacom.pt/template20.jsp?categoryId=58697&contentId=93373 (accessed April 2007)

European Commission. Directive 2002/19/EC of the European Parliament and of the Council on access to, and interconnection of, electronic communications networks and associated facilities (Access Directive) (2002b) URL: http://

www.anacom.pt/template20.jsp?categoryId=58693&contentId=93319 (accessed April 2007)

European Commission. Directive 2002/20/EC of the European Parliament and of the Council on the authorisation of electronic communications networks and services (Authorisation Directive) (2002c) URL: http://www.anacom.pt/template20.jsp?categoryId=58694&contentId =93326 (accessed April 2008)

European Commission. Directive 2002/21/EC of the European Parliament and of the Council on a common regulatory framework for electronic communications networks and services (Framework Directive) (2002d) URL: http://www.anacom.pt/template20.jsp?categoryId= 58691&contentId=93270 (accessed April 2008)

European Commission. Commission Guidelines on market analysis and the assessment of significant market power under the Community regulatory framework for electronic communications networks and services (2002e) URL: http://www.anacom.pt/template_20.jsp?categoryId=58712&contentId= 93378 (accessed April 2008)

European Commission. Communication from the Commission to the Council, the European Parliament, the European economic and social committee and the Committee of the regions on the transition from analogue to digital broadcasting (2003) URL: http://ec.europa.eu/__information_society/topics/telecoms/regulatory/digital_broadcasting/documents/acte_en_vf.pdf (accessed April 2008)

European Commission. What is i2010? (2005a) URL: http://ec.europa.eu/information__society/eeurope/i2010/what_is_i2010/index_en.htm (accessed April 2007)

European Commission. Communication from the Commission to the Council, the European Parliament, the European economic and social committee and the Committee of the regions on accelerating the transition from analogue to digital broadcasting (2005b) URL: http://ec.europa.eu/information_society/policy/ecomm/doc/info_centre/communic_reports/switchover/com_2005_0204_f_en_acte.pdf (accessed April 2007)

European Commission. Communication from the Commission to the Council, the European Parliament, the European economic and social committee and the Committee of the regions: EU spectrum policy priorities for the digital switchover in the context of the upcoming ITU regional Radiocommunication conference 2006 (RRC-06) (2005c) URL: http://eur-lex.europa.eu/LexUriServ/LexUriServ.do?uri=COM:2005:0461:FIN:EN:DOC (accessed April 2008)

European Commission. The Commission's "Broadband for all" policy to foster growth and jobs in Europe (2006a) URL: http://europa.eu/rapid/

pressReleasesAction.do?_reference=_MEMO/06/132&format=HTML&aged=0&language=EN&guiLanguage=fr (accessed April 2007)

European Commission. Bridging the Broadband Gap. Communication from the Commission to the Council, the European Parliament, the European Economic and Social Committee and the Committee of the Regions. Sec (2006) 354 SEC (2006b) p. 355_URL: http://eurlex._europa.eu/Lex.Uri.Servsite/en/com/2006/com2006_0129en01.doc (accessed April 2007)

European Commission. Telecoms: consumers have more choice, but full potential of EU's internal market remains unexploited (2007a) URL: http://ec.europa.eu/information_society/newsroom/cf/itemlongdetail.cfm?item_id=3304 (accessed April 2007)

European Commission (2007b) URL: http://en.wikipedia.org/wiki/European_Commission (accessed April 2007)

European Commission. Directive 2007/65/EC of the European Parliament and of the Council Amending Council Directive 89/552/EEC on the coordination of certain provisions laid down by law, regulation or administrative action in Member States concerning the pursuit of television broadcasting activities (2007c) URL: http://eurlex.europa.eu/LexUriServ/Lex UriServ.do?uri=CONSLEG:1989L0552:20071219:EN:PDF (accessed April 2008)

European Commission. Communication from the Commission to the Council, the European Parliament, the European economic and social committee and the Committee of the regions: Reaping the full benefits of the digital dividend in Europe: a common approach to the use of the spectrum released by the digital switchover (2007d) URL: http://ec.europa.eu/ information_society/policy/radio_spectrum/docs/ref_docs/com/com_dd_en.pdf (accessed April 2008)

European Council. The Lisbon European Council – an agenda of economic and social renewal for Europe. Contribution of the European Commission to the special European Council in Lisbon (2000) URL: http://ec.europa.eu/growthandjobs/pdf/lisbon_en.pdf (accessed April 2007)

European Parliament. Charter of Fundamental Rights of the European Union (2000) URL: http://www.europarl.europa.eu/charter/pdf/text_en.pdf (accessed April 2007)

European Union. Treaty Establishing the European Community (1957) URL: http://europa.eu.int/eur-lex/en/treaties/dat/EC_consol.html (accessed April 2007)

European Union. The Single European Act (1986) URL: http://europa.eu/scadplus/treaties/ singleact_en.htm (accessed November 2006)

EUROSTAT Population and Social Conditions (2007) URL: http://epp.eurostat.ec.europa. eu/portal (accessed April 2007)

International Telecommunication Union. Digital broadcasting set to transform communication landscape by 2015 (2006) URL: http://www.itu.int/newsroom/press_releases/2006/11.html (accessed April 2008)

International Telecommunication Union. ITU World Radiocommunication Conference concludes after four weeks. International treaty sets future course for wireless (2007) URL: http://www.itu.int/newsroom/press_releases\2007\36.html (accessed April 2008)

Lorente S. 'The Global House' eds. Caby L., Vedel Th. Telecommunications. Changing Relationships in an Information Society. TIC Trends in Communication No 3. (1997) Amsterdam: Boom Publishers.

Naisbitt, J. Megatrends. New York, NY: Warner Books (1984)

Reding, V. Telecommunication markets in Europe: Growth and investment need competition (2007) URL: http://ec.europa.eu/information_society/policy/ecomm/tomorrow/index_en.htm (accessed April 2007)

Reding, V. Digital TV, Mobile TV: Let's push for open technologies in Europe and worldwide. DVB World 2008 (2008) URL: http://europa.eu/rapid/pressReleasesAction.do? reference=SPEECH/08/144&format=HTML&aged=0&language=EN&guiLanguage=en (accessed April 2008)

Raycheva L. 'Tracing the Digital Switchover in Enlarged Europe' eds. Urban A., Sapio B. and Turk T. Digital Television Revisited. Linking Users, Markets and Policies. COST Action 298 "Participation in the Broadband Society", Budapest (Hungary) (2008) pp. 155-166.

WTO General Agreement on Trade in Services (2000) URL: http://www.wto.org/English/ tratop_e/serve/audiovisual_e/audiovisual_e.htm#top (accessed April 2007)

Panayiota Tsatsou

Digital Divides in Greece: The Role of Culture and Regulation in Internet Adoption. Implications for the European Information Society

Introduction: objectives and agenda

"Prejudice and ignorance, resulting from the lack of knowledge and information often cause resistance to the introduction of new technologies. This, in turn, leads to limited penetration and exploitation of the technology while, in addition, *it obstructs participation in decision-making procedures* (…)." (emphasis added by author) (Partnership for Democratic Governance and Security 1999).

This statement points to the issues of social ignorance of and resistance to new technologies that bring societal, cultural and decision-making forces to the fore as being significant for the development of the Greek information society. By drawing on this statement, this chapter aims to explore the role of culture and regulation in digital divides in Greece This is not to say that the chapter uncritically adopts the argument that culture and regulation are the only forces driving digital divides in Greece. Rather, it approaches this claim critically by viewing culture and regulation as two possibilities and without overlooking more common-sense factors such as economics, technology and infrastructure.

The following OECD indicators are used to illustrate how digital divides are commonly measured: access lines and channels; mobile and Internet subscribers; broadband subscribers; availability of Digital Subscriber Lines ('DSL'); households with access to the Internet and to a home computer; Internet penetration by size class; Internet selling and purchasing by industry; telecommunication services revenue; telecommunication infrastructure investment; R&D expenditure; trade in ICT goods; contribution of ICT investment to GDP growth; top 50 telecommunications and IT firms[1].

It is evident from the above list that the Internet is considered the key technology in the information society and that emphasis is given to economic and market-oriented indicators of development. Yet what seem to be missing are indicators relating to the ways ordinary people negotiate the meaning, value and

---

1   A full list of the 15 ICT indicators measuring the information society according to OECD standards can be found at www.oecd.org/sti/ICTindicators.

use of Internet-based technologies, as well as the ways in which decision-making mechanisms respond accordingly.

Why is culture one of the two main axes of investigation in this chapter? Generally speaking, the chapter aims to view digital divides from a societal and cultural point of view as opposed to taking a technological and business-oriented approach. National cultures still have an important role to play in determining social integration and the course of global media technologies. People's technological experiences, expertise and integration of technology in their daily lives depend strongly on their daily activities and on the systemic conditions within which these activities take place. Moreover, culture in Greece has historically determined the course of the country's development generally and of its technological development in particular (see Section 4).

Why is regulation the second axis of investigation in this chapter? According to some scholars in the field, the advent of the information society has contributed to the deconstruction of the legacy of the welfare state under the imperatives of liberty and independence (Calabrese 1997, 20). In contrast with neo-liberal views that support deregulation, there continues to be literature arguing that the state has a significant role to play in technological innovation since it significantly influences the availability of resources, establishment of legal frameworks and development of investments (May 2002, 150). On the other hand, the necessity for state moderation has become problematic because the democratic potential of the information society is perceived as clearly serving market goals, competitiveness and trade (Mattelart 2003). Accordingly, the debate on regulation in the information society is considered critical for digital divides, whilst regulation in Greece has also historically been a determining factor of the country's development (see Section 4).

The ultimate aim of the chapter is to explore the possible dialogue between culture and regulation as explanatory variables for digital divides in relation to Internet adoption in Greece. Scant literature exists on the dialogue between the user and decision-makers in the information society. However, this chapter perceives digital divides as being influenced by both socio-cultural and decision-making elements in the field. In Section 2, the chapter presents the grounds on which the case of Greek divides was selected, while in Section 3 the literature in the field is discussed. Section 4 introduces a case-focused discussion of the possible ways in which Greek culture interacts with Internet regulation, influencing the adoption of the Internet in Greece and challenging the dominant discourses on digital divides.

Greek digital divides: a puzzling case and its research implications

Why explore the case of Greek digital divides?
Because the evidence suggests Greek digital divides are distinctive. On one hand, Greece is a long-standing EU member state with one of the highest national development rates across the EU. On the other, Greece has one of the lowest rates in the EU of penetration by the Internet and new technologies, undermining the goal of development and participation in the European broadband society.

More specifically, in the Flash Eurobarometer 250 survey (EC 2006) Greece was at the very bottom of the EU-25 Internet use list, with only 24% of the population using the Internet (ibid, 6). Even at the level of the EU-27, research (EC 2008a, 54) shows that the status of the Greek information society is the same as or even worse than that of new, less socio-economically developed EU member states, and lags behind all other longer standing member states. For instance, in terms of Internet access Greece (22%) is, together with Bulgaria, behind all other member states, while the EU-27 average is 49%. In terms of households in the EU-27 with a broadband connection (ibid, 56), Greece comes in last place, together with Bulgaria, with just 14% of households having a broadband connection, while even Romania (15%) is ahead of Greece and closer to the average level of broadband connections in the EU-27 (36%).

In addition, Greek culture and regulation are presented theoretically and empirically as critical forces in the country's history. From a cultural perspective, it is important to look at particular cultural characteristics when comparing Internet users with non-users in the Greek information society. Greece's general cultural features are greatly reflected in how the Greek information society operates and, more specifically, in ordinary people's decisions not to use the Internet. Indicative of this is that, with regard to the reasons a large majority of Greek people do not use the Internet a 2004, national survey by the National Statistical Service of Greece ('ESYE') concludes that non-appreciation of the Internet is the main force preventing use since 52.62% of non-users argued that the Internet is not useful and that no interesting materials can be found on the Internet (ESYE 2004).

From a regulatory perspective, the regulation of telecommunications in Greece has a long history of delays and inconsistencies. Greece is a country that appears to have problems complying with and implementing EU telecommunications regulations. Regarding implementation of the EU Electronic Communications Regulatory Package, the European Commission's 9th report of 2003 states there were major transposition divergences in most EU member states in key areas of concern from the new regulatory package (EC 2003, 3). Greece was one country that had transposed neither the EU regulatory package nor the e-Privacy Directive by the deadline of 31 October 2003 (ibid, 4). The report expresses concerns about delays and inconsistencies in implementation of the regulatory package in most member states, including Greece: 'The national measures (and drafts in the case of Member States that have not yet transposed)... give rise to some concerns that the Commission considers should be addressed if the objectives of the new framework are to be realized to the full' (ibid, 5). In January 2006 the European Commission sent a formal request to Greece asking for information regarding its compliance with the Court of Justice (CoJ) ruling of 14 April 2005 with respect to the country's failure to implement the liberalisation of electronic communications by the established deadline (ibid).

Hence, the question to be addressed is why the Greek information society diverges from the European information society and whether cultural or regulatory parameters account for this divergence.

The account of digital divides in the literature: why culture and regulation?

The following theoretical discussion develops an understanding of digital divides as a phenomenon embedded in a social context. By reflecting on this wider context and viewing digital divides as developing complex interdependencies with other kinds of exclusion, this chapter aims to justify the importance of identifying the ties between culture and regulation when exploring digital divides and especially in the Greek case.

The complexity and evolution of digital divides: the introduction of culture and regulation parameters

'Just as there are different maps of the physical world, so there are of the internet' (Wyatt et al. 2002, 38). In the same way, the race to the 'information superhighway' is not the same or being run at the same speed for everyone. A major concern regarding the impact of information and communication technologies ('ICTs') is what is conventionally referred to as a digital divide. A fairly general definition of the phenomenon is 'the divide created between those individuals, firms, institutions, regions, and societies that have the material and cultural conditions to operate in the digital world, and those who cannot, or will not adapt to the speed of change' (Castells 2001, 270).

A worldwide debate has taken place over the last two decades concerning the digital divide, its current extent and its variation across social groups[2]. Moreover,

---

2   I adopt the term in the plural, since: 'this is, in fact, a whole series of interlocking "divides" – the gaps that separate segments of society as well as whole nations into those

this debate is increasingly concerned with the impact of the phenomenon on asymmetry in the distribution and effective use of communication resources and power (Wilson 2000), as well as on various aspects of social exclusion. Its social importance as well as its evolving nature have attracted the interest of a growing number of researchers and scholars who point to the importance of the phenomenon, arguing that 'being disconnected, or superficially connected, to the Internet is tantamount to marginalization in the global, networked system' (Castells 2001, 269).

However, the dominant discourses on digital divides increasingly depart from a discussion of 'dystopian' and 'utopian' views of the information society, gradually replacing the term 'digital exclusion' with that of 'digital inclusion' and distinguishing various degrees and levels of inclusion. Nevertheless, most of these discourses have been tackling the various aspects of digital divides by relating them to other social forms of exclusion and largely adopting a monolithic perception of the ways in which digital divides relate to and exacerbate social disparities. In this sense, dominant discourses on digital divides fail to tackle the dialectic between culture, regulation and technology, as will be shown below.

Digital divides discourses: conceptualising 'digital inclusion' and qualitative measurements of exclusion

Theoretical attention was first given to the digital divide in the early to mid-1990s by scholars in the diffusion theory tradition (Rogers 1995). According to this tradition, the acquisition of and access to computers and Internet equipment is a fundamental criterion for overcoming the divides between haves and have-nots (Bradbrook & Fisher 2004; Selwyn 2003, 2004a, 2004b; Warschauer 2003), thus presenting a rather limited conceptualisation of the phenomenon.

Contributions in this tradition were followed by others arguing that broader access to ICTs does not eliminate division or exclusion from current digital opportunities. Since 2000, scholars such as Norris (2001) have presented a relatively more complex picture of digital divides, discarding the dichotomy between haves and have-nots and formulating more insightful approaches whereby weight has also been given to the quality and efficiency of use. The number of works considering how enhanced access might maintain or exacerbate existing divides has increased, while different degrees and qualitative aspects of divides have started to be examined, looking at factors mediating access and use of the Internet such as material, economic, social, cultural and technical factors (Livingstone 2002).

---

who are able to take advantage of the new ICT opportunities and those who are not' (OECD 2000, 3).

From this perspective, scholars such as Selwyn (2004a, 347) have argued that content and resource divides are significant and that access does not determine the existence of divides. Thus, qualitative parameters of a social, cultural and educational character are considered to influence the individual's capability to use the Internet, endowing the concept of access itself, as well as the issue of effective usage through requisite skills, knowledge and support, with greater nuance (van Dijk 1999). These writers have sought to illustrate the fact that the purchase of ICTs is not 'a one-off purchase' (Murdock 2002, 387) and to suggest a 'thicker description of the various shades of information and telecommunications inequalities' (Wilhelm 2000, 69-70).

As a result of these advances in theorisation of the phenomenon, 'digital inclusion' was proposed as an alternative concept to that of 'digital divides' with the intention of highlighting variations or 'gradations in digital inclusion' (Livingstone & Helsper 2007) and refocusing on the physical, digital, human and social forces influencing the social integration of ICTs (Warschauer 2003, 14). In a paper by Livingstone and Helsper (2007, 684), for instance, the concept of 'a continuum of quality of use' allows the identification of inequalities in use while scrutinising the efficiency and benefits of use, as well as the reasons behind non-use.

This graduated approach to digital inclusion constitutes a conceptual progression that has mostly been articulated in writings published after 2000. It constitutes progress as it identifies the variety of capital people have at their disposal and the ways in which capital influences the ability, willingness and effectiveness of people using ICTs. Thus, factors such as material resources and economic capacity, socialisation in the dominant culture, skills and awareness of the prevalent techno-culture, as well as social networks, are all seen as forces shaping our understanding of digital divides (Selwyn 2004a, 352-5).

However, this has only been progress on one front since ICTs equally have the potential to influence the distribution of social, cultural and economic capital. The literature still overlooks the complex interconnections between individuals and decision-makers in the distribution of various forms of capital, and lacks an insightful understanding of digital divides in different socio-cultural, policy and regulatory settings.

This chapter therefore attempts to take the above conceptual progress into consideration and to further extend it, paving the way for a challenging view of the role of society, culture and regulation in the shaping of divides. Besides, as Silverstone (1999, 21) remarks: "The theoretically unsubtle has its value (...). But it misses the nuances of agency and meaning of the human exercise of power and of our resistance. It misses, too, other sources of change: factors that affect the creation of technologies themselves and factors that mediate our responses to them:

society, economy, politics, culture. Technologies, it must be said, are enabling (and disabling) rather than determining."

Digital inclusion in the context of social divides: linearity vs. complexity

The notion of digital inclusion described above indicates the importance of systemic factors in the evolution of divides and provides a link to other forms of social inclusion on the basis of how advantage is taken of ICTs in terms of quality, breadth, duration and efficiency of use (Selwyn 2004a; Livingstone 2002, 10).

Scholars such as Norris have pointed out that the Internet is 'even more important if certain groups and areas are systematically excluded' (2001, 10), stressing that digital divides affect, for example, financial, educational and social divides. This argument illustrates how the relationship between digital and social inclusion/exclusion is commonly perceived in quite a linear way (Cammaerts and Audenhove 2003), overlooking the interdependencies between socio-cultural and political capital and the ways in which people use ICTs.

On one hand, assessing the importance of equal opportunities to access ICTs involves a consideration of possibly harmful effects, on both excluded individuals and social life, of non-participation in the information society. From this perspective, the literature argues that individuals who find themselves digitally excluded become socially, culturally and economically disadvantaged. They are socially marginalised because people without access to communication technologies arguably lack access to a number of mediated communication activities and to alternative means of socialisation and participation in public debates and policy-making processes. In addition, they are culturally excluded because the bulk of information is globally diffused via ICTs in such a way that people deprived of access to informational resources are also deprived of the underlying human right to equal access to information and cultural resources. Finally, the 'have-nots' lag behind economically since they have limited access to information regarding labour markets (Katz & Rice 2002, 19).

On the other hand, as Loader (1998, 3) remarks in his early critique, those who support the view that '...in the long run, it [information and communication technology; the author] will change fundamentally the characteristics of cultures that have evolved over centuries' (Moore 1998, 149) perceive the relationship between ICTs and society in a linear way, with ICTs fundamentally transforming societies and influencing social divisions, diversity and difference. From this perspective, a growing bulk of the literature refers to digital divides as being closely related to social exclusion and economic deprivation, and ICTs are often perceived as deterministically influencing social marginalisation (Loader & Keeble 2004, 37).

There are also somewhat dystopian approaches which predict that new technologies will not have the potential to substantially influence economic deprivation and social disparities because 'the world has always been a place of haves and have-nots and I can see no way that internetworking is going to change this very much' (Haywood 1998, 25).

Further, little attention has been paid to the role of human resistance and mediation in development of the information society. The literature considers culture not as a primary factor but as one of many factors influencing the participation of citizens in the information society[3]. Questions of a shortage of cultural capital could, however, bring issues of social perceptions of and attitudes to ICTs to the fore, issues which are also associated with notions of social participation and citizenship. A characteristic example of the dominant trend in empirical research is Dekkers' study (2003) which concludes that poverty is the most significant factor and where the argument is made that there is a correlation between pre-existing poverty and the low diffusion of ICTs.

Therefore, as Loader and Keeble suggest, a more 'grassroots perspective' is needed on the basis that 'whilst excluded communities and individuals are unable or reluctant to use the technology, their identities and cultures remain invisible' (2004, 35). Digital inclusion should not be seen as a solution to the multi-dimensional problem of social exclusion; it should instead be approached as being in some instances a facilitator and in others a result of policies aimed at combating other structural aspects of social exclusion (Cammaerts, Audenhove & Pauwels 2003, 304). From this perspective, questions are raised about how society and politics can manage technology and the challenges it entails (Slevin 2000, 214). At the core of the problematic lies the 'social embeddedness of technology' (Warschauer 2003, 199), bringing forward the concept of 'perverse integration' (Castells 1998, 74-5) and contrasting with purely technocratic understandings of the information society. The engagement of users with technology entails broader cultural and political consequences (Mansell & Silverstone 1996, 224) and a relatively reciprocal and highly interdependent relationship between technology, society, culture and politics developed over time.

Thus the research literature must call for an examination of digital divides on the basis of the 'cultural ecology' (Loader 1998, 13) of the information society and its interaction with regulation, underlining in particular regulatory schemes which take account of 'cultural ecology'. This complex and interdependent relationship will be discussed in the following section with regard to the case of Greek digital divides.

---

3   See, for example, Frissen's approach, 2003, 20.

The puzzle of Greek digital divides: the role of society, culture and regulation. A historical and pragmatic view

As briefly presented in Section 2, a large majority of people in Greece are still offline, whereas the minority using the Internet chiefly use narrowband. Meanwhile, Greece is one of the countries attempting to make a successful transition to the new liberalised information society and which is simultaneously marked by well-established cultural and long-standing regulatory frameworks.

Society and culture: impeding the Greek information society?

The historical legacies in Greece have categorised the country as belonging to the 'semi-periphery' (Mouzelis 1986). In this context, Greek civil society has historically been marked by an individualistic spirit (Sotiropoulos 1996) and the dominance of clientelism (Mouzelis 1995), characteristics that have been impediments to the evolution of the Greek information society. Likewise, Greece has historically been characterised by a lack of active social networks (Petmesidou 1996), discouraging awareness-raising in Greek society. This has, in turn, entailed significant difficulties for promotion of the information society as the latter relates to the public sector, various social institutions and the population in general.

In addition, social heterogeneity, clientelism and individualism have historically marked Greek society, creating an atmosphere of short-termism that neglects the importance of social inclusion and social transformation through new technological devices such as ICTs. Hence, what has gradually been created is an identity of resistance and techno-phobia that is dominant in both society and the public administration, as shown below.

Culture beyond society: a need for institutional and cultural change?

The picture of an anti-developmental and techno-phobic society has also historically characterised the public administration in Greece, restricting innovation to so-called 'hardware' equipment, while there generally appears to be underinvestment in and underestimation of cultural and social 'capital'. In addition, complex administrative procedures accompanied by a lack of incentive for civil servants have been notable aspects of the top-down character of the Operational Programme Information Society ('OPIS')[4] launched in 2000. The OPIS has failed to touch upon issues of identities of resistance, social ignorance or lack of awareness, instead resulting in the empowerment of individualist identities by a short-sighted public administration.

The initial 1999 White Paper (Greek Ministry of the Economy and Finance 1999) emphasised the socio-political dimension of the information society, reflecting on the particularities of the Greek case, such as a culture of short-term activities. Persistent techno-phobia, a weak IT market, inadequate public administration initiatives and governmental ineffectiveness (Constantelou 2001) contribute to a gloomy picture of the information society in Greece. More drastic state and regulatory action is essential in order to reform the relationship between the state and the economy and the way in which civil society organisations are positioned in decision-making.

Indicatively, a report published by the OECD on regulatory reform in Greece demonstrates the inherent difficulties faced by the country's information society, making more pressing the need for more efficient regulatory reforms through more drastic political leadership: 'although most Greeks will benefit from regulatory reform, the resistance of many protected groups to needed change is hard to overcome' (OECD 2001, 2). The OECD recommends a reform of the Greek civil service in order to permit the establishment of an efficient and transparent regulatory system. It pays particular attention to the existing administrative barriers (ibid, 2-3) and to the tight state control of the economy and of independent regulators which obstructs regulatory reform and the creation of a competitive telecommunications market in Greece (OECD 2002, 57). The OECD therefore highlights the need for 'structural change' (ibid), underlining the criticism found in other literature in Greece that the introduction of ICTs has been driven by the private sector while the public sector is lagging behind (Voulgaris & Sotiropoulos 2002).

In summary, culture in Greece was born in society but goes through the state so appropriate political leadership is required in order for the country's information society to develop.

The Greek information society: past legacies & future prospects. Questioning the EU information society?

In pragmatic terms, the following discussion of the Greek information society illustrates how Greece is positioned within the EU information society and the features that make Greece an interesting case for study.

---

4   More information is available at www.infosoc.gr.

The Greek information society: diverging from the EU information society

Broadly speaking, Greece is lagging behind the EU information society and yet simultaneously it has periodically shown impressively rapid rates of ICT development, thereby presenting quite a puzzling case.

Public telecommunications investment in 1997, when the information society began to develop, was 3.7% in Greece and 5.4% in the EU (Greek 'Information Society' Initiative 1999, 2). However, investment in the Greek information society rose by 27% more than the annual global increase in gross national product in the same period (ibid). The annual growth rate of ICT expenditure between 1992 and 1999 in Greece was very strong and only slightly below the EU average (DDSI 2001, 1). Moreover, in Greece the ICT market was growing rapidly in the early 2000s (EITO 2001, 465), although Greece still had the lowest percentage of network digitisation in the EU (Greek 'Information Society' Initiative 1999, 1).

More recently, EUROSTAT data show that, although ICT expenditure remained the same (2.7% of GDP) in the EU-27 between 2004-2006, Greece was lagging behind with related spending worth 1.2% of GDP in 2006, representing a small decrease from 1.3% in 2004. Strikingly, this percentage share of expenditure on ICT is the lowest across the EU-27. In terms of Internet usage, the Eurobarometer 2005 survey concluded that Greece came last in Internet usage with just 24% of the population using the Internet, although there was an increasing rate of access to the Internet from 15% in 2003/2004 to 24% in 2005 (EC 2006, 14). On the other hand, the same survey showed that mobile telephony in Greece was more common, even among children, than the Internet, with 30% of children owning a mobile phone and 26% using the Internet in 2005, whereas the EU-25 average was 36% and 50%, respectively (ibid, 19). With regard to the share of individuals regularly using the Internet, in 2006 45% of individuals in the EU-27 accessed the Internet at least once a week, whereas the respective percentage in Greece was only 23%, just above Bulgaria (22%) and Romania (18%)[5]. Finally, the latest Eurobarometer 2008 survey (EC 2008b, 9) concludes that Greece is the member state with the lowest Internet use rate since in 2008 84% of Europeans were Internet users, while in Greece the respective percentage was 54%.

The history of the Greek information society: catching up but further ICT diffusion is needed

In attempting to sketch an overall picture of the Greek information society we may conclude that important progress was made in the first few years of this decade,

---

5   For more statistics, see EUROSTAT, at http://epp.eurostat.ec.europa.eu/portal/.

whereas stagnation has appeared in the last three to four years, with Greece now being rated lowest of all in the European Information Society.

On one hand, the 2005 Greek Research and Technology Network survey (GRNet 2005)[6] pointed out the improved picture of ICT diffusion in Greece in the first few years of this decade and this was also reflected in the 2005 Eurobarometer survey which argued that there was a relative shrinking of the digital gap between Greece and the EU (EU 2006, 19). The GRNET survey (2005) illustrates the increasing penetration of ICTs in Greece for the 2001-2003 period and a stagnation in the adoption of new technologies for the 2004-2005 period.

Significantly, in 2005 a five-layered indicator of new technology use rose by only 0.3% (to 13.6%), whereas the percentage of the population not using new technologies decreased by 2.7% (ibid: 125). Moreover, Internet use had increased in 2005 (24.6%) by a mere 0.1% compared to 2004 (24.5%) while remaining lower than in 2003 (25.2%). This tends to show a lack of progress in Internet penetration in Greek society in the last three to four years. On the other hand, in 2005 just 0.7% of Greek households were connected to the Internet via ISDN, 10.8% via ADSL, and 1.4% of those households declared that they were connected to the Internet with the fastest connection, whereas 55.4% of Greek households stated that they did not know or refused to answer the question (ibid, 95). Likewise, computer usage in the 2002-2003 period went up by 1.7%, reaching 34.2% of the overall population in 2003, whereas the decrease of 2% in 2004 and a 2.1% increase in 2005 did not manage to substantially change the overall picture, with only 34.3% of the overall population in Greece using computers (ibid, 5).

According to these figures, as well as those above that position Greece in the European framework, a large majority of Greek citizens are still not users of computers or the Internet.

The Greek information society: digital divides shaped by 'cultural divides?

Beyond the low percentages of Internet use in Greece, it is important to look at particular cultural characteristics when comparing Internet users with non-users so that an explanatory approach is taken to the phenomenon of the low level of Internet adoption in Greece.

The GRNet survey attempted to explore why the majority of citizens in Greece reject ICTs in general and the Internet in particular. The data collected in 2005 indicate that 'I don't need it' remains the most important reason, although the share giving this response dropped slightly in 2004 (29.3%) in comparison to 2003

---

6 In this survey 2,741 face-to-face interviews were conducted from 21 October to 23 November 2005.

(30.7%). On the other hand, a very small increase in lack of interest, from 15.6% in 2003 to 15.8% to 2004, is observed, whereas 'lack of access' was becoming an even less important reason for non-use. With respect to 'cost', the respondents who do not use the Internet seemed to be quite concerned about issues of cost as in 2004 10.3% gave this response, whilst the respective figure in 2003 was just 4.2% (ibid, 77).

A more recent survey (Tsatsou 2009; forthcoming) conducted in 2007 confirms the above observations and concludes that lack of access is not a sufficient explanation of the low Internet adoption rates in Greece (15.1% of Internet non-users reside in connected households). The survey found that 63.4% of Greek[7] non-users of the Internet do not need the Internet and 43.2% are not interested in it, while it argued that the lack of integration of the Internet in people's everyday lives indicates the existence of a 'dismissive culture' in Greece, with non-users being non-interested in and having no need to use the Internet. Along these lines, even a significant number of users were found to be digitally constrained, insufficiently literate and relatively reserved about the Internet and its impact on life (ibid).

Besides, and as the following official statement indicates, Greek citizens suffer from a lack of familiarity with new technologies, emphasising the existence of 'cultural' rather than purely 'digital' divides in the country: "In our country today there is a tendency to distinguish the few (but rapidly increasing in number) users of computers and communication networks such as the internet from the *many who treat the new technologies at best as a mystery and at worst as a danger for their future*" (emphasis added by author) (Greek Ministry of Economy and Finance 2002, 12).

Internet regulation in Greece: new challenges rising to fore

As far as Internet regulation is concerned, the Greek government started to liberalise and privatise the telecommunications market in the early 1990s and in so doing it struggled between two equally important goals: the protection of fundamental rights, such as the right of access and the right to privacy, and the need to develop a legal and regulatory framework that encourages ICT growth (Greek Ministry of Economy and Finance 1999).

The Greek regulator has faced new challenges while the long-lasting shortcomings of the Greek regulatory framework for the information society are increasingly visible: 'first, it is oriented towards regulating "static" situations; sec-

---

7   The scope of the survey is regional as it covered the urban periphery of Attica and the sample was drawn from about half of the Greek population. However, the data were weighted so as to be representative of the whole study population.

ondly, it is primarily concerned with the "material", the "tangible" world, while more and more activities involve "intangible" goods and services' (Greek Ministry of Economy and Finance 2002, 76). These shortcomings hinder the regulator's capacity in the information society (ibid), and the 2002 White Paper acknowledges the need for 'new rules for the protection of data, the protection of privacy, the commercialization of material protected under intellectual property rights, etc' (ibid), as well as the need for 'citizens participation' (ibid, 83).

In addition, although Greek regulation covers a range of policy and regulation areas for the information society, it does so in an incomplete, partial and socially unaccountable way. For instance, in 2001 official terminology in Greece had reportedly not accepted the term 'cyber-crime', and there was no specific and effective regulation for preventing online fraud (DDSI 2001). Elite actors in the Greek information society acknowledge the lack of social accountability of regulation and generally point out the bureaucratic, inefficient, non-modernised and non-technocratic decision-making in the country (Tsatsou 2008, 150-152). Such arguments raise not only the incomplete and static character of regulation in the Greek information society but also the extent to which regulation is influenced by the culture in society, bringing the discussion back to Section 4.2.

Greece diverging from EU Internet law: following the canon or drawing a line of distinctiveness?

The results delivered by regulation in the Greek information society can provide some evidence of the above weaknesses and characteristics. The Greek information society lags behind the European information society not only in terms of new technology penetration but also in terms of regulation in the field. According to the 10th EC report on implementation of the EU Electronic Communications Regulatory Package (EC 2004a), despite the generally positive picture of notifications and legal measures taken in member states, five countries (Belgium, the Czech Republic, Estonia, Greece and Luxemburg) had not transposed the framework one year after the deadline. As a consequence, the Commission launched infringement proceedings for non-notification and proceedings before the European Court of Justice against Belgium, Greece and Luxemburg (ibid, 9). Moreover, EC research (EC 2006; EC 2004b) sheds light on awareness levels and secure Internet use across the EU, reporting that Greek citizens have the lowest level of awareness among all EU users whilst being highly reserved and insecure when going online (ibid).

The delayed and incomplete adoption of the EU regulation in Greece emphasises the issue of divergence across the EU and the question of whether the principles of mediation and subsidiarity can be of use for bridging the gap between EU and national regulatory authorities and monitoring the implementation of Union laws. Nevertheless, Greece remains a distinctive case as it is a country where regulatory insufficiency has been particularly acute; something which, in combination with the abovementioned cultural and broader political characteristics of the Greek information society, raises questions about the role of regulation in fulfilling user and market expectations in the information society and the possible cultural drivers of the insufficient performance of regulation in Greece. These questions must, however, be empirically pursued.

Conclusion

This chapter discusses the phenomenon of the digital divide in Greece and argues that this phenomenon can be seen as the result of cultural and regulatory forces.

Theories and concepts regarding the need for digital inclusion lead to a socio-cultural account of the way in which the Internet is regulated so that a functional link between society, culture and regulation is achieved. Data and evidence concerning the puzzle of the Greek digital divides allow this chapter to apply a socio-cultural and regulatory account to a case study of particular interest that entails significant implications for the future of the EU broadband society as well as for participation in the broadband society overall. Greece is a long-standing EU member state and the failures and delays occurring in the country's information society challenge the vision and rhetoric of a European information society for all.

Nevertheless, due to space limitations this chapter does not report original findings obtained from primary empirical research in Greece. Such primary empirical research has been conducted, consisting in the first phase of interviews with elite actors, in the second phase of a large-scale survey of Internet users and non-users, and in the third phase of follow-up focus group interviews with a sub-sample of surveyed users and non-users. In the empirical part of the study a two-sided examination of the weight carried by culture and decision-making as explanatory parameters of digital divides in Greece is thus pursued. Finally, possible challenges and implications for the future of the European information society conclude the study.

This chapter may therefore be regarded as only an introductory discussion of the issue, paving the way for further and more original work.

Bibliography

Bradbrook G., Fisher J. Digital Equality: Reviewing digital inclusion activity and mapping the way forwards. Citizens Online (2004) URL: http://www.citizensonline.org.uk/site/media/documents/939_DigitalEquality1.pdf (accessed November 2005)

Calabrese A. 'Creative destruction? From the welfare state to the global information society' Javnost/The Public 4(4) (1997) pp. 7-24

Cammaerts B., Audenhove van L. 'Dominant Digital Divide Discourses' eds. Cammaerts B., van Audenhove L., Nulens G., Pauwels C. Beyond the digital divide. Reducing Exclusion, Fostering Inclusion Brussels: VUB Brussels University Press (2003) pp. 7-14

Cammaerts B., Audenhove van L., Pauwels C. 'Beyond the Digital Divide' eds. Cammaerts B., van Audenhove L., Nulens G., Pauwels C. Beyond the digital divide. Reducing Exclusion, Fostering Inclusion Brussels: VUB Brussels University Press (2003) pp. 301-306

Castells M. The Information Age: Economy, Society and Culture Oxford: Blackwell (1998)

Castells M. The Internet Galaxy: Reflections on the Internet, Business, and Society Oxford: OUP (2001)

Constantelou N. In Search of a Vision: Information Society Policies in Peripheral and Middle-Income Countries. STAR Issue Report No. 18 (2001) URL: http://www.databank.it/ star/list_issue/issue.html last (accessed September 2008)

DDSI (IST–2000-29202) European Dependability Policy Environments-Greece. Project funded by the European Community under the "Information Society Technology" Programme (1998-2002) (2001)

Dekkers G.J.M. 'Poverty, Dualisation and the Digital Divide' eds. Cammaerts B., van Audenhove L., Nulens G., Pauwels C. Beyond the digital divide. Reducing Exclusion, Fostering Inclusion. Brussels: VUB Brussels University Press (2003) pp. 35-76

ESYE. Statistics, Athens: ESYE. (2004) URL: http://www.statistics.gr/gr_tables/0800_SFA_3_TB_AN_2004_7_Y.htm (accessed January 2005) (original in Greek)

European Commission. Report on the Implementation of the EU Electronic Communications Regulatory Package. COM (2003) 715 final. Brussels: European Commission, 19.11.2003, (2003)

European Commission Communication from the Commission to the Council, the European Parliament, the European Economic and Social Committee and the Committee of the Regions. European Electronic Communications Regulation and Markets 2004. COM (2004) 759 final. Brussels: European Commission, 2.12.2004, (2004a)

European Commission Illegal and harmful content on the Internet. EB 203/Wave 60.2 survey (November-December 2003). Luxemburg: European Commission (2004b) URL: http://europa.eu.int/information_society/programmes/iap/docs/pdf/reports/eurobarometer_survey.pdf (accessed November 2004)

European Commission Flash Eurobarometer 250: Safer Internet. (December 2005 – January 2006). Publication: May 2006, (2006). Luxemburg: European Commission. URL: http://europa.eu.int/information_society/activities/sip/docs/eurobarometer/eurobarometer_2005_25_ms.pdf (accessed October 2006)

European Commission E-Communications Household Survey. Special Eurobarometer 293/Wave 68.2. Publication: June 2008. Luxembourg: European Commission (2008a) URL: http://ec.europa.eu/public_opinion/archives/ebs/ebs_293_full_en.pdf (accessed January 2008)

European Commission Towards a safer use of the Internet for children in the EU: Analytical report – a parents' perspective. Flash Eurobarometer No 248. Publication: December 2008 Luxembourg: European Commission (2008b) URL: http://ec.europa.eu/information_society/activities/sip/surveys/quantitative/index_en.htm (accessed January 2008)

EUROSTAT Statistics URL: http://epp.eurostat.ec.europa.eu/portal/ (accessed November 2006)

Frissen V. 'The Myth of the Digital Divide' eds. Cammaerts B., van Audenhove L., Nulens G., Pauwels C. Beyond the digital divide. Reducing Exclusion, Fostering Inclusion. Brussels: VUB Brussels University Press (2003) pp. 17-33

Greek 'Information Society' Initiative. Greece in the Information Society. Plan of Regional Development 2000-2006 (1999) URL: http://www.infosoc.gr/content/downloads/spaktp.pdf (accessed December 2004) (original in Greek)

Greek Ministry of Economy and Finance White Paper: Greece in the Information Society, Strategy and Actions (2002) URL: from ftp://ftp.cordis.lu/pub/greece/docs/ wpgreeceinfosoc_mnec_2002_en.pdf (accessed November 2004)

Greek Ministry of Economy and Finance White Paper: Greece in the Information Society, Strategy and Actions Athens, (1999)

GRNet National Survey on New Technologies and the Information Society. Athens (2005) URL: http://www.observatory.gr/page/default.asp?la=1&id183&pl=110&pk=250&ap=101 (accessed December 2006) (original in Greek)

Haywood T. 'Global networks and the myth of equality: trickle down or trickle away?' ed. Loader B.D. Cyberspace Divide: Equality, Agency and Policy in the Information Society London, NY: Routledge (1998) pp. 19-34

Katz J., Rice R. Social Consequence of Internet Use: Access, Involvement and Interaction. Boston: MIT Press (2002)
Livingstone S. Young People and New Media. London: Sage, (2002)
Livingstone S., Helsper H. 'Gradations in digital inclusion: Children, young people and the digital divide' New Media & Society 9(4) (2007) pp. 671-696
Loader B.D., Keeble L. Challenging the digital divide?: a literature review of community informatics initiatives York: Joseph Rowntree Foundation (2004)
Loader B.D. 'Cyberspace divide: equality, agency and policy in the information society' ed. Loader B.D. Cyberspace Divide: Equality, Agency and Policy in the Information Society London, NY: Routledge (1998) pp. 3-16
Mansell R., Silverstone R. eds. Communication by design: the politics of information and communication technologies Oxford: Oxford University Press (1996)
Mattelart A. The Information Society: An Introduction London: Sage Publications (2003)
May C. The Information Society: A Sceptical View Cambridge: Polity Press (2002)
Moore N. 'Confucius or capitalism? Policies for an information society.' ed. Loader B.D. Cyberspace Divide: Equality, Agency and Policy in the Information Society London, NY: Routledge (1998) pp. 149-160
Mouzelis N. 'Modernity, late development and civil society' ed. Hall J. Civil Society: Theory, History, Comparison Cambridge: Polity (1995) pp. 224-249
Mouzelis, N. Politics in the Semi-Periphery: Early Parliamentarism and Late Industrialisation in the Balkans and Latin America London: Macmillan (1986)
Murdock G. 'Review Article: Debating digital divides' European Journal of Communication 17(3) (2002) pp. 385-390
Norris P. Digital Divide: Civic Engagement, Information Poverty, and the Internet Worldwide Cambridge: Cambridge University Press (2001)
OECD Regulatory Reform in the Telecommunications Industry in Greece Paris: OECD (2002)
OECD Greece Set to Reap Maximum Benefits from Regulatory Reform Paris: OECD (2001)
OECD Learning to bridge the digital divide Paris: OECD (2000)
Petmesidou M. 'Social protection in Greece: a brief glimpse of a welfare state' Social Policy and Administration 30 (1996) pp. 324-347
Partnership for Democratic Governance and Security (PDGS) Greece in the Information Society – 9. Regional development in the Information Society (1999) URL: http://www.pdgs.org.ar/Archivo/gr-cap9.htm (accessed November 2006)

Rogers E. M. Diffusion of Innovations vol. 4 New York: Free Press (1995)
Selwyn N. 'Reconsidering political and popular understandings of the digital divide' New Media and Society 6(3) (2004a) pp. 341-362
Selwyn N. 'Technology and social inclusion' British Journal of Educational Technology 35(1) (2004b) pp.127-127
Selwyn N. 'Apart from technology: Understanding people's non-use of information and communication technologies in everyday life' Technology in Society 25(1) (2003) pp. 99-116
Silverstone R. Beneath the bottom line: households and information and communication technologies in an age of the consumer PICT (Programme on Information and Communication Technologies) policy research papers no.17 ESRC (1999)
Slevin J. The Internet and Society Cambridge: Polity Press (2000)
Sotiropoulos D. 'Civil society and the Greek state in the Third Hellenic Republic' in eds. Lyrintzis C., Nikolakopoulos E., Sotiropoulos D. Society and Politics Athens: Themelio, (1996) pp. 118-138 (original in Greek)
Tsatsou, P. Digital Divides in Greece: role of culture & decision-making from a top-down and bottom-up perspective. Implications for the European Information Society. PhD Thesis. London: London School of Economics and Political Science (2009, forthcoming)
Tsatsou, P. 'Digital divides and the role of policy and regulation: a qualitative study' in eds. Avgerou C., Smith M.L., Besselaar P.v.d. Social Dimensions of Information and Communication Technology Policy London: Springer Publishers, (2008) pp. 141-160
Van Dijk J. The Network Society: Social Aspects of New Media London: Sage (1999)
Voulgaris Y., Sotiropoulos D. Information Society, Sociology and Technology Athens: Operational Programme for the Information Society (2002) (original in Greek)
Warschauer M. Technology and Social Inclusion: Rethinking the Digital Divide Cambridge, MA: MIT Press (2003)
Wilhelm A. Democracy in the Digital Age: Challenges to Political Life in Cyberspace. New York and London: Routledge (2000)
Wilson III, E. Closing the digital divide: an initial review Internet policy Institute (2000) URL: http://www.Internetpolicy.org/briefing/ErnestWilson0700.html (accessed February 2004)
Wyatt S., Thomas G., Terranova T. 'They Came, they Surfed, they Went Back to the Beach: Conceptualizing Use and Non-Use of the Internet' ed. Woolgar S. Virtual Society? Technology, cyberbole, reality Oxford: Oxford University Press (2002) pp. 23-40

Vesna Dolničar

Regulating on an Informed Basis: An Integrative Methodological Framework for Monitoring the Digital Divide

Introduction

One characteristic of the diffusion of new information and communication technologies ('ICTs') in developed countries is the high degree of growth involved. Therefore, measuring the dynamics of the digital divide represents one of the greater challenges in information society research. The main objective of the chapter is to demonstrate that an investigation of the digital divide in the temporal perspective requires a wider and more holistic approach; if this requirement is not met, the results could prove to be biased and misleading which could in turn have a strong influence on the policy-making processes. The key concern here is to establish whether the digital divide is expanding, shrinking or stagnating and – based on this – to set (and monitor the implementation of) the policy targets. Within this context, another aim of the chapter is to provide a transparent way of considering different options for regulation and to improve the policy-making process through the development and implementation of an integral methodological approach.

The digital divide concept is encountered in various contexts and is widely discussed in scientific and research studies. Not surprisingly, these are characterised by inconsistencies in the use of the concept and they lack a uniform definition[1]. For the purposes of this chapter, measuring the dynamics of the digital divide is limited to cases of the basic, i.e. the first, digital divide, which is operationalised by differences between individuals in terms of the possibility of Internet access within the domestic environment. The definition of the OECD (2001) was used according to which the digital divide refers to 'differences between individuals, households, companies and regions related to the access and usage of ICTs.' The substantial questions of why, how and with what benefits and consequences individuals are using ICTs should also be addressed more profoundly in future research. However, this chapter aims to provide a competent answer to the question of whether the basic digital divide has been shrinking or expanding over time. This limit is imposed for practical reasons. Likewise, the methodological framework applied is

---

1 For a discussion of the conceptual complexity and ambiguity of the digital divide concept see, for example, Vehovar et al. (2006) where it is demonstrated that the notion of the binary divide is problematic and the multiplicity of the divides was structured within a typology – as well as Haddon (2004).

used to only study one socio-demographic factor (i.e. age). However, the proposed framework for the digital divide study also enables a potential extension to analyses of other types of the digital divide (where motivation, willingness and skills for using new ICTs are studied; for a further discussion see e.g. Dolničar et al. 2002; Vehovar et al. 2006) and other factors, ICTs, units and levels of study.

Measuring the dynamics of the digital divide is one of the most important challenges of information society studies. An overarching question in this respect concerns the dynamics of the diffusion of new ICTs in the future. Some researchers propose that the digital divide will close automatically while succumbing to public policies and the logic of the market. Others, on the other hand, caution against the stagnation and even expansion of the digital divide and point to the existing deeply rooted patterns of social stratification and consequent reproduction and increase of social inequalities. The key question this chapter deals with is measuring the dynamics of ICT adoption; measuring and interpreting the expanding or shrinking digital divide is relatively complex. The chapter therefore focuses particularly on the methodological aspects of the dynamics of the digital divide and on providing a tool for identifying and monitoring the priority issues over time.

Empirical analyses often focus on basic comparisons based, for instance, on absolute or relative differences in percentages of Internet use. They thus offer no substantial insight into the problematic. Therefore, the chapter's main aim is to show that the study of the digital divide in a time perspective requires a broader methodological approach in order to avoid biased or even misleading results. Hence a holistic and multifaceted (not a one-dimensional) answer to the question of whether the digital divide (according to age) is expanding, shrinking or stagnating (based on a secondary analysis of time-series data acquired from the Slovenian Public Opinion Survey) will be provided.

How to establish whether the digital divide is expanding, shrinking or stagnating?

The key question when measuring the dynamics of the digital divide is how to establish whether the digital divide is expanding, shrinking or stagnating. Namely, while calculating the differences between various population segments different statistical measures can give partial and often contradictory views about the size of the digital divide (for illustrative examples see e.g. Vehovar et al. 2006; Sicherl 2007). This often leads to a situation which only allows a partial answer to the key question. In designing a holistic methodological framework for monitoring the digital divide in the time perspective, the chapter's central premise is that (since various statistical measures of the basic digital divide may lead to qualitatively entirely adverse conclusions regarding the estimation of whether the digital divide is growing, shrinking or stagnating) any study of the dynamics of the digital divide based solely on statistical measures is inadequate. Namely, a partial insight into digital divide trends could culminate in suboptimal policy decisions about what actions to take or how to set a certain policy target.

For the purposes of this chapter (and for policy development purposes), the differences will be monitored on the basis of conventional statistical measures of the digital divide (absolute and relative differences) as well as on the basis of temporal distance, i.e. S-time-distance. S-time- distance expresses the time within which the lagging group will achieve the level (e.g. a certain percentage of Internet penetration) that group A is at today. Thus, time-distance generally means the difference in time when two events occurred. The statistical measure S-time-distance measures the distance (proximity) in time between points in time when two series compared reach a specified level of indicator X. The observed distance in time (the number of years, quarters, months etc.) for given levels of the indicator is used as a temporal measure of the disparity between the two series in the same way that the observed difference (absolute or relative) at a given point in time is used as a static measure of disparity. Thus, in addition to a static comparison there exists in principle a theoretically equally universal measure of difference (distance) in time when a given level of the variable is attained by the two compared time series. The new view of information, using levels of the variable(s) as identifiers and time as the focus of comparison and numeraire, is intuitively understandable and can be usefully applied as an important analytical and presentation tool at various levels to a wide variety of substantive fields. As mentioned by Sicherl (2007, 237), S-time-distance enables clear interpretability that 'delivers a broader concept to look at data, to understand and compare situations. This methodology can provide a new insight to many problems, an additional statistical measure, and a presentation tool for policy analysis and debate expressed in time units, readily understood by policy makers, media and general public'. For a more detailed presentation (at conceptual and applied levels) and an in-depth discussion of the time-distance methodology (as developed by Sicherl P.) consult, for example, Sicherl, 2003, 2004, 2005, 2007.

Due to the complex nature of the relationships between the values of these measures, it is advisable that they be presented synchronically, particularly if they necessitate different views of the studied problem. In so doing, the danger of a biased estimation of differences between the studied variables can be avoided. On the other hand, this approach offers protection against potential objections that claim various groups are giving misleading estimates about the size of differences in the adoption of ICT.

Although reporting the three statistical measures is extremely informative, the question about the size of differences remains open; particularly when statistical measures show different results in the direction of a change in the dynamics of the digital divide. Studying the digital divide in relation to all three measures may be more informative and holistic, yet precisely because each of these measures may lead to different conclusions an almost complete relativisation of the problem may be encountered; the seemingly simple question about whether the digital divide is growing or shrinking in most cases (and in most temporal periods in the adoption of ICT) cannot be answered unequivocally.

In the following sections, the values of statistical measures will be monitored in the context of the ICT adoption process where distribution functions, describing the adoption of ICT between particular groups, will be monitored simultaneously. The proposed solution and main argument of this chapter is that, in order to conduct integral monitoring of the dynamics of the digital divide, the following are needed:

(a) a simultaneous three-dimensional monitoring of differences with static absolute and relative differences and with dynamic S-time-distance; and
(b) an explicit consideration of scenarios when forecasting future trends of ICT penetration (e.g. the shape of the diffusion functions, the initial time delay in the early stage of ICT adoption and the final level of ICT penetration).

The diffusion of ICTs and determinist implications of the diffusion of innovation theory

As mentioned above, this chapter seeks to design an advanced approach to measuring the dynamics of the basic digital divide. The proposed holistic methodological framework could contribute to the elimination of imprecise and possibly deceptive interpretations of differences between countries and/or population segments within this field.

In designing a methodological framework and understanding the diffusion and intensity of the adoption of ICT, we depart from the conceptual framework of the diffusion of innovation theory. Everett Rogers, the founder of the diffusion of innovation theory (Rogers 1962), compared diffusion with 'the process in which an innovation is communicated through certain channels over time among the members of a social system' (Rogers 2003, 5). He defined four crucial elements of the process of diffusion of innovation – innovation, communication channel, time and social system.[2] The most relevant process for our research question is time

---

2 For a detailed elaboration of the basic elements of the diffusion of innovation theory, see Rogers (2003, 12-24).

because the study of the digital divide measures 'innovation's rate of adoption in a system, usually measured as the number of members of the system who adopt the innovation in a given time period' (Rogers 2003, 20). With this in mind, we differentiate various population segments in the system. The time element of the diffusion process allows us to classify adopter categories and to draw diffusion curves. Regarding the time needed to adopt an innovation by individuals, Rogers (2003, 410) divides the users of innovations into five categories: innovators, early adopters, early majorities, late majorities, and laggards. It should be emphasised here that these adopter categories are ideal types based on abstractions from empirical investigations (Rogers 2003, 282) and that there are no sharp breaks or discontinuities between adopter categories. Moreover, Roger's categorisation of adopter categories (which has also been extensively applied to ICT users) is nowadays overcome by the notion of 'everyday innovators' (Haddon et al. 2005) and 'humans as e-actors' (Fortunati, this volume). Fortunati (2007) also claims that it is extremely reductive to speak only of users. Instead, 'we should be speaking of individuals/citizens, who may be users, non-users, drop-outs, users of many ICTs, of other technologies or goods' (Fortunati 2007).

As mentioned, the chapter aims to introduce a methodological approach to measuring the dynamics of the digital divide whereby different population segments or countries can be compared. The added value of this approach is that comparisons among different units are more informed and unbiased; however, it should be emphasised that this approach contributes (only) to a more accurate understanding of the digital divide's dynamics and not also to the social (cultural, anthropological, psychological, sociological etc.) factors relevant for explaining the underlying reasons for the differences observed. Of course, this is not to say that we would disregard the importance of studying the individual needs, aspirations, motives and barriers or would underestimate the significant role of users in the ICT adoption process. Thus, we agree with the statement that technology 'should not be seen only as an artefact, but as a social relation, therefore a field of class struggle and cultural development' (Fortunati and Manganelli 2002). Users are not merely passive recipients of technology, they actively engage in it, thereby giving meaning to ICTs (Vehovar et al. 2006).

However, despite the drawbacks of the diffusion of innovation theory (also see Section 2.2), it offers a solid framework for measuring the process of ICT adoption on the structural, aggregate level. Basic characteristics of the diffusion process are thus discussed below. This discussion is then followed by a presentation of the developed methodological approach which critically considers some of the deterministic assumptions of the diffusion of innovation theory (this is done by allowing for different shapes of the diffusion functions – which depict different speeds of adoption within different population segments or countries – the initial time delay in the early stage of ICT adoption and the final level of ICT penetration).

The phenomenon of ICT diffusion among various subjects is normally distributed according to the diffusion of innovation theory. The adoption of innovation usually follows a normal, bell-shaped curve when plotted over time on a frequency basis. When ICTs are diffused in time, coincidental variable t measures the time of the adoption of an ICT (here, the time of adoption should not be conflated with calendar time) and $f(t)$ stands for the probability of a random individual adopting an ICT in a certain time period. If we presume that the time of adopting an ICT is distributed normally with a mean time point T=2008 and a standard deviation of three years, this would then mean that 68% of individuals will have adopted the ICT between 2005 and 2011. On the basis of the mean value and standard deviation the probability that a randomly chosen individual will adopt the ICT in a certain period can be calculated. A normal adopter distribution is divided into five categories by laying off standard deviations (σ) by the average time of adoption (μ). The area lying to the left of the mean time of adoption of an innovation minus two standard deviations, for example, includes the first 2.5% of individuals in a system to adopt an innovation, i.e. the innovators (Rogers 2003). These adopter categories are considered here merely for an illustrative purpose so that the interdependence between time and adoption can be presented in a more understandable way; the methodological approach to be presented later in the text does not otherwise rely on these (or any other) categorisations of the users. We should emphasise here that it is not our intention to indicate that those population segments or countries that accept ICTs at a later stage (so-called late majorities and 'laggards') should in any way be treated in an inferior way. On the contrary, 'each country, each community and each social group will always find its own path towards technology' (Fortunati & Manganelli 2002). Further, Fortunati and Manganelli (2002) added that 'each culture, each society, negotiates the quantity of technology that it needs, in the same way as it decides which technology it needs most, starting from the specific environmental, social and productive conditions in which it lives'. In line with this, we do not imply that all countries, for example, should strive for the highest level of penetration in terms of a specific ICT (this is further discussed in Section 2.2 and also explicitly implemented in our methodological approach).

When the number of adopters is cumulatively added and shown as dependent on time, the result is usually an S-shaped curve (Figure 1).[3] Therefore, according

---

3 F(T) is a cumulative distribution function; it designates a process of ICT adoption and is for the purposes of this chapter also denominated a logistic S-curve or diffusion function because it designates the diffusion of ICT in time.

to Rogers's diffusion of innovation theory, the diffusion of a certain innovation (in this case an ICT) is characterised by an increasing S-curve that represents a cumulative function with regard to the probability density of normal distribution as shown in Figure 1. The S-shaped adopter distribution rises slowly at first, as there are only a few adopters in each time period. The curve then rises to its maximum until half of the individuals in the system have adopted the innovation. It is then increasing at a gradually slower rate as fewer remaining individuals adopt it. Hence, the S-curve can be divided into two parts, i.e. the phase of increasing growth and the phase of decreasing growth; in the initial phase, the values of the function rise faster compared to the second, gradual phase.

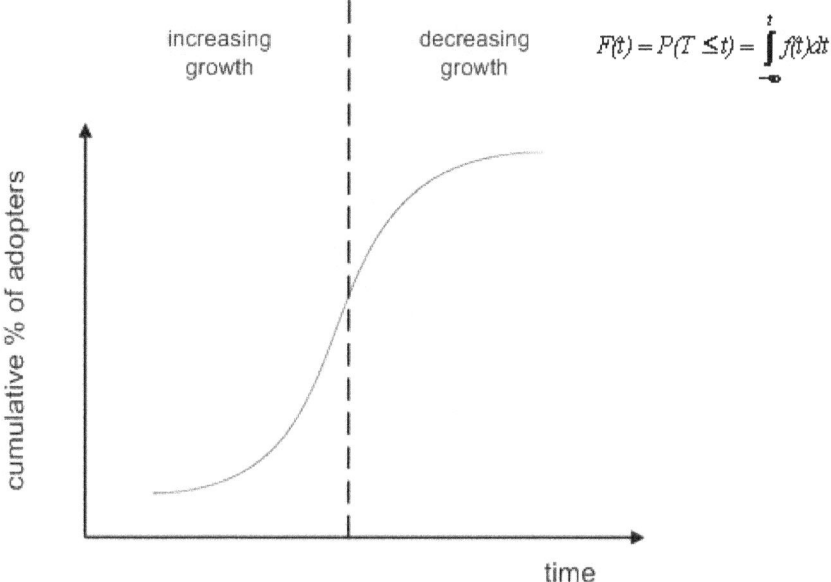

Figure 1: The cumulative S-shaped curve of adoption

The diffusion of innovation theory presupposes that significant differences exist among various social system members with regard to the time component in the adoption of an innovation. In the initial phase of the diffusion process, members of a small category of innovative users (innovators) feature as actors (in terms of the invention and adoption of an innovation) who gradually increase their influence on other individuals, i.e. the imitators. Rogers (2003) uses such social interaction between so-called adopters-pioneers and prospective adopters to explicate the phase of rapid diffusion in the process of the diffusion of an innovation.[4]

In accordance with the diffusion of innovation theory we can assume that the divide between the observed groups is initially growing, starts to shrink when significant parts of the population reach the level of saturation and finally terminates. Roger's S-curve is widely used and has proved to be a relatively accurate description of the adoption of a new ICT, although other, modified shapes of the distribution function are of course possible. Even when the typical S-curve diffusion models are used, the degree of saturation and pace of adoption of an innovation (for instance, an ICT) are not known in advance and it is almost impossible to determine them in the initial phase of adoption. In the following, the diffusion of ICT is discussed and critically elucidated from the perspective of some crucial simplifications of the diffusion of innovation theory, particularly related to the determinism of adoption growth rates and adopter categories.

Form of the diffusion function

In the eyes of policy-makers and consequently wider public opinion, the dynamics of the adoption of ICT are often designated and described by the use of a simplified and deterministic S-curve. Yet, the diffusion of innovative digital technologies, by their very nature diverse and multi-functional, is very much a complex phenomenon; its development in time cannot be easily generalised and uniformly defined by the dynamics of the increase in ICT penetration. The diffusion of innovation theory neglects the fact that this may not be the case in every instance, presuming that after the initial period of slower adoption a phase of a swifter increase in ICT penetration will occur. Norris (2001, 23-24) thus states that the dif-

---

4   Many researchers (mostly in marketing) have modelled the diffusion process taking into account this characteristic of innovation behaviour on the basis of mathematically defined equations of functions of the adoption of innovation. Three of the most often used diffusion models are the model of external influence, the model of internal influence and the model of mixed influence. However, the purpose of our study is not the study of internal or external influences on the adoption of ICT. Rather, it is our aim to study the dynamics of the adoption of ICT and the shape of the diffusion function *in particular population subsegments* (the presented diffusion modelling does not do this). The expected shape of the diffusion function is therefore directly based on Roger's diffusion of innovation theory, which is characterised by a normal distribution. ('Degree of innovativeness is expected to be normally distributed' (Rogers 2003, 272) and the corresponding distribution function is expected to be typically S-shaped; this shape of the diffusion function is close to the models of internal and mixed influence).

fusion of new mass media in developing countries cannot be described by a typical S-curve characterised by a typical increase in the level of growth after a certain point in time but, conversely, by slower (yet steady) growth. Unequal diffusion functions can also be observed in particular population segments within particular countries, in addition to a comparison between countries (global dynamics of the digital divide). One clearly weak point of the diffusion of innovation theory – at least in terms of studying the digital divide – is the S-curve being related to entire populations while neglecting particular population categories. According to Norris (2001), different categories are characterised by various distribution functions that comprise the S-curve typical of an entire population.[5] However, the question also arises of whether the comparison of different distribution functions will enter the so-called normalisation or stratification phase of ICT diffusion in the future; this topic is discussed in more detail below.

The normalisation and stratification model of ICT diffusion

After Pippa Norris, the author of the first influential book on the digital divide, introduced the concept of the normalisation and stratification model of ICT diffusion in 2001, the concept soon started to be used as a critique of the diffusion of innovation theory. The normalisation and stratification model of ICT diffusion is determined by the final level of ICT penetration characteristic of the entire monitored population or particular population segments. The normalisation model can be attributed to monitored categories with a 100% (or nearly 100%) final level of ICT penetration; in categories with a lower final level of ICT penetration in at least one of the categories the situation corresponds to the stratification model.

The normalisation model (see Figure 2) presupposes that differences between groups only grow in the initial phases of adoption. The leading category (e.g. educated, younger individuals or an entire population) usually starts adopting sooner and, of course, it also sooner enters the phase of swiftly increasing growth. However, in the final time period when the adoption of ICT in the leading group enters the phase of saturation, the lagging group/s reach/es higher levels of growth and the differences are eliminated.

---

5   There is a chance that ICT diffusion fails to follow at least an approximation of the normal distribution (apparent in the S-shape of the diffusion function) and could be characterised by, for instance, a bimodal or even a polymodal distribution; this possibility should not be neglected. In principle, this option is allowed; however, later in the chapter we focus on kurtosis and a more or less skewed distribution.

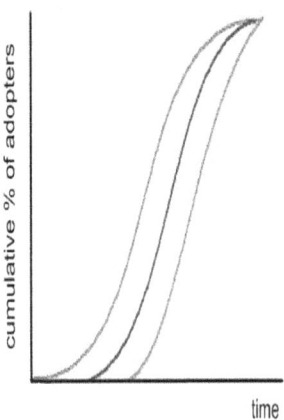

Figure 2: The normalisation model of the diffusion of innovation

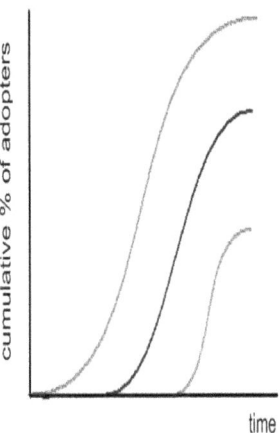

Figure 3: The stratification model of the diffusion of innovation

The stratification model (Figure 3) presupposes that the adoption of an ICT, which is characteristic of monitored categories, is described by similarly formed diffusion functions (an S-curve marked by specific levels of growth in different phases and with saturation). However, apart from the different initial point of adoption, the final point of ICT penetration differs as well. The leading category begins adoption sooner and the final level of ICT penetration is higher; in the lagging category the phase of saturation emerges at a lower level of ICT penetration.

The diffusion of innovation theory with respect to the adoption of an ICT implies that an increase in the cumulative share of adopters among particular categories in the form of the S-curve leads to an understanding of the digital divide as merely temporary differences (between these categories) that will eventually disappear. According to such ideas regarding the dynamics of the digital divide, starting from the position of the diffusion of innovation theory, Compaine (2001) maintains that it makes no sense to study the digital divide as a problematic social phenomenon because the problem will be solved anyway as a consequence of market logic. Thus, Compaine ascertains that the nature of market dynamics itself will eventually lead to elimination of the digital divide – without the intervention or stimulation of policy-makers.

Although the presented understanding of the dynamics of the digital divide is quite common (at least implicitly), it should be noted that the presupposition of the self-elimination of the digital divide usually includes an essential (in our opinion questionable) condition that market logic alone leads to elimination of the digital divide (supply and demand). This argument is based on the so-called 'trickle-down' principle (van Dijk 2005), which explains the adoption of new technologies as a gradual process. This process first entangles the higher and only later lower social (income, employment, educational) strata (this also applies to other technological innovations). In the long run, 'the digital divide should not necessarily and self-evidently lead to universal social inclusion' (Hüsing & Selhofer 2004, 23). Van Dijk (2005), Hüsing and Selhofer (2004) and Norris (2001) maintain that it is quite probable that certain categories will never reach an equal final level of penetration of an ICT compared to the level of the general population.

On the other hand, the data show that certain media (radio, TV, telephone) in developed countries have reached an (almost) total level of 100% penetration (see Schement & Scott 2000). Huysmans and De Haan (2003, 35) thus estimate – on the basis of an analogy with the penetration of telephone and TV sets – that there is a significant probability that a further diffusion of PCs and the Internet will reduce the differences between population categories.

Generally speaking, new media are more expensive than traditional media because they become out-dated sooner and have to be constantly up-dated with additional and supplemental hardware and software (Rogers 2003, 13; van Dijk 1999, 150). Moreover, it seems that lower hardware prices are compensated for by relatively expensive software and programmes. In order to use interactive audiovisual services the user has to purchase an end-user licence in addition to high-performance hardware. Besides, more and more Internet contents must be paid for. Therefore, the basic argument of the trickle-down principle – that computers and Internet connections are becoming cheaper by the day and eventually accessible to all – should be mitigated to a large extent.

A lower final level of ICT penetration among some population segments (or even the entire population) may be expected in technologically more advanced ICTs because computer hardware and software and network connections and services require a greater input, i.e. engagement regarding both material assets, and digital skills and time. This may also present great an obstacle for adopting a certain technological innovation. Among the important factors that influence the adoption of an innovative ICT one may, of course, also or mainly find ICT characteristics relating to hardware and software design and/or the contents offered. If individuals (regardless of their socio-demographic characteristics) fail to perceive a new ICT as useful (they do not expect it to satisfy their needs and fulfil their expectations, or they perceive the ICT as user-unfriendly or dangerous etc.), it seems very likely that individuals will not adopt the new ICT even if it were available free of charge and delivered to their home. Therefore, it is important to draw a line of distinction between individuals who cannot afford it or are insufficiently acquainted with its potential benefits and advantages and those who reject a new ICT out of principal or for specific reasons (for them all the more valid). Thus, we should take into account that 'probably the main factor influencing innovation adoption rates is that users often adapt technology to their own needs or desires, transforming the technological artefact in both its purpose and meaning and, ultimately, when passing from the early adopters to the majority, also in its design' (Fortunati, this issue).

Similarly to van Dijk, we expect that in the long run the digital divide will not be completely eliminated relative to more advanced ICTs; moreover, even risk-free or progressive segments will most probably not reach a 100% penetration level of some (more specialised) ICTs:

> Basic computer and Internet adoption will continue to grow but advanced multimedia machines, high-speed Internet connections, and their applications probably will not reach the adoption rate of the telephone in the developed countries for the next two decades at least. We do not have to mention the developing countries – here, population wide diffusions of the old mass media are not even a realistic prospect (van Dijk 2005, 63–64).

Of course, as happens in real life, the complete, 100% adoption of an innovation is never reached. This is particularly characteristic of ICT because technological development dictates swift changes. In cases of larger technological and innovation achievements the existing technology may be completely substituted by an innovation in the process of adopting this technology.[6] Therefore, the so-called

---

6   The incessant development and upgrading of ICT and new technologies as substitutes of their predecessors demands a dynamic study of ICT (van Dijk & Hacker 2003) that acknowledges that late adopters and laggards are still in the phase of adopting the 'old'

'trickle-down' principle seems to be an inappropriate line of thought for studying the adoption of ICTs.

The research approach based on non-determinist definitions of the diffusion process

Now that the critical objections to the classic diffusion of innovation theory have been discussed, it is time to outline the theoretical foundations of the study of the dynamics of the digital divide.

The objects of this study are two of the key simplifications (that relate to the determinist definition of the diffusion process) of the diffusion of innovation theory: the shape of the distribution function and the final level of ICT penetration of compared segments. Alongside these two characteristics of the adoption of ICT, we also study the initial time delay among the compared segments as an equal characteristic. We thus compare (first taking theoretical values of the diffusion functions, then real empirical data) how the digital divide – in relation to the three statistical measures – changes in time if the three characteristics of ICT adoption are varied:

- Regarding the shape of the distribution function the process of ICT diffusion may be expected to be shown in various growth levels not defined by a normal distribution (typical symmetric S-curve). This is true of the entire period of adoption and particular phases of the adoption of ICT. Therefore, we can differentiate between normal distribution, leptokurtic or platykurtic distribution and a positively/negatively skewed distribution. The presumption is that the diffusion of ICT in time has to be monitored in various population segments because such disaggregated monitoring enables a deeper insight into trends of ICT adoption within the entire population. We established how the distribution functions that are valid for the entire population are differentiated in particular population segments.
- The final level of trends penetration of ICT that defines the normalisation or stratification model of ICT diffusion significantly influences the relationship

---

technology, while the early adopters are already in the phase of adopting a new ICT (which substitutes the old one). For instance, the VCR was substituted by the DVD player already during the phase of adopting the former. Once the ICT adoption comes to a near halt (at a point, for instance, of 60%) and when such stagnation lasts for some time, we assume this point to be the point of 100% penetration. The dynamics of the digital divide are therefore only observed in the population that adopted ICT until a certain point in time (VCR); from that point onward, the adoption of DVD players is monitored.

between the statistical measures and the interpretation of the dynamics of the digital divide. In the fifth chapter we will observe the increasing values of statistical measures of the digital divide (according to the diffusion of innovation theory) in the normalisation and stratification models. The two final levels of ICT penetration (50% and 70%) will be varied. Similarly, by designing scenarios we will represent cases which are expected to lead to self-elimination of the digital divide (the normalisation model) and cases where a less optimistic course of ICT diffusion will be represented (although particular distribution functions are still within the typical ICT adoption S-curve). We will also establish whether the existing data perhaps imply the normalisation or stratification model of ICT adoption in particular socio-demographic groups.
- The third monitored characteristic of ICT adoption is the initial time delay between the compared groups. Most authors who talk about the normalisation and stratification models (Hüsing & Selhofer 2004; Norris 2001; van Dijk 2005) presuppose that the normalisation and stratification models are characterised by an initial time delay between the leading and lagging groups. Here, however, the initial point of ICT adoption is understood as a characteristic independent of either model of ICT adoption. In the normalisation model the studied population segments may lack the initial time delay (e.g. two groups started adoption at the same point or period). In the stratification model only the various different-sized models have been varied, while the possibility that a delay never occurred was not anticipated. When dealing with empirical data on Internet adoption in Slovenia we determined the initial time delay at a 5% level of Internet penetration.

Basic elements of the methodological framework for the study of the digital divide

According to the presumption, that absolute and relative differences and time distance are a function or manifestation of the form of distribution functions, the time delay and the final level of ICT penetration, we shall examine how measures of the digital divide vary in cases of particular types. To that end, a methodological framework has been designed[7].

---

7 Because of lack of space we do not present the methodological framework in detail; the description of the basic elements of applied methodological approach can be found in Dolničar (2008).

Typology of relationships among the three statistical measures of the digital divide

In order to more accurately define the relationships between absolute differences, ratios and S-time-distance, a so-called standard typology of relationships among the statistical measures of the digital divide is introduced. Since each of the three studied measures may increase, decrease or remain constant, the direction of change of absolute and relative statistical measures and S-time-distance can be combined in 27 ways, which can also be equated with the potential relationships between the three measures.

The typology of potential relationships between the measures is designed in such a way that one statistical measure corresponds to one of the three possible directions of movement (i.e. increase, decrease or constant)[8].

Figure 4 shows the case where the two compared subjects or population segments (or only a section of the time period of the compared subjects) are characterised by a distinctive combination of trends of increasing and decreasing growth (these trends could be part of a diffusion function).

When two subjects are characterised by different trends (as presented above) the relationship between the statistical measures changes three times, at time points T3, T5 and T8 (these changes are represented by the vertical dashed line). While in the first and last time periods all three statistical measures are increasing (the period until T3) or decreasing (the period after T8), the relationships between measures of the digital divide in the middle period are more complicated. In the period between T3 and T5, the S-time-distance and absolute differences are increasing, while the differences in ratios are decreasing; in the third time period (between T5 and T8) only the S-time-distance is increasing while the absolute and relative differences are decreasing.

When studying the digital divide and comparing two subjects or population segments regarding the dynamics of adoption of a certain technology, it is unfeasible to discuss one time period (as presented above) alone; several relationships emerge between two static and one dynamic measures. With the increasing number of various combinations of trends – with regard to particular diffusion functions and combinations of the two studied functions – the complexity of the relationships also rises.

---

8   The typology of all potential relationships between statistical measures is introduced in Dolničar (2008).

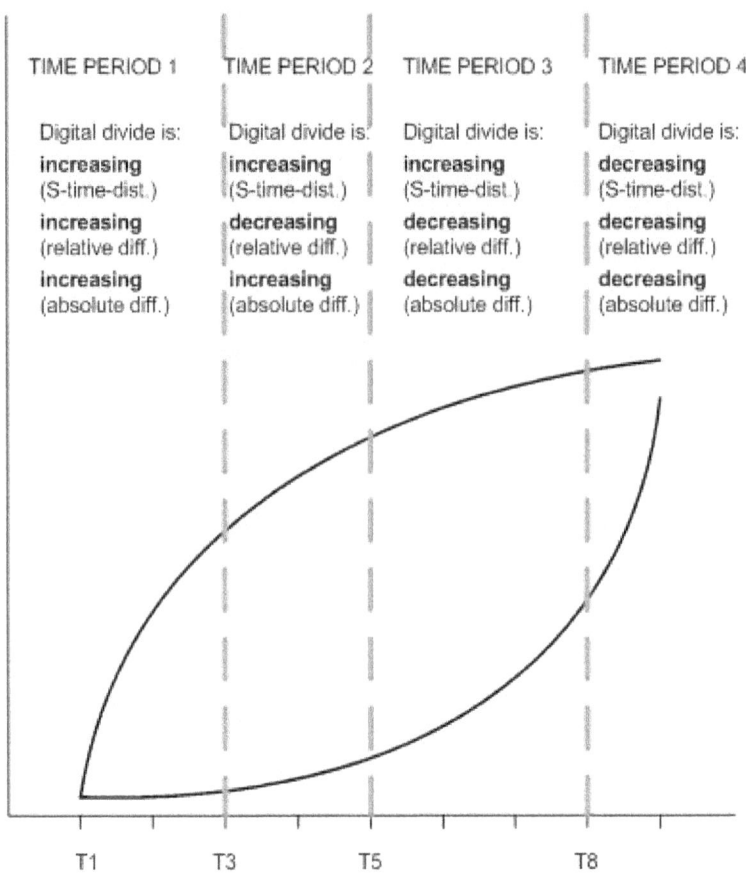

Figure 4: Comparison of two trends (increasing and decreasing growth) as part of the diffusion functions and corresponding digital divide, measured by three different statistical measures

The key question of the empirical part will be the problem of identifying the type of digital divide in terms of the shape of the diffusion function, the initial time delay and the final level of ICT penetration. Thus, a change in the digital divide can be accurately interpreted and situated, and the role of the statistical measures correspondingly explained. In so doing, we can avoid incorrect interpretations of the digital divide growing or shrinking. These misinterpretations stem from monitoring only one phase in the development of the digital divide and are based on observing particular statistical measures.

Typology of combinations of two diffusion functions

In order to make the monitoring of the digital divide systematic and consistent with regard to the values of the three statistical measures, a typology of combinations of two distribution functions is introduced, alongside the varying of three mentioned characteristics of the diffusion process (i.e. shape of the diffusion function, initial time delay and final level of ICT penetration)[9].

Here, let us briefly mention that *type* is a chosen typical case; it denotes a combination of two diffusion functions which are determined by varying the three characteristics of the diffusion process. Three types were discerned (Type A, Type B and Type C), among which the latter two are further structured as Type B1 and Type B2, and Type C1 and Type C2. In deploying the key and their respective subtypes designed to designate pre-defined probability distributions the diffusion of ICT in time is described using theoretical and artificially generated values. By doing this, it was established that the changing (increasing or decreasing) of statistical measures (absolute differences, ratios and time-distance) is influenced not only by the shape of the probability densities and corresponding distribution functions but also by the initial time of adoption of the two compared segments and the final level of ICT penetration. In all three basic types (A, B and C), where appropriate, the existence and size of the time delay, and the final level of ICT penetration have been varied, in addition to various degrees of kurtosis and skewness.

We demonstrated, for example, that even in the case of the most rudimentary example of monitoring the delayed diffusion of innovation where both probability densities are equal and normally distributed, no one-dimensional or uniform conclusions can be drawn regarding the size of the digital divide. We demonstrated that the reason behind this is that innovation diffuses with different intensity in different periods (see e.g. Vehovar et al. 2006; Dolničar 2008).

This typology thus serves as a framework for examining how the digital divide (in terms of the three statistical measures) changes in the case of different types (of combinations of diffusion functions). It is also useful for investigating in which way the three characteristics of the diffusion process influence the relationships between the statistical measures. A drawback of this typology is that it is limited to 14 ideal typical cases (empirical reality cannot be analysed completely). However, scenarios can be used for determining certain types (e.g. by choosing the saturation or normalisation model) and on this basis it is easier to estimate what the dynamics of the digital divide (according to an individual statistic measure) will

---

9   Also this typology – alongside with the key terms that facilitate an understanding of this typology and the influence of distribution – functions on the relationships between statistical measures have been defined in Dolničar (2008).

be in the future. This enables a more informative interpretation of the relationships between the statistical measures. The next chapter demonstrates how an elaborated framework can be applied not only to theoretical simulations of diffusion functions, but also to real empirical data.

The digital divide in Slovenia: three scenarios for a case study on age

The in/existence of an initial time delay in the monitored groups can already be monitored in the first phase of the diffusion of ICT. Yet it is impossible to determine this for the other two characteristics of the diffusion process (shape of the diffusion function and final level of ICT penetration that is in two or more groups defined by the normalisation or stratification model). In Slovenia, the entire population reached an approximately 50% Internet penetration level in March 2005. This means that the Internet has been adopted (presupposing a normalisation model that accepts a 100% final level of penetration) by approximately one-half of all potential adopters. Thus, one of the biggest problems of studying the digital divide is insufficient information about the expected intensity of future ICT diffusion. A key question is which directions a particular population segment will take in the future, i.e. what will be the shape of the diffusion function since the last measuring. A particular projection of the development of diffusion functions offers an answer to this question.

Thus, the purpose of this sub-section is to provide scenarios of Internet adoption in Slovenia; the entire population will be compared with the older age group. Various scenarios will be presented below; we believe that their implementation is probable (being aware, of course, that such projections of diffusions of the Internet in the future are uncertain; thus, each scenario is open to change)[10].

The essential characteristic of scenarios as methods that propose multiple possible future outcomes led to adoption of this technique in anticipating probable future concepts in the field of Internet diffusion and in relation to age in Slovenia. Approaching the deterministic presumptions of the diffusion of innovation theory sceptically (hence the introduction of the two key models of diffusion of innovation – alongside the normalisation model we introduce the stratification model – and the focus on various shapes of the diffusion functions), we anticipate

---

10 Scenarios are understood as a form of a qualitative technique of forecasting. They are narrative descriptions of possible future events and as such they imply no prediction of the future (Chermack et al. 2001). Scenarios may be defined as blueprints of the future, based on schematic descriptions of some crucial presumptions. This is a probable and simplified description of the potential course of the future and is based on understandable and meaningful presumptions about crucial relationships and factors (see Chermack 2005; van der Heijden 1997).

that it makes no sense to predict only one course of events and the final outcome. On the contrary, it seems viable to outline and present several alternative possible drafts of the future. According to Bouwman and van der Duin (2003, 8), this is the first condition for using scenarios as methods of future research.

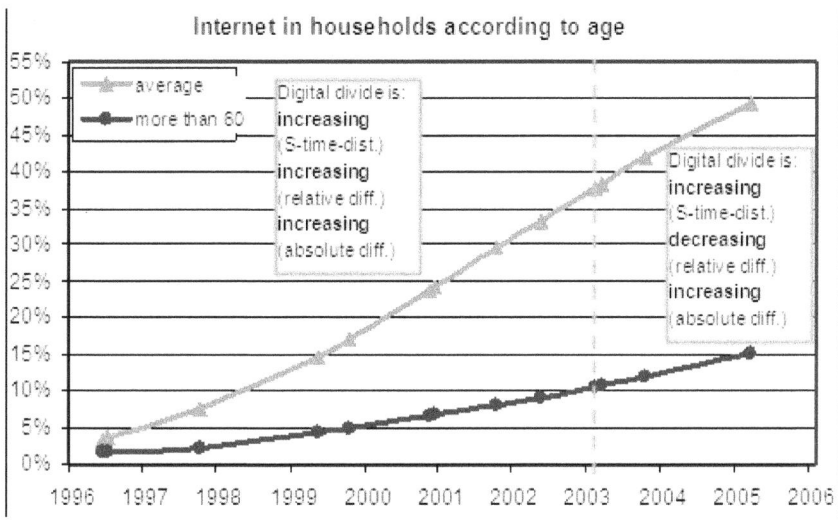

Figure 5: Diffusion of the Internet in Slovenian households among the entire population and among the older population in the 1996 to 2005 period

The monitoring of the adoption of the Internet in households regarding age in the period between June 1996 and March 2005[11] showed that considerable differences exist among individuals above 60 years of age and the entire population regarding all three statistical measures (Figure 5). With respect to household Internet access, the older population segment lagged behind the entire population by

---

11 In this chapter the study of the digital divide is focused on the basic digital divide where the measure of the divide is household Internet access and the units of observation are Slovenian residents. Data are acquired from the Slovenian Public Opinion Surveys conducted by the Public Opinion and Mass Communication Research Centre at the Faculty of Social Sciences of the University of Ljubljana.
Here, only one aspect of the application is discussed; in Dolničar (2008) empirical data for the diffusion of eight ICTs in Slovenia are presented: the Internet, personal computer, mobile, hi-fi, VCR, video camera, TV set and landline telephone. The diffusion of these technologies was monitored – based on available past measurements and the presence of a particular technology – in the period between 1973 and 2005. The digital divide according to Internet access was studied with respect to 13 socio-demographic variables.

33 months in October 1999; by the end of the monitoring period (March 2005) the delay had extended to 67 months. Regarding the relative differences, the digital divide between the entire population and its older segment was slightly increasing since May 2002. After that date, the elderly started to reach an ever-greater share of ICT penetration within the general population and the delay began to wane, relatively speaking. Despite the intermittent smaller decreases and increases in value ratios, in the entire monitored period the relative differences between the groups are maintained. This is so, as the elderly reached 31% of the mean value of the entire population in both 1997 and 2005. Over the nine monitored years, the divide between the entire population and the elderly increased by 32.7% in terms of absolute differences. The digital divide between individuals above 60 years old and the overall population is constantly increasing regarding the absolute differences.

According to Slovenian Public Opinion Survey data, in March 2005 the Slovenian population reached a level of 49.5%[12] Internet penetration (i.e. household Internet access). Only one of the three characteristics of the diffusion process that influence the relationships between the statistical measures – the existence of an initial time delay – can be determined on the basis of empirical data at less than 50% of ICT penetration. Therefore, in the following three possible combinations of the movement of the distribution functions are presented. Based on values that determine the intensity of Internet adoption in the future, we will be able to estimate – in addition to the time delay between the observed segments – the other two characteristics: the shape of the probability density function and the final level of Internet penetration. Two key scenarios for Internet diffusion are presented below: one with the normalisation model and the other with the stratification model (where we will consider two variations).

The normalisation model

In predicting the diffusion of the Internet in the monitored groups we have been determining cumulative relative functions. Hence, the shape of the probability density was defined as a derivative of the distribution function. Prior to that, we had to estimate the values of the distribution functions (i.e. cumulative relative frequencies of the diffusion of the Internet in households) that can also be assigned to a sequence of uniform time periods for the period between 1996 and 2005 because time intervals vary during the measurements of ICT penetration, varying from one month to more than a year.

---

12 The percentage of those who have household Internet access (49.5%) is based on corrected values that result from a smoothening procedure based on trendline; the initial value was 47.8%.

Thus, Figure 6 includes cumulative relative frequencies that are valid for the diffusion of the Internet in Slovenian households among the entire population and among the older population segments in the period between 1996 and 2005. Although these values are based on real data gathered in the Slovenian Public Opinion Survey, the estimated values are presented in regular time intervals, i.e. one year. Apart from the already known empirical data, on the right side of the vertical line data we present one of the possible scenarios for the diffusion of the Internet in the period between 2006 and 2020.[13]

We examined how many times the relationships between the statistical measures change. Figure 6 shows the entire process of adoption of the Internet applicable to the entire population and the segment of over 60-year-olds. The bold orange vertical line at time point March 2005 differentiates real, measured data from potential anticipated values. The anticipated values present the scenario of adoption of the Internet according to the normalisation model. Each of these distribution functions is characterised by two trends. In both cases, the increasing growth is followed by decreasing growth; the decreasing growth trend is marked in lighter red and blue colours. Regarding the entire population, on one hand the increasing growth turns decreasing close to 50% Internet penetration (to be more exact, 44.8% in March 2004), in line with the theoretically defined normal distribution. On the other hand, the older population segment would, if the normalisation model were to be deployed, reach decreasing growth only towards the end of the process of adoption (as shown in Figure 6, this would occur in March 2005 at a level of 76% Internet penetration).

Let us now examine which relationships between statistical measures of the digital divide are characteristic of the household diffusion of the Internet in the entire and older population groups, respectively. Changes in relationships between the statistical measures are presented in the chart below with a dashed vertical line – these changes occur three times. The digital divide is increasing with regard to all three monitored statistical measures in the initial monitoring period and decreasing in the final period. In the intermittent period, on the other hand, first the relative differences begin to decrease and are later followed by decreasing absolute differences. Such a sequence equals the comparison between the theoretically defined diffusion functions of Type C_2 designating the comparison of the normal and the negatively skewed probability density functions.

---

13 Very different time horizons are used in forecasting, usually classified as short-term, mid-term and long-term forecasts. The 'real' time horizon varies regarding the studied research problem. The longer the time horizon, the greater is the possibility that unforeseen factors or external influences appear. This may lead to a less accurate forecast. For forecasting the diffusion of the Internet, a time frame of 14 years was taken (from 2006 to 2020). Considering other classifications of forecasts' time horizons (see Albright 2002; Weingand 1995) this fits into mid-term predictions.

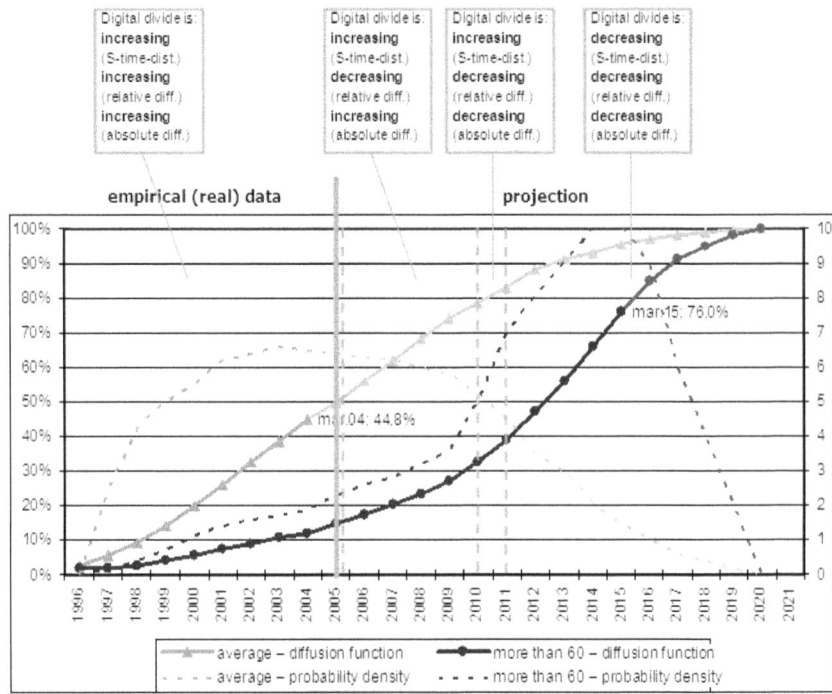

Figure 6: Projection of diffusion of the Internet in Slovenian households in the entire population and the older population for the entire period of diffusion (1996-2020); normalisation model

The following section presents a projection of the diffusion of the Internet among the entire population and the older segment of the population, assuming that the diffusion corresponds to the stratification model.

The stratification model

The stratification model designates all comparisons of the two segments that describe Internet diffusion, where one segment reaches a lower level of final Internet penetration compared to the leading segment. Also in this instance, the values valid for a particular segment have been estimated for one-year time intervals (this also means the monitored period, not only the projected values).

Since the comparison entails the entire population and part of it (i.e. the older segment of the population), the leading population segment clearly cannot reach a 100% Internet penetration level (this could only be the case if the comparison were to entail the youngest and older population segments). According to data from the Statistical Office of the Republic of Slovenia, in December 2005 there were 1,671,145 Slovenian citizens older than 17 (who comprise our target population with regard to the pattern of the Slovenian Public Opinion survey). In the overall population, 413,180 (24.7%) are 60 years of age (and above); this percentage has been rounded off to 25%. Presuming that the older segment of the population will reach a 80% final level of Internet penetration, it is reasonable to expect that (provided all other segments will reach a 100% Internet penetration) the entire population will reach a 95% Internet penetration level.[14]

Designing the scenario of Internet diffusion up until 2020 and presuming the stratification model, we have taken into account (according to the description of characteristics of the stratification model of ICT diffusion) the S shape in both distribution functions (Figure 7). Thus, each function comprises two trends: increasing growth and decreasing growth. Here, the point of inflection, namely the transition from one trend to another in the entire population occurs just before the second half of the process of adoption (regarding the time and level of penetration), while in the lagging group (older population) decreasing growth only occurs towards the end of Internet adoption.

The presented compared segments again correspond with relationships among the statistical measures also characteristic of a combination of theoretical diffusion functions in the stratification model of Type C. The above figures show that the diminishing relative differences between the two segments (starting in 2005) are a result of the trend transition from increasing to decreasing growth. Considering the anticipated scenario, absolute differences are expected to begin to decrease in 2009, with the start of a period of a swifter increase in the lagging segment compared to the entire population (the latter is, with a 70% Internet penetration level, far into the phase of decreasing growth).

If we were to use the stratification model where it would be presumed that the oldest population segment would reach a mere 50% Internet penetration level by 2020, the differences between the entire population and individuals above 60 years of age with regard to all three statistical measures would of course be significantly greater. However, this case is particularly interesting because it illustrates con-

---

14 This percentage is arrived at by means of a simple calculation which presupposes that the older population (25% of the entire population) is reaching an 80% Internet penetration level ($0.25 * 0.8 = 0.2$) and the rest of the population is reaching a 100% penetration level ($0.75 * 1 = 0.75$); the sum of both products represents 95% Internet penetration within the entire population.

stant absolute differences in the final time period. Identical absolute differences (and with them the perseverance of the digital divide) occur when both segments evolve at the same pace, but with varying levels of Internet penetration. However, this bears no significance for the S-time-distance values which are incessantly (even in the final period) increasing in both examples of the stratification model.

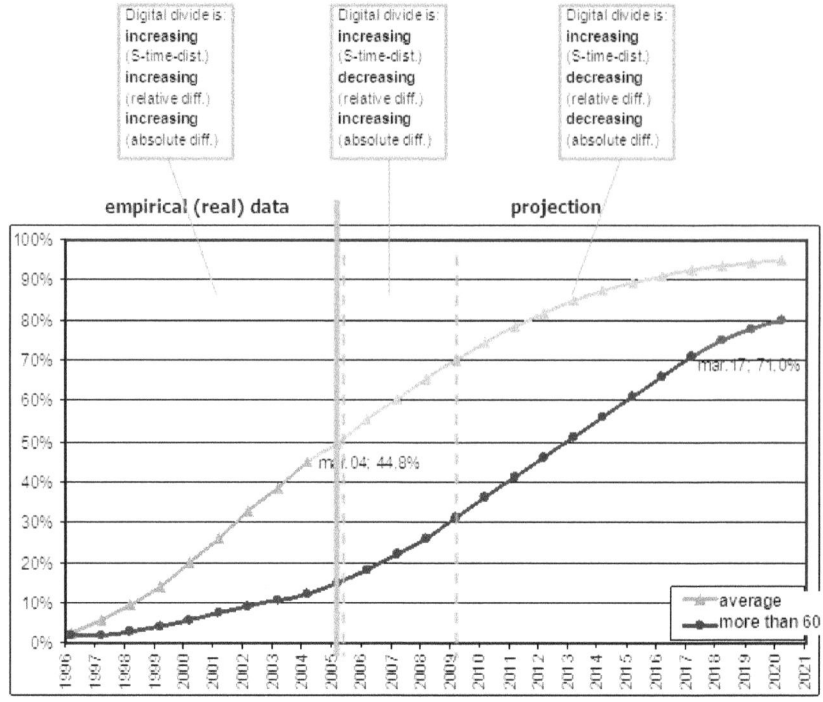

Figure 7: Projection of diffusion of the Internet in Slovenian households in the entire population and older population for the entire period of diffusion (1996-2020); stratification model (older segment reaches a level of 80% Internet penetration)

Based on the overview of the three possible scenarios of Internet diffusion regarding age, it can be maintained that monitoring the relationships between the statistical measures is only viable over the entire period of Internet adoption and not only regarding the past and present trends of the divide. Thus, for instance, the growing digital divide between some most-at-risk groups (one of those is surely the older part of the population) and the entire population is to be expected in the initial period (this can be attributed to the initial time delay in ICT adoption). It is important, however, for us to monitor in which period the so-called inflection point will occur in the entire population (in line with the diffusion of innovation theory this can be expected at a level of about 50% Internet penetration). Decreasing differences in Type C can be expected precisely when the decreasing growth of the leading subject occurs. Of course, a shrinking divide with regard to the relative differences does not mean that the lagging subject may be expected to catch up with the entire population. This is a mere reflection of the leading subject being in the phase of decreasing growth. As explicated in the second scenario (Figure 7), even based on the decreasing absolute differences, the last, final period of ICT adoption should not be misinterpreted as the ultimate elimination of the divide. In establishing whether the diffusion of the Internet among various subjects may imply the normalisation or stratification model, the S-time-distance seems crucial. As mentioned, it is reasonable to expect that the time differences between the subjects or segments in Type C will increase in the initial and intermittent periods; the key question is whether the differences will start to diminish or not. If a reduction of the S-time-distance does not occur, the stratification model may be brought into play.

Simulated and real cases were used to show that in the changing dynamics of the digital divide it makes sense to design multiple scenarios and thus provide various views on possible trends of ICT diffusion. Although the scenarios always express subjective anticipations and presuppositions, they are nevertheless valuable for establishing the future potential dynamics of the digital divide and, in addition, for monitoring the dynamics of the digital divide from the perspective of the growing or shrinking differences of present and future inequalities. By designing scenarios (and along with them the shapes of diffusion functions), the characteristics of growth of the digital divide – defined as crucial for explaining the notion of the dynamics of the digital divide (in addition to statistical measures) – can be clearly determined.

Conclusion: The role of the proposed approach in policy assessment and policy-making

Substantial effort has been devoted around the world to developing indicators to support policy-making and the development and implementation of the necessary data-collection procedures. However, little attention is being paid to the better utilisation of the existing data to improve knowledge-building and better usage for policy-making through the application of analytical methodologies and innovative visualisation and presentation formats. This chapter has introduced a methodological framework for benchmarking, monitoring and regulating the dynamics of the basic digital divide on the national and international levels. The proposed approach should be seen and used as an additional, complementary view which offers a more holistic insight into the dynamics of the digital divide and empowers public authorities to consider various policy options and regulate digital inequalities on an informed basis. Thus, the suggested analytical framework offers a practical tool for setting the targets and for monitoring success in achieving those targets.

We departed from the conceptual framework of the diffusion of innovation theory, emphasising and analysing two (according to our findings) crucial elements of the theory. Yet, they are also problematic for monitoring the dynamics of the digital divide due to their determinist-normative nature. These elements (perhaps inadequately thematised by the diffusion of innovation theory) refer to the shape of distribution functions which designate the diffusion of ICT and the final level of ICT penetration in compared groups. Regarding the shape of the distribution function, it was expected that the diffusion of ICT may unravel over various growth phases not necessarily congruent with a normal distribution (in the cumulative shape this means the S-curve symmetric diffusion function). Accordingly, we differentiated between the normal distribution, kurtic distribution and skewed distribution. Thus, unlike classical studies of the diffusion of innovation theory we departed from the presumption that ICT diffusion in time has to be monitored in various population segments; such disaggregated monitoring enables a profound insight into ICT adoption trends among the entire population. Another critically evaluated key element taken from the diffusion of innovation theory that was also included in the design of our methodological framework can be noted in the implicit theoretical presumption that the digital divide will shrink by itself; the entire population (with all its segments) is supposed to reach a 100% level of ICT penetration. On the contrary, this study of the digital divide considered more potential final levels of ICT penetration. Therefore, alongside the usual normalisation model a stratification diffusion model was introduced.

By considering the abovementioned characteristics of the diffusion process we acquire a more holistic insight into the dynamics of changes in ICT adoption in studied segments, particularly where the three statistical measures (absolute differences, relative differences and S-time-distance) display different possibilities regarding the direction of change of the digital divide. Namely, the reporting of results based on all three measures yields a more informative and holistic insight into the studied dynamics – however, the question about the size of the differences may remain unanswered. This can lead to a methodological quandary, an utterly blurred field that gives no uniform answer to the question about the growing or shrinking digital divide while three contradictory answers are possible. Because of the complex relationships between the statistical measures it is recommended: (a) to present all of them so as to avoid potentially one-sided, partial estimations of the disparities; and (b) to interpret the extent of the digital divide according to the presumption that statistical measures are a function, namely a manifestation, of the shape of the distribution functions, time delay and final level of ICT penetration. If one does not explicitly use the broader framework outlined here, there is a possibility that in political debate and policy formulation 'various interest groups would intentionally look only at the measure which will suit their particular interest' (Sicherl 2007). It is usually the case that 'both supporters and opponents of various policies use lessons selectively to gain advantage in the struggle to get their ideas accepted' (Dolowitz & Marsh 1996, 346). Public decision-makers, citizens and the media are 'perhaps inevitably exposed much more to the views of advocates – those who administer programs or receive benefits from them – than the views of critics or neutral observers' (Wolman 1992, 32). If the basis of successful policy-making is an objective, unbiased and encompassing understanding of the trends under investigation, policy-makers need to be aware of the different views.

Even though the developed methodological approach allows for the better interpretation, presentation and communication of the results to policy-makers and to the public, our intention is not to promote the digital divide as a policy issue wich can benefit specific country governments or the development industry. On the contrary, multinational companies, particularly ICT suppliers, also have a very specific interest in the interpretation of digital divide measures. Since digital divide trends interfere with complex economic, social and political issues it is extremely important to minimise all potential methodological shortcomings. Thus the methodological approach introduced here directly contributes to the avoidance of any potential manipulation of the results.

References

Albright R. 'What can past technology forecast tell us about the future?' Technological Forecasting and Social Change 69 (2002) pp. 443–464

Bouwman H., van der Duin P. 'Technological forecasting and scenarios matter: Research into the use of information and communication technology in the home environment in 2010' Foresight 5 (2003) pp. 6–19

Chermack T. J. 'Studying scenario planning: Theory, research suggestions, and hypotheses' Technological Forecasting and Social Change 72 (2005) pp. 59–73

Chermack T. J., Lynham S. A., Ruona W. E. A. 'A review of scenario planning literature' Futures Research Quarterly 17 (2001) pp. 7–31

Compaine B. M. ed. The digital divide: facing a crisis or creating a myth? Cambridge, MA: MIT Press (2001)

De Haan J. 'IT and Social Inequality in the Netherlands' IT&Society 1 (2003) pp. 27–45

Dolničar V. Merjenje dinamike digitalnega razkoraka [Measuring the Dynamics of the Digital Divide]. Ljubljana: Faculty of Social Sciences (2008)

Dolničar V., Vukčevič K., Kronegger L., Vehovar V. 'Digitalni razkorak v Sloveniji' [Digital Divide in Slovenia] Družboslovne razprave 40(XVIII) (2002) pp. 83–106

Dolowitz D., Marsh D. 'Who Learns What from Whom: a Review of the Policy Transfer Literature' Political Studies 44 (1996) pp. 343–357

Fortunati L. 'Understanding Mobile Phone Design' ed. R. Pertierra. The Social Construction and Usage of Communication Technologies. Asian and European Experiences Diliman, Quezon City: The University of the Philippines Press (2007) pp. 20–47

Fortunati L., Manganelli 'A. A review on the Literature on Gender and ICTs in Italy' eds. K.H. Sørensen & J. Stewart Digital Divides and Inclusion Measures. A Review of Literature and Statistical Trends on Gender and ICT Trondheim/Edinburgh: NTNU. (2002) pp. 137–170

Haddon L. Information and Communication Technologies in Everyday Life: A Concise Introduction and Research Guide Oxford: Berg (2004)

Haddon L., Mante E., Sapio B., Kommonen K-H, Fortunati L., Kant A. eds. Everyday Innovators. Researching the Role of Users in Shaping ICTs Dordrect: Springer (2005)

Hüsing T., Selhofer H. 'DIDIX: A Digital Divide Index for Measuring Inequality in IT Diffusion' IT&Society 1 (2004) pp. 21–38

Norris P. Digital divide: civic engagement, information poverty, and the Internet worldwide Cambridge, New York: Cambridge University Press (2001)

OECD Understanding the digital divide Paris: OECD Publications (2001)

Rogers E.M. Diffusion of Innovations 1st ed. New York: The Free Press (1962)

Rogers E.M. Diffusion of Innovations 5th ed. New York: The Free Press (2003)

Schement J., Scott, S.C. 'Identifying temporary and permanent gaps in universal service' The Information Society 16 (2000) pp. 117–126

Sicherl P. Different Statistical Measures Provide Different Perspectives on Digital Divide Paper presented at the 6th Conference of the European Sociological Association, Murcia URL: (http://www.sicenter.si/pub/Sicherl_Digital_divide_Murcia.pdf) (2003) (accessed January 2009)

Sicherl P. A 'New Generic Statistical Measure in Dynamic Gap Analysis' The European e-Business Report Luxembourg: European Commission (2004)

Sicherl P. 'Analysis of Information Society Indicators with Time Distance Methodology' Journal of Computing and Information Technology 13 (2005) pp. 293–298

Sicherl P. 'The inter-temporal aspect of well-being and societal progress' Social Indicators Research 84 (2007) pp. 231–247

van der Heijden K. Scenarios: The Art of Strategic Conversation New York: Wiley (1997)

van Dijk J. A. G. M. The Deepening Divide: Inequality in the Information Society Thousand Oaks: Sage (2005)

van Dijk J., Hacker K. 'The digital divide as a complex and dynamic phenomenon' The Information Society 19 (2003) pp. 315–326

Vehovar V., Sicherl P., Hüsing T., Dolnicar V. 'Methodological Challenges of Digital Divide Measurements' The Information Society 22: 5 (2006) pp. 279–290

Weingand D. E. 'Futures Research Methodologies: Linking Today's Decisions with Tomorrow's Possibilities' Paper presented at the 61st IFLA General Conference Istanbul, Turkey (1995)

Wolman H. 'Understanding Cross-national Policy Transfers: the Case of Britain and the US' Governance 5 (1992) pp. 27-45

Authors

Vesna Dolničar, Ph.D., is a Teaching Assistant in the field of Social Informatics and Methodology and a Researcher at the Centre for Methodology and Informatics, Faculty of Social Sciences, University of Ljubljana. She is pedagogically engaged in several courses (e.g., Survey Methodology, Internet in Everyday Life, Practical Training in Research Methodology) and has been actively involved in (inter)national research projects related to the field of measuring, monitoring and understanding the information society and the specific needs and motives of potentially excluded groups. She is currently a national correspondent for the 6th Framework Programme project SOPRANO and a member of the Action COST 298. She has authored several scientific papers (e.g., The Information Society), a scientific monograph and two chapters in monographs of the publishers Wiley and Greenwood.

Leopoldina Fortunati is a Professor of the Sociology of Communication at the Faculty of Education of the University of Udine. She has conducted several researches in the field of gender studies, cultural processes as well as information and communication technology. She is the author of many books and, together with J. Katz and R. Riccini, the editor of *Mediating the Human Body. Technology, Communication and Fashion* (Erlbaum 2003) and, with P. Law and S. Yang, of *New Technologies in Global Societies* (World Scientific 2006). She is very active at the European level especially in the COST action networks. Fortunati is associate editor of the journal *The Information Society* and serves as a referee for many outstanding journals. She is the co-chair with Richard Ling of the International Association *The Society for the Social Study of Mobile Communication* (SSSMC) which seeks to facilitate the international advancement of cross-disciplinary mobile communication studies. Her works have been published in 11 languages: Bulgarian, Chinese, English, French, German, Italian, Japanese, Korean, Russian, Slovenian, and Spanish.

Julian Gebhardt studied Sociology, Communication Science and Psychology (M.A.) at the University of Augsburg (Germany). From 2000 till 2007 he worked as a Researcher and Lecturer at the University of Erfurt, Department of Media and Communication Studies, where he also defended his Ph.D. on telecommunicative actions in everyday life. He has conducted a series of industry-funded research projects in the field of designing, using and adopting new communication technologies. His subjects of interest are Interpersonal and Mediated Communication, Mobile Communication, Media and Cultural Change, Everyday Life and Qualitative Research Methods. He is the first Speaker of the Division Sociology of Media and Communication of the German Communication Association (DGPuK) and represents Germany in the European Study Group COST 298 'Participation in the Broadband Society'. Gebhardt has published a number of articles, co-edited books and a monograph, e.g., *Telekommunikative Handeln im Alltag. Eine Sozialphänomenologische Analyse Interpersonaler Medienkommunikation* (VS Verlag 2008) and *Mobile Kommunikation. Perspektiven und Forschungsfelder* (Peter Lang 2005) together with Joachim R. Höflich.

Hajo Greif holds a Ph.D. in Philosophy from the Darmstadt University of Technology obtained within the 'Technology and Society' graduate school. After a visiting fellowship at the Science Studies Unit, University of Edinburgh, Scotland and a stipendiary fellowship at the IAS-STS, Graz, Austria, he became Co-ordinator of the Information and Communication Technologies Research Unit at the Inter-University Research Centre for Technology, Work and Culture (IFZ), Graz in 2005. Since spring 2009, he has been holding an assistant professorship at the University of Klagenfurt. Greif's areas of specialisation are the philosophy and social studies of science and technology as well as the analytical philosophy of the mind and language. His main research fields are technology and human agency, risk perception and risk policies in the field of ICTs, theories of information, the philosophy of Artificial Intelligence, and methodological issues in Science and Technology studies. His recent publications include: 'On the Very Idea of an Information Society', in *Contributions of the Austrian Ludwig Wittgenstein Society* (ALWS 2007).

Amparo Lasen is a Lecturer on Political Sociology and Social Movements at the University Complutense of Madrid. She holds a Ph.D. from La Sorbonne, has been an Academic Visitor at the Department of Sociology of the London School of Economics and has been a Researcher at the Digital World Research Centre of the University of Surrey. Her main research interests are the social implications of ICTs, especially mobile telephony, regarding the constitution of subjectivities, the material aspects of identity, the affective dimensions of the shared agency between people and devices and the multiple manifestations and implications of the presence of mobile phones in urban spaces. Her recent publications include: the edited collection (with Lynne Hamill) *Wireless World: Mobiles – Past, Present and Future* (Springer 2005) and 'How to Be in Two Places at The Same Time:

Mobile Phone Uses in Public Places', in *Mobile Communication in Everyday Life: Ethnographic Views, Observations and Reflections* (Frank & Timme 2006).

Oana Mitrea is a sociologist with interests in Communication Studies and Science and Technology Studies. She has worked as a Research Project Manager at the Romanian Institute for Public Opinion (IRSOP), Bucharest, specialising in qualitative research on political and advertising communication and quantitative studies on consumption. Mitrea completed her doctoral studies in sociology at the University of Bucharest (2002) and the Darmstadt University of Technology (2005). She was a Fellow of IAS-STS (2004-2005) where she explored the social construction and effects of wireless communication technologies. Since 2005, Mitrea has been working as a Researcher in the Information and Communication Technologies Research Unit at the Inter-University Research Centre for Technology, Work and Culture (IFZ), Graz, Austria. Her main fields of activity are the intertwining of mobile services, ubiquitous devices and transport systems; the psychological and symbolic dimension of technology; technology effects at the micro and macro levels. She has published widely in German and English on these topics. Most recently, her paper 'Mobile Learning Visionen – Mobiltelefonie als Dispositiv zur orts- und zeitunabhängigen Kollaboration in Lernsystemen' appeared in *Learning Communities, Das Internet als neuer Lern- und Wissensraum* (Campus Verlag 2008).

Giuseppina Pellegrino is a Lecturer in Social Communication and a Researcher in Sociology of Culture and Communication at the University of Calabria (Italy). She received a Ph.D. in Science, Technology and Society from the same university and visited the Research Centre for Social Sciences at the University of Edinburgh and the Lancaster University Centre for Mobilities Research. Her main research interests concern Science and Technology Studies, especially the sociology of technology in organisations, mobile and ubiquitous communication, media and everyday life, communication and gender issues, science and technologies in the laboratory. Her latest publications include 'Rhetoric, Practice, and Context-Sensitivity in Sociotechnical Action: The Compass Case', in *Issues and Trends in Technology and Human Interaction* (IRM Press 2007).

Gregor Petrič is an Associate Professor for Social Informatics at the Department for Informatics and Methodology and a Researcher at the Centre for Methodology and Informatics (both Faculty of Social Sciences, University of Ljubljana). He is the leading co-ordinator of the reform of Social Informatics undergraduate study and lectures in Introduction to Social Informatics, Internet in Everyday Life and Public Opinion Research. His research interests encompass measuring and explaining Internet-related social phenomena, social networks, web and hypertext, technology mediated social relationships and public opinion. He has published his work in domestic and international journals such as the International Journal of Public Opinion Research, and The Information Society.

Andraž Petrovčič is a Ph.D. candidate at the Faculty of Social Sciences, University of Ljubljana and currently holds the position of young researcher at the Centre for Methodology and Informatics. His research interests span the social aspects of mobile telephony to Internet-related social phenomena. His current work focuses on emerging forms of technologically-mediated sociality in late modernity as well as sociological and communication aspects of social action within online communities. To investigate these issues Andraž Petrovčič has been involved in the project Social and Cultural Aspects of Virtual Life-styles funded by the Slovenian Research Agency (J5-7029-0582). Since 2006 he has been a member of COST action 298 on Participation in the Broadband Society.

Lilia Raycheva, Ph.D., is a member of the Council for Electronic Media (the regulatory authority for radio and television broadcasting in Bulgaria) and a member of the Standing Committee on Transfrontier Television at the Council of Europe. For over 30 years she has been on the regular staff at the Faculty of Journalism and Mass Communication of the St. Kliment Ohridski University of Sofia, where she has served as Vice-Dean for Scientific Research and International Affairs and Head of the Radio and Television Department. Her portfolio includes a number of TV programmes (one of them aired for nearly 30 years). She has successfully participated in a number of international projects and networks on mass media issues. Her scientific interests include: ICTs' impacts, communication issues, media developments, regulatory practices, media professional standards. She has been extensively published, including chapters in edited books of publishers such as Greenwood, Sage, Hampton, Nordicom etc.

Panayiota Tsatsou is a Lecturer at the Swansea University. Previously she was affiliated with the Department of Media and Communications at the London School of Economics and Political Science (LSE), where she defended her Ph.D. project dealing with digital divides in Greece and focusing on the role of culture and decision-making. Her research is financially supported by the Hellenic Republic State Scholarships Foundation (I.K.Y) and the foundation's programme of research scholarship. She has also been working as a Tutorial Fellow and Research Assistant at the LSE, being involved in a wide range of teaching and research in media and communications studies. More specifically, beyond her research on digital divides her scientific interests include research on children and new media technologies as well as research on policy and regulation in digital business technologies.

Vasja Vehovar is a Professor of Statistics at the Faculty of Social Sciences of the University of Ljubljana. He is the Principal Investigator of the RIS (Research on the Internet in Slovenia) project and was the principal investigator of the EU Fifth Framework WebSM project within which the leading website related to the methodology of web surveys (www.websm.org) is maintained. He has published work in several international journals (e.g., the International Journal of Electronic Commerce, Journal of Official Statistics, New Media & Society, and Journal of the American Statistical Association) and with international publishers (e.g., Springer, Wiley, Westport) on a wide range of statistical issues (sampling, non-response, the use of ICT in survey research) and methodological issues regarding the measurement of ICT.

Olga Vershinskaya received her doctoral degree in Economics and has received advanced training in Sociology. Currently she is Head of the Social Problems of ICT Dissemination Department at the Institute for Socio-Economic Studies of the Population at the Russian Academy of Sciences, where she has worked since 1988. Vershinskaya served as a Deputy Director of the Institute for five years (2000-2005). The areas of her research interest range from informational, cultural and psychological aspects of social dynamics to the social consequences of ICT dissemination. In 2007 she published *A Human Being in an Electronic World* (Nauka).

Jane Vincent is Visiting Fellow with the Digital World Research Centre (www.dwrc.surrey.ac.uk) in the Faculty of Arts and Human Sciences at the University of Surrey. Jane researches the social practices of mobile communications users, in particular children's use of mobile phones on which she has completed two studies for the DWRC, and older people's emotional attachment to mobile phones which is the topic of her doctoral thesis. Vincent joined the DWRC in 2001 after over 20 years in the European mobile communications industry. She regularly publishes in journals and books and makes presentations at international telecommunications industry events. Her works have been appeared in outstanding international journals such as Knowledge Technology and Policy, and Information, Communication & Society. She is the co-editor (together with Leopoldina Fortunati) of the book entitled *Electronic Emotion: The Mediation of Emotion via Information and Communication Technologies*, released in 2009 by Peter Lang, Oxford.

Matthias Werner studied Political Science, Social and Economic History, and Economics at the universities of Bonn and Hamburg. From 2002 to 2005 he was a Ph.D. student at the Institute for Technology Assessment and Systems Analysis (ITAS), Karlsruhe. Since December 2005, he has been working as a Researcher in the Information and Communication Technologies Research Unit at the Inter-University Research Centre for Technology, Work and Culture (IFZ), Graz, Austria. His main fields of activity are modes of governance in technology development, especially in ICT development, the order and politics of knowledge in the information/knowledge society, ICT use in politics and ICT-related political practices. With Oana Mitrea and Hajo Grief he edited *Information und Gesellschaft: Technologien einer sozialen Beziehung* (VS Research 2008).

Vsevolod M. Zherebin is a Professor of Economics and works at the Institute for Socio-Economic Studies of the Population at the Russian Academy of Sciences. He is the author of 211 publications, including books, book chapters, and scholarly articles. His areas of interest have encompassed: economic cybernetics, economic information systems, living standards of the population, and household economics. At present they include: the phenomenon of information, the evolution of information, the information society, the information resources of households. His latest publications include: 'The phenomenon of information – one more attempt of interpretation', *The Economic Science of the Modern Russia*, 2007, No. 2; 'Evolution of information is the way to the formation of the information society', *Social and Demographic Policy*, 2007, N7; 'Informatization is coming to the Russian families', *Problems of Statistics* (2008).

Participation in Broadband Society

Edited by Leopoldina Fortunati / Julian Gebhardt / Jane Vincent

This series publishes peer-reviewed monographs and edited volumes by internationally renowed scholars in the field of the 'social use of information and communication technologies (mass media included)', 'communication studies' and 'science and technology social studies'. It provides an editorial space specifically dedicated to the collection of work that integrates new research regarding theoretical discourse, methodologies and studies from multiple disciplines such as sociology, anthropology, psychology, geography, linguistics, information science, engeneering and more.

The editors particularly welcome texts elaborating new theories, original methodological approaches and challenges to existing knowledge. Proposals aimed at scholars, professionals and operators working in the diverse field of participation in broadband society are invited from all disciplines.

Vol. 1 Leopoldina Fortunati / Jane Vincent / Julian Gebhardt / Andraz Petrovčič / Olga Vershinskaya (eds.): Interacting with Broadband Society. 2010.

Vol. 2 Julian Gebhardt / Hajo Greif / Lilia Raycheva / Claire Lobet-Maris / Amparo Lasen (eds.): Experiencing Broadband Society. 2010.

www.peterlang.de

www.ingramcontent.com/pod-product-compliance
Ingram Content Group UK Ltd.
Pitfield, Milton Keynes, MK11 3LW, UK
UKHW021822140426
5217IPUK00004B/52